The Biblical Case

Against Infant Baptism

Cliff Hellar

Our goal is to provide high-quality, thought-provoking books that foster encouragement and spiritual growth. For more information regarding bulk purchases, other IP books, or our publishing services, visit us online or write to adam@ichthuspublications.com.

The Biblical Case Against Infant Baptism
ISBN 13: 978-0692609859
ISBN 10: 0692609857

Publishing services provided by:

ICHTHUS
PUBLICATIONS

www.ichthuspublications.com

Printed in the United States of America

Contents

Introduction   ix

Part 1—THE KEY PASSAGES

1 Luke 18:15-17 // 17

2 1 Corinthians 7:13-14 // 25

3 Acts 2:38-39 // 29

4 Romans 11:16-24 // 35

5 Ephesians 6:1, 4 // 40

6 The Key Paedobaptist Text: Genesis 17:7-8 // 42

Part 2—THE ORDINANCES

7 Ordinances or Sacraments // 55

8 Baptism and the Lord's Supper // 59

9 The Relationship of Baptism to Circumcision // 63

10 The Significance of Circumcision // 70

11 What Covenant does Circumcision Belong to? // 87

12 Signs and Seals // 90

Part 3—BAPTISM

13 The Purpose of Baptism // 101

14 Anabaptism or Rebaptism // 110

15 Household Baptism // 119

16 Repentance: Baptism, The Baptism of John // 126

17 Disciple Baptism // 137

Part 4—THE COVENANTS

18 Definition, Number, and Headship // 149

19 The Mosaic Covenant—of Works or of Grace? // 158

20 Circumcision—A Type of Spiritual Circumcision // 199

21 The Old Covenant and Circumcision // 203

22 Who are under the Covenant of Works? // 208

23 The Abrahamic Covenant // 217

24 The Two Covenants within the Abrahamic Covenant // 226

25 The New Covenant—The Covenant of Grace // 233

26 Who are Members in the Covenant of Grace? // 236

27 Dr. Murray's Questions // 242

Part 5—THE CHURCH

28 Definition and Membership // 251

29 The Commonwealth of Israel and the Church // 259

30 The Characteristics of the Nation of Israel // 261

31 The Commonwealth of Israel Not the Church // 267

32 The Inconsistencies of Infant Church Membership // 285

Part 6—A THEOLOGY OF INFANTS

33 Regeneration of Infants // 293

34 State of Those Who Die in Infancy // 299

35 Infants and the Covenant // 305

36 Infants in the Light of Romans 5 // 307

37 Infants and the Church // 313

38 Infants and Scripture // 315

39 Infants and the Promises // 323

40 One Way of Salvation // 335

41 A body of Truth // 341

Part 7—THE DOCTRINES IN REGARD TO INFANTS

42 The Doctrine of Election and the Remnant // 347

43 Reconciliation // 356

44 Regeneration, Calling, and Faith // 366

45 Regeneration, Faith, and the Holy Spirit // 370

46 Faith and Union with Christ // 371

47 Conversion and Repentance // 375

Part 8—THE ILL EFFECTS OF INFANT BAPTISM

48 It Opposes the Doctrines of Grace // 381

49 It Brings the Unregenerate into the Church // 384

50 It Produces Carnally Secure Hypocrites // 398

51 Discipline is Lacking // 400

52 It Encourages a Trust in the Name // 404

53 It Tends to Formalism // 406

54 It Tends to Superstition // 409

55 Children are Regarded as Safe // 411

Introduction

I WORK AS A MISSIONARY in Papua New Guinea with a remote tribal people in the highlands. They were unreached with the gospel when we first came among them in 1962. My wife and I have been doing literacy work, teaching, evangelizing, planting churches and translating the scriptures into their language since then.

I had been brought up in an independent church that was baptistic but not affiliated with any denomination. I first came into contact with what is called Calvinism or the doctrines of grace during my missionary training in the United States. These doctrines were a great and glorious revelation to me and changed the gospel I witnessed and taught. I became a follower of the teaching of the Reformers and Puritans. Along with their ringing doctrine they were nearly all Paedobaptists.

The earliest Missions and the largest Missions in Papua New Guinea are Paedobaptist. The book *Operation World* says of the people of Papua New Guinea that, "Today over 96% claim to be Christian."*

Probably that whole number have been baptized. The overwhelming majority of those baptized are unregenerate which means that baptism is a major problem for evangelical work in this country. I will speak more in detail about this later. Because of this background and since we had Paedobaptist friends I began to study infant baptism. I have been studying and writing for the last six years whenever I had time between mission work and during furlough. This will explain some of the personal notes in this book since they were written over this long time span.

To study a doctrine in the New Testament the word is usually looked up in a concordance and then studied in detail from the verses found along

---

* p. 439.

with other cross-references. When the word baptism is looked up in a concordance and all the verses studied it is found that,

> "It is true that there is no express command to baptize infants in the New Testament, no express record of the baptism of infants, and no passages so stringently implying it that we must infer from them that infants were baptized."*

Therefore it is reasonable to draw the conclusion that infant baptism is unscriptural. "No, not so," say the Paedobaptists, "our proof for the baptism of infants is found in the Old Testament in the Abrahamic covenant of circumcision." This seems strange since no one was baptized in the Old Testament record and baptism is a New Testament ordinance. However, to look at this argument our study needs to be extended to include circumcision and the covenants, particularly the Abrahamic covenant. But this, too, does not cover the whole Paedobaptist position since they believe all the infants of believers belong to the Church.

Thus, the study must be extended to include the church and who belongs to it. This requires study of other relevant doctrines such as original sin, its imputation and further various doctrines associated with it and with salvation. My wife began to wonder if I would ever finish. Infant baptism touches all these things so it necessarily becomes a major doctrine. From my viewpoint—please excuse my frankness—Paedobaptism is a *major error* that makes an assault even on the doctrines of grace such as original sin, the depravity of man, regeneration, the perseverance of the saints, election, the inviolability of the Covenant of Grace, the promises, conversion, reconciliation, faith, union with Christ, etc.

You say how can this be since the Paedobaptist fathers such as Owen, Goodwin, Edwards and later Hodge, Murray, among many others, were the great teachers and defenders of that Reformed faith? That certainly is true. They were truly great and good men. Yet, I believe they took a different stance when defending infant baptism than when defending the great

---

* Warfield, *Studies in Theology,* 399.

doctrines of our faith. Because of this I use their teachings on the doctrines to combat their errors when speaking about infant baptism. As you will see, they are my main helpers to stand against infant baptism. Nearly all my quotes are from these men. This may seem quite surprising for it means that I think they contradict themselves. I trust I have been fair to those great men and that I have honestly stated their case and mine. The reader will decide.

There is a danger attached to the teaching of men who towered above us, who are leading scholars with impeccable credentials, and were highly gifted to serve the Church. The danger is that because we highly respect them and love them for their humility, godly lives, and service to the Church we will accept their teaching because they taught it. Pastor Albert Martin, on a tape of the Trinity Pulpit, said that,

> "Infant baptism is practiced as a humble but misguided deference to godly and learned men of the past and present. Today men of spiritual stature practice infant baptism. Too, a mark of humility is submission to others, to be teachable. However, 'One is your teacher' (Mt. 23:8) and He is the final authority. God alone is over the conscience. No man is our lord. Our one and true Lord said, 'Teaching them to observe all things that I have commanded you' (Mt. 28:20). We must yield our conscience to no man but only to the word of God. The people of Berea did not accept teaching just because the great apostle Paul taught it but rather, 'searched the Scriptures daily to find out whether these things were so' (Acts 17:11)."

Note that the Holy Spirit commended them in the same verse by having Luke write, "They were more noble than those in Thessalonica."

In God's providence I met in a local church in New Jersey, which we both came to attend, an Australian young man whom I had previously met when I went to the Sydney Harbor park to meet in the open air where he regularly preached. He had access to tapes by Greg Nicols who had taught the adult Bible class when he was an elder at Trinity Church of Essex Fells. He copied about 60 tapes on infant baptism for me. These tapes are excellent and I am indebted to Greg Nicols and his teaching for many things I have written. Had he written them in a book my writing would be needless.

I trust I have not been too impudent in writing against great and good men. I feel like Jonathan Edwards who found himself differing with his grandfather, who preceded him as pastor of the same church. He defended himself in the introduction of his treatise, "Inquiry Concerning Qualifications for Communion." I add it here because I think it is pertinent to my introduction:

"My appearing in this public matter on that side of the question, which is defended in the following sheets, will probably be surprising to many; as it is well known, that Mr. Stoddard, so great and eminent a divine, and my venerable predecessor in the pastoral office over the church in Northampton, as well as my own grandfather, publicly and strenuously appeared in opposition to the doctrine here maintained.

However, I hope it will be not taken amiss that I think as I do, merely because I herein differ from him, though so much my superior, and one whose name and memory I am under distinguishing obligations, on every account, to treat with great respect and honor. Especially may I justly expect, that it will not be charged on me as a crime that I do not think in every thing just as he did, since none more than he himself asserted this scriptural and Protestant maxim, that we ought to call no man on earth master, or make the authority of the greatest and holiest of mere men the ground of our belief of any doctrine in religion. Certainly we are not obliged to think any man infallible, who himself utterly disclaims infallibility. Very justly Mr. Stoddard observes in his Appeal to the Learned, p. 97. 'All Protestants agree, that there is no infallibility at Rome; and I know nobody else pretends to any, since the apostles' days.' And he insists, in his preface to his sermon on the same subject, that it argues no want of a due respect in us to our forefathers, for us to examine their opinions. Some of his words in that preface contain a good apology for me, and are worthy to be repeated on this occasion. They are as follows:

It may possibly be a fault (says Mr. Stoddard) to depart from the ways of our fathers: but it may also be a virtue, and an eminent act of obedience, to depart from them in some things. Men are wont to make a great noise, that we are bringing in innovations, and depart from the old way but it is beyond me, to find out wherein the iniquity doth lie. We may see cause to alter some practices of our fathers, without despising them, without priding ourselves in our wisdom without apostacy, without abusing the advantages God has given us, without a spirit of compliance with corrupt men, without inclination to superstition, without making disturbance in the church of God: and there is no reason, that it should be turned as a reproach upon us. Surely it is commendable for us to examine the practices of our fathers; we have no sufficient reason to take practices upon trust from them. Let them have as high a character as belongs to them; yet we may not look upon their principles as oracles. Nathan himself missed it in his conjecture about building the house of God. He that believes principles because they affirm them, make idols of them. And it would be no humility, but baseness of spirit, for us to judge ourselves incapable to examine the principles that have been handed down to us. If we be by any means fit to open the mysteries of the gospel, we are capable to judge of these matters: and it would ill become us, so to indulge ourselves in case, as to neglect the examination of received principles. If the practices of our fathers in any particulars were mistaken, it is fit they should be rejected; if they be not, they will bear examination. If we be forbidden to examine their practice, that will cut off all hopes of reformation."*

---

* Jonathan Edwards, *Works*, Volume 1, 431.

Part 1

The Key Passages

1

Luke 18:15-17

"Then they also brought infants to Him that He might touch them; but when His disciples saw it, they rebuked them. But Jesus called them to Him and said, 'Let the little children come to Me, and do not forbid them; for of such is the kingdom of God. Assuredly, I say to you, whoever does not receive the kingdom of God as a little child will by no means enter it' " (Luke 18:15-17).

These verses, as everyone who is knowledgeable about infant baptism knows, are used by Paedobaptist writers probably more than any others to defend infant baptism. As a general observation on the whole incident as it applies to infant baptism I believe Strong's statement is pertinent. He wrote, "None would have forbidden if Jesus and his disciples had been in the habit of baptizing infants."[*]

Let us look at the account. We first want to look at the phrase "of such is the kingdom of God." Who is Christ speaking of? John Murray says,

> "It might readily be thought that our Lord had in mind only such children as could come to Jesus of their own accord and were of sufficient age and understanding to answer to the description of Matthew 18:6, 'these little ones who believe in me.' All doubt, however, is removed by Luke 18:15, for there we are informed that the children were babes (brephe), that is to say, little infants. Hence our Lord's word to the effect that 'of such is the kingdom of God' applies to little infants and not solely to children of more advanced

---

[*] Strong, *Systematic Theology*, 951.

years and intelligence."*

A careful reading of the above three verses I think will show that Dr. Murray errs. First, verse 15 reads, "and they brought to him also infants." Matthew and Mark in the parallel accounts say they brought little children. Luke gives added information: "Even infants, says Luke, were included."† That is they brought children to him and also infants. The Greek word translated "also" or "even" is *kai*, a conjunction, usually translated "and". It connects words or terms. Thus the implied information in verse 15 is that they brought children and infants.‡

To whom does the phrase "of such is the kingdom of God" refer? Does it refer to the infants or the others? We note that our Lord uses a different word from infants when he says, "let the little children (*paidia*) come unto me." He does not speak of the infants but the little children. This is underlined when he says, "forbid them not," *i.e.*, the little children. He does not say do not forbid those who bring the infants. He says don't forbid the little children who desire to come to me. He gives as a reason for not forbidding these little children to come to him: "for of such is the kingdom of God." John Murray wrote, "It is necessary to note the class of which Jesus had been speaking, it is distinctly and only the infant class,"§ but Jesus had not been speaking of the infants. He had been speaking of the little children. Dr. Murray writes, "the infant class alone provides us with the antecedent of the (word) *toiouton* (of such)."** Antecedent in this case refers to the preceding noun *toiouton*, ("of such"). The noun that "of such" refers to is little children. Our Lord did not speak about the infants. His interest was mainly in the little children who were of their own accord coming to him. These are the ones that Christ refers to as "of such is the kingdom of God." He is not referring to infants. Dr. Murray acknowledges this by saying,

---

* Murray, *Christian Baptism*, 62.

† Hendriksen, *Luke*, 829.

‡ For similar constructions see Matt. 5:46, Mark 1:27, Luke 10:17, Gal. 2:17, etc.

§ Murray, 64.

** *Ibid.*

"It was with little children the disciples were concerned, it was with little children Jesus was concerned, the disciples to forbid them and Jesus to receive them. Little children were in the focus of attention and interest, and it is therefore of the little children themselves that Jesus proceeds to speak."[*]

It should be emphasized that Christ was not speaking of infants. As Dr. Murray says, "Little children were in the focus of attention and interest," not infants.

The word for little children is *paidion* defined by Strong, "a child, or infant, or as half-grown." (In this context it does not mean infants since another word *brephe* is used for infants to distinguish them). Others define it as immature or a child that has not reached maturity. It should be noted that this Greek word is used for a girl of twelve years of age in Mark 5:39, 40, 41. For example, "Then He took the child (*paidion*) by the hand . . . she was twelve years of age" (5:41, 42).

Bannerman in *The Scripture Doctrine of the Church*, says, "Jesus called them—the babes—unto Him . . . ,"[†] but this is a mistake. Jesus did not call the unconscious infants to him who were unable to come. He called the little children to Him. "Jesus called them to Him and said, 'Let the little children come to me.' " The ones whom Christ called to Him are the ones he told his disciples not to hinder but to let them come to him. Bannerman continues, "Our Lord counted it 'a call' to the babes, although it reached them only through their parents." No. The Lord did not "call" unconscious infants to himself through their parents. He called the little children to himself and they heeded that call and came. It was a real call and a real coming. Bannerman further says, "He counted it as 'their coming' in some real sense, 'unto Him' when they were brought in their mother's arms." No, Christ did not "count" their coming in some real sense when they were brought. The little children came in a real sense but not as unconscious infants brought in their mother's arms. They were not brought. They came! They came willingly and consciously.

---

[*] Murray, 63.
[†] p. 32.

What does the phrase, "for of such is the kingdom of God," mean? It can mean it belongs to such children or it consists of such children. Parallel verses such as Matthew 5:3, "theirs is the kingdom of heaven" would point to the meaning that they receive the kingdom; it belongs to them. Verse 17 of this context seems to define it as meaning to "receive the kingdom of God."

Please carefully consider the sentence in verse 17, "Whosoever shall not receive the kingdom of God as a little child shall in no wise enter therein." This tells us that children are not in the kingdom of God by physical birth but rather they receive it. It is not as an infant they receive it but by a conscious, intelligent act. Dr. Lloyd-Jones preaching on Romans 5:17 and the phrase "they which receive" says,

> "The contrast is that while on this Christian side we actively and voluntarily receive and believe, we are unconsciously involved in the sin of Adam. This is not a point of contrast that occurred to me personally; it is part of John Calvin's exposition. Calvin says that one of the contrasts here is brought out in the phrase 'they that receive', denoting the activity of faith. . . . We were unconsciously involved in Adam; here we consciously embrace the gift of salvation—and every man who is a Christian does just that."*

Note that Calvin calls it "the activity of faith" and Lloyd-Jones calls this receiving a conscious embracing of salvation. The children who receive the kingdom are not passive but actively receive it. How do they receive it? They receive it the only way anyone receives spiritual blessing; by faith. Without faith a man or child can receive nothing. James referring to the doubter, the man without faith says, "Let not that man think that he shall receive anything of the Lord" (Jas. 1:7).

Some may have doubts that such little children as came to Christ could receive the kingdom by faith. However, this verse is an ellipsis. That is it omits words needed to complete the sense. When Christ says, "whosoever shall not receive the kingdom as a little child" we can rightly add the words

---

* Lloyd-Jones, *Romans*, "Assurance," 261.

"receives it", that is, "receives the kingdom as a little child receives it." How must a person receive the kingdom to enter into it? Would you deny that he must receive it by faith? Well, that is the same way a little child receives it. And the same way a little child receives it is the way that all must receive it. There is but one way. "Whosoever shall not receive the kingdom as a little child (receives it) shall in no wise enter into it."

A further proof that little children are able to believe and receive the kingdom is found in Matthew chapter 18. This chapter immediately precedes chapter 19 that includes the parallel portion we are considering. The same Greek word is used in Matthew 18:2-5 and in Matthew 19:13-14 for "little children" or, in the singular "little child". Christ speaking of little children says, "But whoever causes one of these little ones who believe in Me . . ." (Matt. 18:6). Note that these little children believe. Thus, such little children as were brought to Christ for his blessing and came to him are able to believe so that "to such is the kingdom of heaven."

Others may doubt a little child's capacity to receive the kingdom. Charles H. Spurgeon was the pastor of a large Baptist church that had many children who were full members. He had much experience with children. He said in one of his sermons,

> "Upon this subject, if I were at this moment to deal with facts alone, and not with mere opinion, I could spend the whole morning in giving details of young children whom I have personally conversed with, some of them very young children indeed. I will say broadly that I have more confidence in the spiritual life of the children that I have received into this church than I have in the spiritual condition of the adults thus received. I will even go further than that, and say that I have usually found a clearer knowledge of the gospel and a warmer love to Christ in the child-converts than in the man-converts. . .
>
> If you want to know what faith in Jesus is, you must not look to those who have been bemuddled by the heretical jargon of the times, but to the dear children who have taken Jesus at his word, and believed in him, and loved him and therefore know and are sure that they are saved. Capacity for believing lies more in the child than in the man. We grow less rather than more capable of faith; every year

21

brings the unregenerate mind further away from God, and makes it less capable of receiving the things of God. No ground is more prepared for the good seed than that which as yet has not been trodden down as the highway, nor has been as yet overgrown with thorns. Not yet has the child learned the deceits of pride, the falsehoods of ambition, the delusions of worldliness, the tricks of trade, the sophistries of philosophy; and so far it has an advantage over the adult. In any case the new birth is the work of the Holy Ghost, and he can as easily work upon youth as upon age."[*]

What do we learn from these three vital verses? We learn that little children can and do receive the kingdom. We learn that they should never be prevented or hindered from coming to Christ but rather brought to Christ. We learn that Christ rebuked the disciples for forbidding "little children" to come to him. He never mentions the infants. Is our concern foremost with little children who are of understanding years and able to exercise faith? Christ was not usually displeased but in the parallel account in Mark we read in verse 14, chapter 10 that he was "much displeased" with His disciples. Christ knew that the children needed salvation or they would perish. What a great sin it is to hinder a person from coming to Christ and particularly a child. That Christ looks on children being hindered or prevented from coming to Him as a great sin shows that He didn't see them as safe in the Covenant of Grace but needing conversion.

Dear brethren, all children are in Adam until they believe. As Spurgeon says when he preached on this portion,

> "If you indulge in the novel idea that your children do not need conversion, that children born of Christian parents are somewhat superior to others, and have good within them which only needs development, one great motive for your devout earnestness will be gone. Believe me, brethren, your children need the Spirit of God to give them new hearts and right spirits, or else they will go astray as other children do. Remember that however young they are, there is

---

[*] Spurgeon, 570-71.

a stone within the youngest breast; and that stone must be taken away, or be the ruin of the child. There is a tendency to evil even where as yet it has not developed into act, and that tendency needs to be overcome by the divine power of the Holy Spirit, causing the child to be born again. Oh, that the church of God would cast off the old Jewish idea which still has such force around us, namely, that natural birth brings with it covenant privileges! Now, even under the old dispensation there were hints that the true seed was not born after the flesh, but after the spirit, as in the case of Ishmael and Isaac, and Esau and Jacob. Will not even the church of God know that 'That which is born of the flesh is flesh; and that which is born of the Spirit is spirit'? 'Who can bring a clean thing out of an unclean?' The natural birth communicates nature's filthiness, but it cannot convey grace. Under the new covenant we are expressly told that the sons of God are 'born, not of blood, nor of the will of the flesh, nor of the will of man, but of God.' Under the old covenant, which was typical, the birth according to the flesh yielded privilege; but to come at all under the Covenant of Grace ye must be born again. The first birth brings you nothing but an inheritance with the first Adam; you must be born again to come under the headship of the second Adam."[*]

By application; are we doing anything to prevent little children from coming to Christ? Are we doing all we can to bring them to Christ? Or are we bringing them to the font rather than to Christ? I know of no greater hindrance to children coming to Christ in repentance and faith than infant baptism. How rarely do we ever hear of a little child being converted in a Paedobaptist church. Why is this? Isn't it because many Paedobaptists believe children do not need conversion but rather treat them as Christian. Dr. J. W. Alexander in a letter written in March 1845 and quoted by D. Kingdon writes, "Ought we not daily to say (in its spirit) to our children—'you are Christian children—you are Christ's—you ought to think and feel and act as such.'" Nothing could be more deadly nor more calculated to make hypocrites of little children. If we assume they are all saved the great motive for earnestness in bringing them to Christ is lost. Are the children of

---

[*] *Ibid.*, 569.

believers as John Murray writes, "(1) among Christ's people and members of His body; (2) members of his kingdom and therefore have been regenerated; (3) that they belong to the church"?[*]

If you believe so then surely you will not plead with your children as brands needing to be plucked from the fire with all haste. Instead of them being alerted to their danger of being "dead in trespasses and sin" and "shapen in iniquity," they are comforted that they are covenant children, not born in sin but born into the kingdom. What could in a greater way lead to carnal security, deadness and unconcern? Often none are so hardened in sin and unbelief as those baptized as infants. We should rather tell them to flee from the wrath to come and flee to Christ in faith for He receives little children. Yea, "of such is the kingdom of God." What a great lack of urgency we see everywhere but particularly where it concerns the salvation of little children. Let us earnestly exhort them to seek him early for "those that seek me early shall find me" (Prov. 8:17, KJV).

---

[*] Murray, 65.

2

1 Corinthians 7:13-14

"And a woman who has a husband who does not believe, if he is willing to live with her, let her not divorce him. For the unbelieving husband is sanctified by the wife, and the unbelieving wife is sanctified by the husband; otherwise your children would be unclean, but now they are holy" (1 Corinthians 7:13-14).

A major argument that the Paedobaptists use to prove infant baptism comes from 1 Corinthians 7:14. The argument is that the children of believers, or even the children of one believer are not unclean, "but . . . are holy." Thus, as the Directory for the Public Worship of God prepared by the Westminster Assembly says of such children, "They are Christians and federally holy before baptism, and therefore are they baptized." The formula for the Baptism of Children of the Christian Reformed Church says, "Paul said that children of believers are holy (1 Cor. 7:14), so our children are given the sign of baptism."

R. R. Booth argues, "These 'holy, cleansed' children must receive the cleansing sign of baptism to mark them off from the 'unholy' or defiled children of unbelievers, just as circumcision performed this task in the Old Testament."[*]

Paedobaptists hold that the holiness of the children is different to the holiness of the unbeliever who is sanctified by his believing spouse. They go to the Greek words to maintain this. They say that being sanctified is inferior to being holy. In English holiness and sanctification are different words but

---

[*] Booth, *Children of the Promise*, 134.

in Greek they are the same. The Greek family of words are *hagios* (holy) an adjective, *hagiazo* (to make holy, or sanctify) a verb, and *hagiasmos*, *hagiosune*, and *hagiotes* (holiness or sanctification) nouns. Thus, all these words are closely linked. To sanctify is to make holy and a holy one is a saint or a sanctified one.

The intimate connection of the words is illustrated in 1 Corinthians 1:2, ". . . to those who are sanctified (*hagiasmenois*) in Christ Jesus called to be saints (*hagiois*)." The point is that the sanctification or separation of the unbelieving partner is the same as the sanctification or separation of the children. It says "the unbelieving husband is sanctified by (or in) the wife, and the unbelieving wife is sanctified by (or in) the husband." The preposition is *en* (in) in the Greek. The relation of marriage being one flesh is even closer and more intimate that the parental relationship. Thus, the unbeliever is sanctified "in" the believing spouse. "Otherwise your children would be unclean but now they are holy." Thus, the sanctification of the children is based on or is an outgrowth of the sanctification of the unbelieving spouse; "otherwise your children would be unclean."

If such a holiness entitles the children to baptism it would also entitle the unbelieving spouse to baptism. Since the conjugal relation has a oneness of flesh that the parent child relationship does not have we see that the unbelieving spouse is sanctified by the believer and then from that relationship the children are holy. The children's holiness comes from the sanctification of the unbelieving parent, see verse 14. If this holiness is covenant holiness such that it brings the children into the church why doesn't it do the same for the unbelieving spouse? No, the unbelieving spouse is not holy as belonging to the church but as being under the sanctifying influence of the believer. Likewise, the children are not holy as belonging to the church but as being under the sanctifying influence of the believer.

The context of this verse is a chapter on marriage. The purpose of the immediate verses (13 to 16) are to convince those who are married to unbelievers not to divorce them. The reason given as to why they should not divorce them is that they may be the means of saving their unbelieving spouses if they stay with them. "How do you know, wife, whether you will save your husband? Or how do you know, husband, whether you will save your wife?" (1 Cor. 7:16).

Paul in this chapter is not dealing with baptism at all. He was not arguing for infant baptism. He was not arguing for infant baptism even in a roundabout way. The problem in chapter 7 was marriages that were divided through one of the partners being saved. See verses 12 and 13. Should there be divorce? Paul's answer is no because the unbelieving spouse is sanctified by the believing partner. What is this sanctification or holiness of the unbeliever? It is not the "sanctification by the Spirit" from the world and unto salvation for this is accompanied by "belief in the truth" (1 Thess. 2:13). Nor does this sanctification make the unbeliever morally or inwardly holy. Rather, it is the sanctifying or setting apart of the unbelieving spouse and children into the realm of the gospel's influence through the believing partner.

The verb *hagiazo* that is used here means to sanctify, make holy, to separate. Because the spouse and children come under the sanctifying influence of the gospel it is said that they have been sanctified or separated into a state of privilege. The believer's prayers, tears, exhortations, teaching and invitations have often led to salvation of the unbelieving spouse and/or children. This is particularly so if this is backed up by a loving, godly example. In this sense the unbelieving spouse and children are sanctified by the family relationship even as the temple sanctified the gold connected with it (Matt. 23:17) and so they are called "holy." This sanctified state of privilege is not a proper ground for baptism or admission into the church but it does separate or set apart "for the operation of the grace of God in salvation through the witness of the believing partner."[*]

Rather than these verses implying infant baptism they seem to rather indicate that infant baptism was not practiced in apostolic times. As B. B. Warfield commenting on this verse wrote, "No doubt capable of an interpretation on the supposition that the practice (infant baptism) did not exist and is scarcely a sure foundation concerning it."[†] And, as Olshausen

---

[*] Kingdon, *Kingdom Children of Abraham*, 90.
[†] *Studies in Theology*, 398. Quoted by T. E. Watson, *Baptism Not for Infants*, 38.

agreed, "It is moreover clear that St. Paul could not have chosen this line of argument, had infant baptism been at that time practiced." Jacobi, quoted by Strong, calls this text, "a sure testimony against infant baptism since Paul would certainly have referred to baptism as a proof of their holiness, if infant baptism had been practiced."*

---

* Strong, 951.

3

Acts 2:38-39

"Then Peter said to them, 'Repent, and be baptized every one of you in the name of Jesus Christ for the remission of sins, and ye shall receive the gift of the Holy Spirit. For the promise is unto you, and to your children, and to all that are afar off, even as many as the Lord our God shall call.'" (Acts 2:38-39).

P rof. Murray, in his writings on baptism, makes the following claim in regards to children and the promise spoken of by the apostle Peter in the books of Acts:

> "The promise is to the children as well as to the parents and that, in respect of this property, the children are included with their parents . . . Now what does this imply? It demonstrates that Peter, in the illumination and power of the Spirit of Pentecost, recognised that there was no suspension or abrogation of that divine administration whereby children are embraced with their parents in God's covenant promise."[*]

Thus, Prof. Murray is saying that the promise of the Abrahamic Covenant, "to you and your seed," is referred to and repeated by Peter with the words, "The promise is to you and your children." He makes salvation due to heredity. The implication then is as R. R. Booth writes, "If the children of believers are embraced by the promises of the covenant as certainly they are, then they must also be entitled to receive the initial sign of the covenant,

---

[*] Murray, 70-71.

which is baptism. This is affirmed by Peter in Acts 2:38, 39."[*] Mr. Booth believes that all the children of believers are embraced by the Covenant of Grace. This seems to mean then that all the children are elect and will be saved or what are the promises of the covenant? That they will all be saved is contrary to experience. Most Paedobaptists are quick to acknowledge this: "It must be admitted that the fact that the children of believers are included in the Covenant of Grace does not imply that all children of believers, without exception, are elect persons who shall receive eternal life."[†]

Do these verses in Acts teach that all children of believers are in the Covenant of Grace? No, for none are until they enter the covenant by spiritual birth. All, having been born in sin and in Adam their covenant head, continue in that state under the covenant of works until they are united by faith to Christ, the head of the Covenant of Grace. Physical birth did not nor does it save.

The Paedobaptists take these verses to mean that the children of these Jews were in a position of special privilege since the children of believers are in the Covenant of Grace with their parents. However, these parents were not believers so that even by the Paedobaptist reasoning their children were not in the covenant. Peter is preaching the gospel to the unsaved urging them to repent and to save themselves from that corrupt generation. The parents were not believers.

Were these children to obtain the promise through being the seed of believers? Was the promise to come through heredity? Not at all. They had to receive it through repentance just as much as the fathers. In fact, they had to receive the promises the same way the Gentiles, those afar off, had to receive them. Being circumcised and in the covenant of circumcision gave no special privilege.

Dr. Murray continues,

> "We may well regard Pentecost as that which brought to fruition the inauguration of the new dispensation. Nothing could advertise more

---

[*] Booth, 59.
[†] Vos, "Blue Banner Faith and Life," January – March 1959, 37.

conspicuously and conclusively that this principle of God's gracious government, by which children along with their parents are the possessors of God's covenant promise, is fully operative in the New Testament as well as in the Old than this simple fact that on the occasion of Pentecost Peter took up the refrain of the old Covenant and said, 'The promise is to you and to your children.' It is the certification of the Holy Spirit to us that this method of the administration of the Covenant of Grace is not suspended . . ."*

He says, "children along with their parents are the possessors of God's covenant promise." Is this true? If it is true how could any children of believers ever be lost? Can God's promises fail? No, children are not possessors of God's covenant promise until they repent as Peter commands. These children were no more linked to their parents to obtain the covenant promise than the Gentiles were linked with them. All without exception could only receive the promise by faith. As Galatians 3:13-14 says, the blessing of Abraham comes to the Gentiles by faith just as it does to the Jews. It doesn't come because Jews are in the Abrahamic covenant by heredity.

"Christ has redeemed us from the curse of the law, having become a curse for us (for it is written, 'Cursed is everyone who hangs on a tree'), that the blessing of Abraham might come upon the Gentiles in Christ Jesus, that we might receive the promise of the Spirit through faith . . ." (Gal. 3:13-14).

These verses in Acts are not a promise of special privilege to a special people. Nor is it an unconditional promise that automatically comes to believers' children. Rather it is a promise to everyone. It excludes no one. That is, the promise is to everyone who fulfills the condition of the promise, "Repent, and be baptized every one of you . . ." Does this mean that all the children are "entitled to receive the initial sign of the covenant, which is baptism" simply because they are children of believers as Mr. Booth says? Assuredly not. They were not children of believers and also baptism is not

---

* Murray, 71.

the promise. Repentance and baptism are the conditions of the promise. The baptism is repentance-baptism which *excludes* all infants.

What is the promise? "Ye shall receive the gift of the Holy Spirit." This is the context of Peter's sermon. His text was not Genesis 17:1-8 but Joel 2:28-32. Peter preached God's promise quoting Joel, "In the last days, God says, I will pour out my Spirit on all people. Your sons and daughters will prophesy ..." (Acts 2:17). Does this apply to infants?

The command to repent and be baptized was to all in verse 38. However, verse 39 emphasizes that the promise will be fulfilled to a certain people, "even as many as the Lord our God shall call." It is important to see that this phrase qualifies all the preceding phrases, that is the three groups: you, your children, and those afar off. None will obtain the promise apart from God's call. For whom He calls He justifies. "Those he predestined, he also called; those he called, he also justified ..." (Rom. 8:30).

C. H. Spurgeon's commented on this verse thusly:

> "But it is written, saith one, 'That the promise is unto you, and to your children.' Dear friends, there never was a grosser piece of knavery committed under heaven than the quotation of that text as it is usually quoted. I have heard it quoted many times to prove a doctrine which is very far removed from that which it clearly teaches. If you take one-half of any sentence which a man utters, and leave out the rest, you may make him say the opposite of what he means. What do you think that text really is? See Acts 2:39: 'The promise is unto you, and to your children, and to all that are afar off, even as many as the Lord our God shall call.' This grandly wide statement is the argument on which is founded the exhortation, 'Repent, and be baptized every one of you.' It is not a declaration of privilege special to anyone, but a presentation of grace as much to all that are afar off as to them and to their children. There is not a word in the New Testament to show that the benefits of divine grace are in any degree transmitted by natural descent: they come, 'to as many as the Lord our God shall call,' whether their parents are saints or sinners. How can people have the impudence to tear off half a text to make it teach what is not true?
>
> No, brethren; you must sorrowfully look upon your children as

born in sin, and shapen in iniquity, 'heirs of wrath, even as others'; and though you may yourself belong to a line of saints and trace your pedigree from minister to minister, all eminent in the church of God, yet your children occupy precisely the same position by their birth as other people's children do; so that they must be redeemed from under the curse of the law by the precious blood of Jesus, and they must receive a new nature by a work of the Holy Ghost. They are favoured by being placed under godly training, and under the hearing of the gospel; but their need and their sinfulness are the same as in the rest of the race. If you think of this, you will see the reason why they should be brought to Jesus Christ—a reason why they should be brought as speedily as possible in the arms of your prayer and faith to him who is able to renew them."*

And here is a final quotation from John Reisinger:

"It is not accidental that hyper-Calvinism and a strong 'covenant seed' concept go hand in hand. It is impossible to think and speak in terms of 'covenant children' and 'non-covenant children' and not wind up with two different 'gospels', one for the 'covenant child' that includes God loves you for sure, and one for the 'pagan child' that cannot include 'God loves you' until we are first sure that they are of the elect.

I think it can be proven historically that one of the major problems created by using Acts 2:39 as a proof text for infant baptism is that it confuses the message of the gospel of grace to all men. The 'Seed' in Acts 2 is neither natural Jews nor the children of believing parents. The Seed in this whole chapter is our Lord Jesus Christ Himself. He is the true Seed to whom the promises were made and the message of this chapter, and especially verse 39, is that the promise to the seed has been fulfilled—the Messiah Redeemer has come—believe in Him and be saved whoever you are.

The gospel of grace is to be preached to 'whosoever believeth,' not just one nationality or group and their physical children. There is no such thing as a 'covenant community' inclusive of all 'physical'

---

* Spurgeon, 569-70.

33

children now that the prophecy of Joel has been fulfilled. No one group any longer has any special claim or privilege because of birth. There is only *one* status before God—*guilty*, regardless of who your parents are, and there is only *one* gospel message to every guilty sinner—*repent* and *believe.* This is the one message we must preach to the children of believers as well as the children of unbelievers.

This is what Peter is declaring in Acts 2:39! Do not destroy the universal offer of the gospel by twisting these words into a 'promise to Christian parents.' "*

---

* Reisinger, *Abraham's Four Seeds*, 86.

4

Romans 11:16-24

"If the root is holy, so are the branches. And if some of the branches were broken off, and you, being a wild olive tree, were grafted in among them . . ." (Romans 11:16-24).

John Flavel, a Puritan, comments on this passage,

> "It is clear to me, beyond all contradiction, from Rom. 11:17, 'If some branches be broken off, and thou being a wild olive-tree, wert grafted in amongst them, and with them partakest of the root and fatness of the olive tree;' I say I can scarce desire a clearer scripture light than this text gives, to satisfy my understanding in this case, that when God brake off the unbelieving Jews from the church, both parents and children together, the believing Gentiles, which are as truly Abraham's seed as they were, Gal. 3:29, yea, the more excellent seed of Abraham, were implanted or ingrafted in their room, and do as amply enjoy the privileges of that covenant, both internal and external, for themselves and for their infant-seed, as ever any member of the Jewish church did or could."*

It is taught by the Paedobaptists from this scripture of the figure of the olive tree that the olive tree is the Jewish church and that it continues under the new covenant. "The good olive tree was not uprooted but pruned, and

---

* Flavel, *The Works of Flavel*, 3:545.

new branches were grafted in."* This is supposed to teach that the New Testament church was a continuation of the Old Testament church such that infants are included in the church and so should be baptized. I have dealt with this question under the heading, "The Commonwealth of Israel and the Church."

In this passage the New Testament church is distinct from the Old Testament "church" and in fact is seen to be grafted into the place of the Jewish nation. It is not a continuation of the Jewish "church."

Goodwin comments,

> "He speaks of their engrafting, not into the Jews' church, as proselytes were of old, that they should be members of that church as if it still stood; but instead of the Jews' church, considered as broken off, and these growing up of themselves on the Jews' stock, to be a church of themselves unto God, entire and distinct from that of the Jews, in the room therof."[†]

The teaching seems to be that the natural branches signify Abraham's seed or the nation of Israel. Due to unbelief the nation was broken off. Only the remnant is left. In their place Abraham's spiritual seed or Gentile believers are grafted in. Then the figure is extended to graft in the natural branches, the nation of Israel, if they would turn from their unbelief.

This makes it clear that only believing branches are joined to the olive tree. Objections could be made that this makes the tree to be drastically changed from that which included unbelievers to that which no longer includes unbelievers and so changes the identity of the tree. Quite so! The branches that were previously joined to the tree by nature are cut off and now only believers, not believers and their seed, are joined to the tree by a supernatural, contrary to nature, act of God. This is a drastic change! Indeed as Ephesians 2:15 says it is a new creation!

Infant membership in the church is argued from this portion. However, the very changes that occur to the tree do away with that argument. The

---

* Booth, 85.
† Goodwin, *Works*, Volume 9, 434.

natural branches have been cut off, that is, membership is not through descent. It is not the natural branches that are now joined to the tree. Now, only believing branches are joined to the tree. Infant membership is done away with. Faith is substituted for natural descent.

It may then be asked what the tree signifies. Some commentators say the tree signifies the Church. However, this seems impossible since at first the tree includes many branches that are not joined to the tree by faith but only naturally as natural branches. This would make the church to consist of mostly unbelievers. Other commentators say the tree signifies the nation of Israel but this would mean that the Gentile believers become part of the nation of Israel when they are grafted into the tree.

I believe both sets of commentators are partly right and partly wrong. The tree is both Israel and the Church. It signifies the nation of Israel before the branches were broken off and it signifies the Church after they were broken off and only believing branches (believing Jews) remain and wild olive branches (believing Gentiles) are grafted in. When were the natural branches broken off? They were broken off when the Jewish nation was rejected after they had rejected their Lord and crucified Him. They were rejected and replaced by another nation, the Church, that would bear the fruit of the kingdom, "The kingdom of God will be taken from you and given to a nation bearing the fruits of it" (Matt. 21:43). This is the nation born "in one day, born at once" (Isa. 66:8) at Pentecost. This rejection of Israel made way for the Church to be formed and to take the place of Israel. This is signified by the natural branches being broken off and wild branches being grafted in their place.

Yet, since the believing Jews remain Jew and Gentile are joined, "creating the one new man from the two" (Eph. 2:15). Notice it is one new man. It had never existed before. It is a new creation. The Church could not exist before that time since the Church was created "one body through the cross" (Eph. 2:16). It had to be "built on the foundation of the apostles and prophets (New Testament prophets)" (Eph. 2:20). Before his death Christ spoke of the Church in the future tense.

I agree with many commentators that the root of the tree signifies the patriarchs; Abraham, Isaac and Jacob; who are both the root of natural Israel and also spiritual Israel, the Church. Thus there is in that sense continuity. Believers being "Christ's are Abraham's seed and heirs according to the promise" (Gal 3:20). Thus the fatness that New Testament believers partake of is the promise to Abraham.

However, there is also discontinuity since the tree has been changed drastically from all Jews by natural birth being part of the tree to all unbelieving Jews broken off so that now the tree only includes believers. No longer does birth automatically join to the tree but only faith. Our Paedobaptist brethren that disregard this discontinuity fail to give the work of Christ its due prominence for it was the cross and resurrection that brought this cataclysmic change. Things did not continue as they were. The redemption obtained by the Savior introduced the most revolutionary thing in history.

Haggai describes this change by God saying, "I will shake heaven and earth . . . I will shake all nations" (Hag. 2:6-7). The time this historical shaking of the world and heaven would occur was defined by Haggai, "I will shake all nations and the desired of all nations will come" (Hag. 2:7, NIV). Historically the Church has given a Messianic interpretation to this verse. The "desired" or "Desire of All Nations" (see NKJV) is undoubtedly the Lord Jesus Christ. He is the one who came to the temple built in the days of Haggai filling it with glory. As Malachi wrote, "the Lord, whom you seek will suddenly come to his temple, even the Messenger of the covenant, in whom you delight" (Mal 3:1).

Mr. Booth wrote, "The Lord has been steadfast in bringing his plan to pass in a smooth and unbroken fashion, showing his redemptive concern for individuals, families, and society."*

However, this shaking of all things is further explained in Hebrews to mean the removal of the things that are shaken: "But now He has promised saying, 'Yet once more I shake not only the earth but also heaven.' Now this, 'Yet once more,' indicates the removal of those things that are made, that the things which cannot be shaken may remain" (Heb. 12:26-27).

The Puritan theologian John Owen wrote of this great "commotion and

---

* Booth, 35.

alteration,"

> "Take the words metaphorically for great changes, commotions, and alterations in the world, and so were they accomplished in him and his coming ... But as we observed before, it is the dealing of God with the church, and the alterations which he would make in the state thereof, concerning which the apostle treats. It is therefore the heavens of Mosaical worship, and the Judaical church-state, with the earth of their political state belonging thereunto, that are here intended. These were they that were shaken at the coming of Christ, and so shaken, as shortly after to be removed and taken away, for the introduction of the more heavenly worship of the gospel, and the immovable evangelical church state. This was the greatest commotion and alteration that God ever made in the heavens and earth of the church, and which was to be made once only."[*]

Rather than God's plan of redemption, particularly during the time of the crucifixion and resurrection, being depicted as "a smooth and unbroken" line it should rather be depicted as a jagged line traced by a seismograph during a major earthquake until it jumps off the graph. Let us not minimize the effects of the coming of Christ but rather magnify them. Hallelujah for the cross! What has He wrought?

---

[*] Owen, *Hebrews*, Volume 7, 365-66.

5

Ephesians 6:1, 4

"Children, obey your parents in the Lord, for this is right. And you, fathers, do not provoke your children to wrath, but bring them up in the training and admonition of the Lord" (Ephesians 6:1, 4; also, Colossians 3:20-21).

D r. Murray writes in regard to these verses,

"In these passages the apostle Paul includes the children among those who are addressed as saints. In the contexts of both passages exhortations are being given to the various classes of saints—wives, husbands, fathers, servants, masters. . . . It is necessary, therefore, to understand that the children are reckoned as saints in terms of the salutation in both epistles and that they are not regarded as belonging to any different category in respect of the Saviourhood and Lordship of Christ."*

His assumption seems to be that these children are members of the church and so were previously baptized as infants. However, we would expect that believers' children would come with their parents to the public worship even if they were unsaved and nonmembers and so come under the teaching and exhortation. Yet, it does seem that these children were believers since the motive given in the command, "Obey your parents in the Lord," is meant to move the believing children by their relation to the Lord. They were exhorted as mature and responsible believing children able to be moved by the motive, "For this is well pleasing unto the Lord." There is no reason

---

* Murray, 66-67.

to believe these children were joined to the church as infants rather than as believers who were baptized on their confession of faith.

6

The Key Paedobaptist Text: Genesis 17:7-8

"And I will establish my covenant between me and thee and thy seed after thee in their generations for an everlasting covenant, to be a God unto thee, and to thy seed after thee. And I will give unto thee, and to thy seed after thee, the land wherein thou art a stranger, the land of Canaan, for an everlasting possession; and I will be their God" (Genesis 17:7-8).

T he above verses are the key portion in the infant baptism controversy. The Westminster Confession of Faith uses these two verses as proof verses for infant baptism. Dr. Vos, the editor of the "Blue Banner Faith and Life," says, "The real proof of infant baptism depends on the truth that the children of believers are included in the Covenant of Grace."[*]

He uses Genesis 17:7-10 as supporting verses.

John Owen says,

"This covenant was, that God would be 'a God unto Abraham and to his seed;' which God Himself explains to be his infant seed (Gen. 17:12), that is, the infant seed of every one of his posterity who should lay hold on and avouch that covenant as Abraham did, and not else."[†]

Again and again the words "to you and your seed" are quoted to support

---

[*] Vos, 37.
[†] Owen, *Works*, Volume 16, 261-62.

the concept of infant baptism.

The Heidelberg Catechism (1563), which is appealed to by the Dutch and German Reformed churches, also uses the argument taken from the covenant with Abraham. Question 74 to be used on the Lord's Day 27 is, "Are infants also to be baptized?" Answer: "Yes, for since they, as well as adults, are included in the covenant and Church of God . . ." Their proof verse is Genesis 17:7.

Likewise, Calvin's argument for infant baptism is, "But if the covenant still remains firm and steadfast, it applies no less today to the children of Christians than under the Old Testament it pertained to the infants of the Jews."*

To highlight and to spotlight what I believe to be the error of this teaching I would like to simplify the argument into a syllogism, that is a major premise, a minor premise and a conclusion.

> MAJOR PREMISE: The Covenant of Grace as given to Abraham includes all of God's people and remains for all time.
> MINOR PREMISE: Infants were included with their parents in the Covenant of Grace given to Abraham.
> CONCLUSION: The infants of believers are included with their parents in the Covenant of Grace in the New Testament Church.

I grant the major premise. It is quite true that all God's people, believers in all ages, are in the Covenant of Grace. I deny the minor premise that infants are included in the Covenant of Grace in the Abrahamic Covenant. To disprove this premise I want to look at who were included in the Covenant of circumcision and what is the promise of the Covenant of Grace.

All Abraham's physical seed were included in the Abrahamic Covenant of circumcision.

There were no exceptions as to who was included in the Abrahamic Covenant of circumcision. It was every Jewish infant. It was the whole nation. The command is absolutely clear, "Every male child among you shall

---

* Calvin, *Institutes*, Book IV, chapter 16, 1328.

be circumcised" (Gen. 17:10). Further, "every male child in your generations . . ." (Gen. 17:12). "My covenant shall be in your flesh for an everlasting covenant" (Gen. 17:13).

From these verses we see that there was no qualification except birth for circumcision. It was not dependent on the faith of the parents nor even on their outward morality. "Every male child among you shall be circumcised." This was God's command! This is why Ishmael and Esau were circumcised and their children after them. The children of the faithful and unfaithful, the godly and the ungodly, were circumcised. And this was to be done "throughout their generations," even for all time. This covenant of circumcision included all Abraham's descendants, the whole Jewish nation.

What is the promise of the Covenant of Grace?

The promise of the Covenant of Grace is, "I will be God to you and to your seed after you" (Gen. 17:7), and "I will give unto thee and to thy seed after thee the land . . ." (vs. 8). As Calvin well says, "the primary promises, which contained that covenant . . . were spiritual and referred to eternal life."* They were spiritual promises. The promise of "being God to you and to your seed" includes all the promises within it. No spiritual promise is lacking to those in the Covenant of Grace. It is "every spiritual blessing in the heavenly places in Christ" (Eph. 1:3).

John Owen addresses this, "Whoever hath an interest in any one promise has an interest in them all, and in the fountain-love from whence they flow. He to whom any drop of their sweetness floweth may follow it up unto the spring."†

All the promises are sure and are certain to everyone in the Covenant of Grace.

As Calvin says, "they refer to eternal life." Everyone in the Covenant of Grace obtains all the blessings in it including eternal life. Not one person in the covenant can be lost. It is a sure covenant. The promises cannot fail for they are made by Him who cannot lie. The Covenant of Grace is not a legal covenant as the covenant of law so it is not conditional. All the conditions

---

* *Ibid.,* 1334.
† Owen, *Works,* Volume 11, 233.

are met for all those in the covenant by the Surety of the Covenant, our blessed Lord. Praise the Lord!

John Owen's proof of this is unassailable. For a full and powerful presentation that all the promises are sure and unconditional I would turn you to Owen's treatise on the doctrine of the saint's perseverance, volume 11 of his *Works*. I will just quote a few of his arguments.

"Saith he, then, to believers, those whom he taketh into covenant with him: 'This is my covenant with you' (in the performance whereof his all-sufficiency, truth, and faithfulness, with all other his glorious attributes, are eminently engaged), 'I will be your God' (what that expression intends is known, and the Lord here explains, by instancing in some eminent spiritual mercies thence flowing, as sanctification, and acceptance with him by the forgiveness of sins), 'and that for ever, in an everlasting covenant, I will not turn away from you to do you good.' This plainly God saith of himself, and this is all we say of him in the business, and which (having so good an author) we must say, whether men will hear or whether they will forbear. Whether it be right in the sight of God to hearken unto men more than unto God, let us judge. Truly they have a sad task, in my apprehension, who are forced to sweat and labour to alleviate and take off the testimony of God.'"*

"We affirm, (1) That the promise God made unto, or the covenant he makes here with, his people, is distinguished from or opposed unto the covenant that was broken, upon this account, that that was broken by the default of them with whom it was made, but God would take care and provide that this should not fail, but be everlasting, Jer. 31:32; 32:40; Heb. 8:8, 9. (2) that the intendment of God in this promise, and the administration of this covenant, with means and power mentioned therein, is the abiding of his saints with him, or rather, primarily and principally, his abiding with them, notwithstanding all such interveniences as he will powerfully prevent from even interposing to the disturbance of that communion he

_____

* *Ibid.*, 208-09.

taketh them into. 'I will,' saith he, 'make an everlasting covenant with them, that I will not turn away from them, to do them good.'"*

"This promise being by the prophet and apostle insisted on as containing the grace whereby, eminently and peculiarly, the new covenant is distinguished from that which was abolished, if the grace mentioned therein be only the laying a powerful and strong obligation on men to duty and obedience, upon the account of the gracious and bountiful dealing of God with them, both as to their temporal and spiritual condition, I desire to know wherein the difference of it from the old covenant, as to the collation of grace, doth consist, and whether ever God made a covenant with man wherein he did not put sufficient obligations of this kind upon him unto obedience; and if so, what are the 'better promises' of the new covenant, and what eminent and singular things as to the bestowing of grace are in it; which things here are emphatically expressed to the uttermost."†

"I pray, to what end, is all this noise? As though any had ever asserted that God promised to continue his love and gracious acceptation always to his saints, and yet took no care nor had promised that they should be continued saints, but would suffer them to turn very devils. It is as easy for men to confute hypotheses created in their own imaginations as to cast down men of straw of their own framing and setting up. We say, indeed, that God hath faithfully promised that he will never leave nor forsake believers; but withal that he hath no less faithfully engaged himself that they shall never wickedly depart from him, but that they shall continue saints and believers. Yea (if I may so say), promising always to accept them freely, it is incumbent on his holy Majesty, upon the account of his truth, faithfulness, and righteousness, to preserve them such as, without the least dishonour to his grace and holiness, yea, to the greatest advantage of his glory, he may always accept them, delight in them, and rejoice over them; and so he tells us he doth, Jer. 31:3, 'Yea, I have loved thee with an

---

* *Ibid.*, 220.
† *Ibid.*, 221.

everlasting love; therefore with loving-kindness have I drawn thee.' He draws us with kindness to follow him, obey him, live unto him, abide with him, because he loves us with an everlasting love."

"That these promises of God do not properly, and as to their original rise, depend on any conditions in believers, or by them to be fulfilled, but are the fountains and springs of all conditions whatever that are required to be in them or expected from them, though the grace and obedience of believers are often mentioned in them as the means whereby they are carried on, according to the appointment of God, unto the enjoyment of what is promised or continued in it.'"

All right, I have tried to clear the ground. So let us try to gather up these thoughts. First, the covenant of circumcision was with all Abraham's natural seed. Secondly, the promises of the Covenant of Grace are spiritual promises and include eternal life. Thirdly, the promises are "sure to all the seed."

Our argument is that spiritual promises were not made to Abraham's natural descendants. The spiritual promises are only made to his spiritual seed. Therefore, his natural descendants are not in the Covenant of Grace for all in the Covenant of Grace receive all the spiritual promises; including eternal life. But did every male who was circumcised receive eternal life? Obviously not. The nation as a whole were unfaithful and never received the spiritual promises.

How can it be that the whole nation of the Jews was in the Covenant of Grace since God effectually saves all in the Covenant of Grace. Why then were they not saved? Why then are they now "enemies concerning the gospel"? Why is it that "Israel has not obtained what it seeks"? Why did they then not "submit to the righteousness of God"? They did not because the whole nation of Israel is not included in the Covenant of Grace. They failed of the promises and "stumbled at that stumbling stone." See Romans 9-11 from which I have quoted the above and where Paul thoroughly explains who the true Israel is and why the physical seed failed to obtain the promise. They will all be put to shame. But none in the Covenant of Grace will be put

---

* *Ibid.*, 237.

to shame. No, the carnal seed are not the heirs of promise! They are of the law. The promise is "given to those who believe."

Then, with whom besides Abraham was the Covenant of Grace made? Paul tells us in Galatians 3:16, "Now to Abraham and his Seed were the promises made. He does not say, 'And to seeds,' as of many but as of one, 'And to your Seed,' who is Christ." Paul quotes part of the promise to Abraham to show us to whom it was made. The phrase he quotes from the Old Testament is, "And to your seed." What verse or verses are these words taken from? They are taken from Genesis 17:7-8 and Genesis 13:15. This phrase, "and to your seed," is found in these three verses. This phrase is not found elsewhere in the promises given to Abraham. It is not in another verse. What is the promise referred to? God's promise "to be a God unto you, and to your seed after you" and to give the land "to you and to your seed." It is the spiritual promise of the Covenant of Grace. To whom was it made? Paul explains that it was not to seeds, that is it was not to Abraham's descendants. Rather it was to one seed or one descendant "who is Christ."

The translations such as the NASV and the NIV that use the word "descendants" rather than "seed" to translate the Hebrew word "zera" use the wrong word in Genesis 13:15 and 17:7-8. The word used has to be ambiguous in regard to number. That is, it has to be a noun that can mean either singular or plural. The collective noun seed is such a word. *Offspring* is also a good translation. Unless such a word is used Paul's argument is not comprehensible. In Galatians 3:16 Paul is saying that in the phrase "and to your seed," as found in Genesis 13:15 and 17:7-8 the word seed is not referring to plural "seeds" but is referring to one "seed"; that is one descendant. Paul identifies this one descendant as Christ. If the word seed is replaced by the word descendants Paul's argument becomes nonsense in Galatians 3:16. Thus, the phrase "and to your seed" that the Apostle Paul quotes from Genesis 17:7-8 cannot be translated "and to your descendants." The vital truth Paul teaches is that the promises of the Covenant of Grace made to Abraham were not made to his natural descendants (plural) but to his one descendant (singular) even Christ.

Paul does not mean that seed is in the singular therefore it refers to one individual. He knew it is a collective noun and thus can mean more than one.

But as John Brown says, " It is just as if he had said, 'In the passage I refer to, the word seed is used of an individual, just as when it is employed of Seth, Gen. 4:25, where it is called another seed.' "* Thus, Genesis 17:7-8 refers to Christ and his spiritual seed not to Abraham's natural seed.

I cannot say it better than Hendriksen who said,

"However, in keeping with the point which he is driving home, namely, that God promised salvation not to Abraham's physical descendants but to true believers, to them all (whether Jew or Gentile) and to them alone, he is saying that this great blessing is concentrated in one person, namely, Christ. It is in him alone, that all these multitudes of believing Jews and Gentiles are blessed. It is in this sense that seed is singular, definitely not plural. It is true that the physical descendants of Abraham inherited the physical land of Canaan, according to God's promise (Gen. 12:7; 13:15; 15:18; 17:8; 24:7), but even Abraham already knew that there was more to this promise than appeared on the surface. The promised country on earth was the type of 'the better country,' the heavenly, reserved for believers in the Lord Jesus Christ, for them all and for them alone, as is beautifully stated in Heb. 11:8-16. Now the one and only heir of that 'country' is Christ, for he is the Son by nature. It is by his grace that believers, as children by adoption, are joint-heirs with him, (Rom. 8:17). And as for the basic promise, expressed from the beginning in spiritual terms, the promise according to which God assures Abraham that he will be his God and that in Abraham's seed all the nations of the earth will be blessed, (17:7; 22:18), is it not very obvious that this promise also, in its fulfillment, was centered exclusively in one person, namely, Christ? The many are blessed in the One!"†

And again,

"Accordingly, Paul's intention in writing, He does not say, 'And to

---

* Brown, *Galatians*, 59.
† Hendriksen, *Galatians*, 135.

the seeds,' as (referring) to many, but as (referring) to one, 'And to your seed,' which is Christ," is to show, that God's promise to Abraham, in its richest, spiritual meaning, was to be fulfilled in connection with one—and not more than one—definite person, Christ the true seed; b. that all those—and only those—who are 'in him' are saved; c. that had the case been otherwise, that is, had the promised blessings been dispersed indiscriminately among an indefinite aggregate of individuals, such plurality would have been definitely indicated; and d. that being thus concentrated unchangeably in the one seed, Christ, nothing, not even the law, is able to nullify this promise, the truth to which the apostle gives further expression by continuing in verse 17.""

John Stott argues in his commentary on Galatians,

> "God's purpose was not just to give the land of Canaan to the Jews, but to give salvation (a spiritual inheritance) to believers who are in Christ. Further, Paul argues, this truth was implicit in the word God used, which was not the plural 'children' or 'descendants', but the singular 'seed' or 'posterity.' a collective noun referring to Christ and to all those who are in Christ by faith (verse 16)."[†]

> "So every sinner who trusts in Christ crucified for salvation, quite apart from any merit or good works, receives the blessing of eternal life and thus inherits the promise of God made to Abraham."[‡]

The Paedobaptist theologians when writing of infant baptism say the promise of the Covenant of Grace in Genesis 17:7-8 was to all Abraham's natural seed who were thus in the Covenant of Grace. Paul says, not so. It was not to his natural descendants but to his one descendant, even Christ.

Why have the Paedobaptist theologians failed to use Paul's explanation of seed? A large part of their failure is because they do not use the New

---

[*] *Ibid.*, 137.
[†] Stott, 88.
[‡] *Ibid.*, 89.

Testament to explain the Old Testament. They tend to rather read the Old Testament into the New. Galatians 3 and Romans 4 explain to whom the Abrahamic Covenant was given and its spiritual meaning but these portions are largely ignored in the Paedobaptist presentation of infant baptism.

Finally, let us state once again: None of Abraham's natural descendants were or are in the Covenant of Grace by natural birth. The Covenant of Grace is to Abraham's spiritual descendants who enter it by spiritual birth not natural birth. The Covenant of Grace was made with Christ and to all those "in Him." But all Abraham's natural seed were born in Adam not in Christ. Only believers, who are Abraham's true seed, as Galatians 3 abundantly proves, are in the Covenant of Grace. They and they alone, are "the heirs of promise" for the promise is "given to those who believe."

Part 2

THE ORDINANCES

7

Ordinances or Sacraments

I prefer to call Baptism and the Lord's Supper "ordinances" rather than "sacraments." The word sacrament comes from the Latin, *sacramentum*, which means *sacred*. The word "sacrament" is not found in Scripture. It was applied to all things sacred and the Roman Catholic church has seven sacraments. The word sacrament, at least to some people, speaks of the Roman Catholic sacraments. For that reason I think the word ordinance is more suitable—and also because Christ ordained Baptism and the Lord's Supper, so that we can call them ordinances.

In the book, *The Seceders*, published by Banner of Truth, it is written of J. C. Philpot that, "He maintained that Baptism and the Lord's Supper were not sacraments at all, i.e., immediate channels of divine grace, but ordinances 'which may or may not be attended with a divine blessing, but are not channels of spiritual life.' "*

Generally, people who call Baptism and the Lord's Supper sacraments believe they are channels of grace. As Hodge wrote under the heading Doctrine of the Reformed Church, "The first point clearly taught on this subject in the Symbols of the Reformed Church is that the sacraments are real means of grace, that is, means appointed and employed by Christ for conveying the benefits of his redemption to his people."†

Baptists would deny that they are immediate channels of divine grace and so call them ordinances. We would agree with Zwingli and the

---

* Philpot, 118.
† Hodge, *Systematic Theology*, Volume 3, 499.

Remonstrants.

> "According to the doctrine of Zwingle afterwards adopted by the Remonstrants, the sacraments are not properly 'means of grace.' They were not ordained to signify, seal, and apply to believers the benefits of Christ's redemption. They were indeed intended to be significant emblems of the great truths of the Gospel. Baptism was intended to teach the necessity of the soul's being cleansed from guilt by the blood of Christ and purified from the pollution of sin by the renewing of the Holy Ghost. They were further designed to be perpetual memorials of the work of redemption, and especially to be the means by which men should, in the sight of the Church and of the world, profess themselves to be Christians."*

Lloyd-Jones in his book, *The Church and the Last Things*, says on page 30 that, "a sacrament conveys grace." He then illustrates this by an engagement ring and says, "that when the young woman receives the engagement ring, she feels she has received something additional, something extra."

If this is all that Paedobaptists mean by the sacraments being a "channel of grace" and that they "convey grace" we could agree. Baptism, like an engagement ring, can subjectively strengthen assurance. However, Paedobaptists believe that baptism conveys objective grace in a positive way to an infant. Grace is in the baptism. He receives something. He has gained something the unbaptized infant does not have. The baptism has operated of itself. The grace is in the act of baptism. It acts and does something. This is surely very close to grace *"ex opere operato"* that Lloyd-Jones so strongly opposes on page 28 of his book. The Paedobaptist view makes a sacrament a necessity since it is required to convey grace and be a channel of spiritual life. This I deny and would agree with J. C. Philpot that it is an ordinance "which may or may not be attended with a divine blessing." Certain it is that spiritual life does not come through the channel of baptism. Does baptism convey life to the dead? As to Baptism being a sign and seal I would direct

---

* Hodge, 498.

the reader to the section, "Signs and Seals" later in this book.

DEFINITION

The Westminster Shorter Catechism defines a sacrament,

> "A sacrament is an holy ordinance instituted by Christ; wherein, by visible signs, Christ and the benefits of the New Covenant are represented, sealed, and applied to believers." [Berkhof agrees and adds the words, "and these, in turn, give expression to their faith and allegiance to God."]*

We can see that this definition of sacrament is incompatible with infant baptism because of the phrase, "applied to believers." Infants, also, do not "give expression to their faith and allegiance to God" through infant baptism so that infant baptism contradicts the above definition of a sacrament and is inconsistent with its purpose. The baptism of believers is declaratory. The Lord's Supper is declaratory. Infant baptism is not declaratory. Therefore, since the purpose of the sacraments is declaratory, infant baptism is inconsistent with its purpose.

EFFICACY

Hodge states that "the sacraments are effectual as means of grace only, so far as adults are concerned, to those who by faith receive them. It is affirmed that their efficiency in conveying grace, is due solely to the blessing of Christ and the cooperation of his Spirit; and that such efficiency is experienced only by believers."†

Since its efficiency "is experienced only by believers" infants receiving it is only an empty form. It has no efficacy to infants.

---

* Berkhof, *Systematic Theology*, 617.
† *Ibid.*, 500.

VALIDITY

Hodge wrote something is valid if it avails for the end intended. As to the validity of baptism he said, "It involves on the part of both the administrator and the recipient the profession of the Christian religion."[*] "If a man receives the ordinance of baptism, he must intend to profess his faith in the gospel and to accept the terms of salvation therein presented."[†] An infant does none of these so that his baptism is invalid.

Thus we see that infant baptism is inconsistent and incompatible with the definition of a sacrament, with the efficacy of a sacrament and with the validity of a sacrament.

---

[*] *Ibid.,* 523.
[†] *Ibid.,* 524.

8

Baptism and the Lord's Supper

We hold that there are two ordinances. There is a unity in these two as well as harmony and coherence. This means that the same people should be recipients of both ordinances because a participation in them signifies that salvation has been applied to the recipients. Thus believers' baptism and believers' communion are consistent. If it is believed that infants are saved then infant baptism and infant communion are consistent. Infant baptism and believers' communion is inconsistent no matter what is believed.

Because Paedobaptists are inconsistent to give baptism to infants but not the Lord's Supper their arguments that condemn believers' baptism also condemn believers' communion, (which they support). Likewise, their arguments that support infant baptism likewise support infant communion, (which they deny).

They argue for infant baptism by using the analogy of circumcision. The analogy of the Passover is an argument for infant communion. Circumcision, they argue, is a long settled institution so infants should be baptized. The Passover, which was participated in by the whole family, was also a long settled institution. Nothing explicitly forbids infant baptism so infant baptism is practiced. However, nothing explicitly forbids infant communion but it is not practiced. They say a credible profession of faith is not required for baptism but they require it for communion. They say they baptize infants, not on their confession of faith, but on God's covenantal promise. Why then is a confession of faith needed for communion? Isn't the promise sufficient? Why deny the covenantal meal to those whom they say belong to the covenant?

Dr. Murray argues vigorously that the greater privileges under the New Testament include infant baptism. This argument, if it is valid, would be equally valid for infant communion. Paedobaptists say that we make ourselves judges of men's hearts if we require a credible profession of faith for baptism but they require a credible profession of faith for communion. They argue that believers' infants belong to the church so they should be baptized. If they belong to the church shouldn't they have the privilege of its communion meal?

Dr. John Murray's reasoning to forbid children's communion is, "that the very things signified by the Lord's Supper involve intelligent understanding on the part of the participant."[*] This is our argument against infant baptism. He goes on to say, "The things signified by baptism, however, do not necessarily involve intelligent understanding and baptism may therefore be administered to those who are incapable of such understanding." This is quite inconsistent. Since "baptism signifies union with Christ in his death, burial and resurrection" (Dr. Murray's statement), it necessarily involves intelligent understanding to make it more than an empty form.

Dr. Murray wrote concerning the inconsistency of infant baptism and believers' communion:

> "At the outset it should be admitted that if Paedobaptists are inconsistent in this discrimination, then the relinquishment of infant baptism is not the only way of resolving the inconsistency. It could be resolved by going in the other direction, namely, that of admitting infants to the Lord's supper. And when all the factors entering into this dispute are taken into account, particularly the principle involved in infant baptism, then far less would be at stake in admitting infants to the Lord's supper than would be at stake in abandoning infant baptism in the divine economy of grace."[†]

---

[*] Murray, footnote on p. 78.
[†] *Ibid.*, 77.

It is evident that Dr. Murray would never have relinquished infant baptism. It does seem better to relinquish the error of infant baptism to be consistent rather than to add another error, infant communion, to be consistent. Yet for the health of the evangelical Paedobaptist churches it is much better for them to be inconsistent and refuse infant communion for this would not require a profession of faith for full communicant membership and would inevitably lead to an empty formalism bringing in the unregenerate into full membership.

However, by having communicant and confederate membership they divide the local church and in practicality they have a church within a church. In fact it is much like a Baptist church within a Paedobaptist church. During the time of the Reformation there came about what has been called "*ecclesiola in Ecclesia*" or a little church in the church. Luther himself was moved in that direction as were many others.

Lloyd-Jones wrote about that:

> "Luther's relationship to the Anabaptists is a most fascinating one; it is a kind of ambivalent relationship. He reacted against them, and yet in a sense he admired them and was a little bit jealous of the wonderful discipline that they were able to exercise in their own churches. He had to admit that there was a quality of life in their churches which was absent in the churches to which he belonged. So he reacts in two ways to them; he has got to discipline his people against them, and yet he wishes to have in his church the kind of thing that was working so well in their churches. He seemed to be failing to reform the whole church; well then, the best he could do was second best, which was to gather together the people who are truly Christian into a kind of inner church."[*]

Why did these movements occur? I believe there were a number of reasons but the foremost was because the churches included many who were Christian in name only. How did so many unregenerate get into the churches? Many entered through infant baptism. The issues immediately

---

[*] Lloyd-Jones, *The Puritans: Their Origins and Successors*, 133-34.

after the Reformation were: What is the church? What is a Christian? Who should be admitted to church membership? These questions are vital questions for today.

The Reformers failed to bring back the New Testament church. They tried to work with the situation as they found it and so thought of an *"ecclesiola in Ecclesia"* because of the dead wood in the churches. They did not go back to the New Testament and try to put the New Testament pattern into practice. May God help us to humbly, in love, and with courage to go back to the New Testament.

9

Relationship of Baptism to Circumcision

This relationship goes to the heart of the issue of infant baptism. This is the very foundation of the argument for infant baptism as given by Paedobaptist theologians and as held forth in their catechisms and confessions.

A representative of the Dutch Reformed position is Dr. Berkhof who writes, "In the new dispensation baptism is by divine authority substituted for circumcision as the initiatory sign and seal of the Covenant of Grace."[*]

This is repeated in the "Form for the Baptism of Infants," which says, "Since, then, baptism has come in the place of circumcision, the children should be baptized as heirs of the kingdom of God and of His covenant."

The Heidelberg Catechism states under Question 74,

> "Are infants also to be baptized?" Answer: "Yes; for since they, as well as adults, are included in the covenant and Church of God, and since both redemption from sin and the Holy Spirit, the Author of faith, are through the blood of Christ promised to them no less than to adults, they must also by baptism, as a sign of the covenant, be ingrafted into the Christian Church, and distinguished from the children of unbelievers, as was done in the old covenant or testament by circumcision, instead of which baptism was instituted in the new covenant."[†]

---

[*] Berkhof, 633.
[†] *Psalter Hymnal*, 33.

Dr. Berkhof sums up their position, "It will be observed that all these statements are based on the commandment of God to circumcize the children of the covenant for in the last analysis that commandment is the ground of infant baptism."* That is a significant statement.

Professor Murray is a good representative for the Presbyterian position. His argument is basically the same as the Dutch argument. It is found on pages 49-50 of his *Christian Baptism*. His first point starts with circumcision as commanded in Genesis 17:1-14. Their argument in a simplified form is:

- Infants were commanded to be circumcised and so "are included in the covenant and church of God." Proof text: Genesis 17:1-14.

- Circumcision had the same spiritual significance as baptism. Proof text: Romans 4:11.

- Circumcision has been replaced by baptism. Proof text: Colossians 2:11.

- Their conclusion is: therefore, infants of believers should be baptized.

As an aside, if eating the Passover is substituted for circumcision in the above argument and if the argument is valid for baptism of infants then it is also valid for infant or children's communion. Why then do our Paedobaptist friends reject children's communion without a New Testament revocation? The Passover, too, was a "long settled institution" as was circumcision. Be that as it may, I would like to examine the three points of the Paedobaptist argument as written above.

Point 1. For the conclusion taken from the three points to be valid (assuming at present that points two and three are true) it would be necessary to state in point one that only believers' children were circumcised.

However, all Jewish infants, without exception, were to be circumcised. It had nothing to do with the spiritual condition of the parents. Is that true of infant baptism? The parallel of circumcision and infant baptism fails in this first point.

---

* Berkhof, 638.

Since the church, according to Professor Murray, "consists of those who are united to Christ and are members of his body. It is the communion of saints. And it is precisely that body of believers in fellowship with Christ and with one another," * then it is evident that the infants that were circumcised were not included in the church. None were believers when circumcised and the overwhelming majority later evidenced by their life that "they were a rebellious nation." If only God's elect are in the Covenant of Grace then very few of the circumcised infants in Israel were ever in the Covenant of Grace. As Paul writes, "They are not all Israel who are of Israel nor are they all children because they are the seed of Abraham" (Rom. 9:6-7).

Point 2. According to the Paedobaptist position: Circumcision had the same spiritual significance as baptism. Their proof verse is Romans 4:11, "And he received the sign of circumcision, a seal of the righteousness of the faith which he had while still uncircumcised, that he might be the father of all those who believe, though they are uncircumcised, that righteousness might be imputed to them also."

The argument depends on the significance of circumcision to Abraham being the same to all who are circumcised. Does it carry the same significance to everyone or was Abraham unique such that circumcision had a specific purpose in regard to him that it does not have in regard to others? Why was Abraham circumcised? This verse says, "he received the sign of circumcision . . . that he might be the father of all those who believe, though they be uncircumcised." Abraham has a unique place in the history of redemption.

"To Abraham we grant this transcendent privilege that he had the peculiar honor to be 'the father of all the faithful.' "†

He, and he alone, is "the father of all those who believe." The phrase (*eis to einai*) means in order that, "because 'eis' with the infinitive, commonly expresses design, but also because the whole context shows that the apostle intends to bring in view the purpose of God in the justification of Abraham."‡

---

* *Ibid.,* 42.
† Goodwin, 429.
‡ Hodge, *Romans,* 117.

Note, circumcision is a sign in regard to "the purpose of God in the justification of Abraham." It was a sign of his paternity of his spiritual seed.

Thus, it was a sign that Abraham is "the father of all them that believe though they are uncircumcised." The true descendants of Abraham are not the circumcised but believing Jews and believing Gentiles. To Abraham circumcision was "a seal of the righteousness of the faith." It confirmed that he was justified. It was not such a seal to the circumcised unbelieving Jews for they were not justified.

Why was circumcision "a seal of the righteousness of faith" to Abraham? It was a seal of the righteousness of faith to Abraham because Abraham had faith. It was "a seal of the righteousness of the faith which he had while still uncircumcised." It was not such a seal even to Isaac or Jacob for when circumcised they did not have faith and, of course, it was not such a seal to the unbelieving Jews. Therefore, circumcision did not have the same spiritual significance as baptism.

Point 3. The third point in the Paedobaptist position is that circumcision has been replaced by baptism. Their proof verse is Colossians 2:11, "In Him you were also circumcised with the circumcision made without hands, by putting off the body of the sins of the flesh, by the circumcision of Christ."

It should be noted that physical circumcision is not mentioned in this verse. Since it is not mentioned it is not teaching that baptism replaces physical circumcision. The circumcision that is spoken of is "circumcision made without hands." All Jewish circumcision was made with hands. Colossians 2:11 is not talking of that circumcision but of spiritual circumcision. This spiritual circumcision is called, "the circumcision of Christ," that is it is Christ who is the subject of circumcision, he produces it, he effects it. Thus, this spiritual circumcision of Christ is contrasted with the physical circumcision of Moses. The circumcision "made without hands" is of God. It is nothing less than regeneration, effected by Christ "through faith the working of God, who raised Him from the dead" (Col. 2:12), having been, "made alive together with Him" (vs. 13).

This spiritual circumcision occurs at conversion when the believer puts off "the body of the sins of the flesh." Since this is pictured in water baptism

Paul goes on to say, "buried with Him in baptism, in which you also were raised with him."

> "The putting away of the old nature was openly declared in Christian baptism, which is the visible covenant-seal of the new Israel, just as circumcision was of the old. The picture of being buried beneath the water and rising again is a vivid portrayal of the same truth as that which circumcision has been declaring; for the old man is buried that the new man may rise." (Op. Cit. In loc.)[*]

Therefore, we can say that circumcision and baptism are similar symbols and symbolize the same thing in regard to believers. Circumcision, as we will see later, had a different meaning when given to Jewish infants. Does this mean that baptism has superseded circumcision? Yes, in regard to believers but no, in regard to unbelievers and infants. What has come in the place of physical circumcision is spiritual circumcision. The shadow is bodily circumcision, the substance is spiritual circumcision not baptism.

God's great Old Testament promise was, "And the Lord your God will circumcise your heart and the heart of your descendants, to love the Lord your God with all your heart and with all your soul, that you may live" (Deut. 30:6). This promise was fulfilled to the Colossians. All in the Colossian church were circumcised spiritually and it was through faith. Therefore, no infants belonged to the Colossian church.

This portion further brings forth the truth that the ones baptized were previously circumcised in Christ that is they were regenerate. This regeneration is evidenced "by the putting off the body of the sins of the flesh." This excludes all infants for none give any evidence of regeneration.

The Paedobaptist position, regarding Colossians 2:11-12 is given by Warfield in his *Selected Shorter Writings*.

> "Helpfully Paul believed that circumcision and baptism were but two symbols of the same change of heart and declares when speaking to a Christian audience that in Christ you were also circumcised. But

---

[*] Carson, *Commentary of Colossians and Philemon.*

how? With a circumcision not made with hands in putting off the body of the flesh, that is, in the circumcision of Christ. But what was this Christ ordained circumcision? The apostle continues, 'having been buried with him in baptism, in which you also were raised with Him . . . from the dead.' Hence, in baptism they were buried with Christ and this burial with Christ was the circumcision which Christ ordained."

Warfield says "baptism . . . was the circumcision which Christ ordained." He seems to be talking about physical circumcision since he begins by calling it a symbol of a change of heart. However, Colossians 2:11-12 is not talking about physical circumcision but "circumcision made without hands." The circumcision of Christ in verse 11 is not physical circumcision ordained by Christ but spiritual circumcision of heart done by Christ.

"The apostle adds, in conclusion, that this is the circumcision of Christ. First, because our Lord and Saviour has expressly instituted it in his gospel, commanding us to be born again, to deny ourselves, to change our deportment, to put on a simplicity and humility like that of little children, and to break all the ties which fasten us to the flesh and the world, if we will follow him and have part in his kingdom. This is the first and most important instruction contained in the Scriptures. Secondly, it is the circumcision of Christ, because it is he alone who is the author of it, and effects it in us; neither is there anything besides his gospel which can unclothe man of this body of the sins of the flesh; for it is impossible that a soul on whom the doctrine of Jesus Christ has been imprinted by the power of the Holy Ghost should fail to renounce the world and the flesh."*

I think Warfield had a misconception of the identity of circumcision in the text. He identifies physical circumcision with baptism but the text says that baptism is related not to physical circumcision but spiritual circumcision.

I would like to sum up our investigation into the three points of the

---

* Daille, *An Exposition of the Epistle to the Colossians*, 317.

Paedobaptist position that they take from Genesis 17:1-14, Romans 4:11 and Colossians 2:11-12. The former (Gen. 17:1-14) does not teach that infants of believers were circumcised but, rather, that all Jewish infants were circumcised without regard to any spiritual qualification. Romans 4:11 teaches that circumcision was "a seal of the righteousness of faith" to a believer but not to unbelievers. Colossians 2:11-12 teaches that baptism is related to spiritual or heart circumcision and does not mention physical circumcision at all. In each case their textual exegesis is inadequate and faulty.

The Old Covenant sign was circumcision and this marked out Israel after the flesh. The New Covenant sign is spiritual circumcision and this marks out the spiritual Israel, the church. "We are the circumcision" (Phil. 3:3). There are two kinds of circumcision just as there are two kinds of Jews. The Jewish nation although circumcised in the flesh was uncircumcised in heart. In contrast all God's true people are circumcised in heart.

> "For he is not a Jew who is one outwardly, nor is that circumcision which is outward in the flesh; but he is a Jew who is one inwardly, and circumcision is that of the heart, in the Spirit, and not in the letter, whose praise is not from men but from God" (Rom. 2:28-29).

10

The Significance of Circumcision

Circumcision is called a sign and also a seal. In Abraham's case it was "a seal of the righteousness of the faith." This is the very heart of the gospel; justification by faith. Abraham was accepted by God and justified by faith. He was accounted righteous by faith. Circumcision was thus a seal and sign of the Covenant of Grace. Abraham's election, calling and faith are documented in the scriptures and here in Romans 4 it is emphasized that he believed before being circumcised. Abraham was in the Covenant of Grace, as are all believers. Everyone in the new covenant is regenerate. Everyone is a believer. There are no unbelievers in the Covenant of Grace. It is made up of only believers; not believers and their children.

We could call Abraham's circumcision Believers' Circumcision. As such it was the forerunner of Believers' Baptism. Believers' Baptism has replaced Believers' Circumcision. They are parallel. Some of the parallel features are:

- Abraham was circumcised as an adult.
- Abraham was circumcised while a believer
- Abraham's circumcision followed his faith.
- Abraham was in the Covenant of Grace when circumcised.
- Abraham had been called and justified before he was circumcised.
- To Abraham circumcision was a sign of the Covenant of Grace.
- Circumcision was "a seal of the righteousness of faith" to Abraham.

- Circumcision was received voluntarily.
- Circumcision was received consciously.
- Circumcision carried spiritual promises.
- The qualification for circumcision was faith.

None of the above applied to infant circumcision. It may be said that Abraham is the only example we find in the scriptures of a believer being circumcised in the Old Testament. The usual circumcision was circumcision of infants which had another meaning from Abraham's circumcision. Infant circumcision was corporate, external and physical while Abraham's circumcision was individual and spiritual in emphasis.

IN REGARD TO ISHMAEL

A question of great importance is: Why was Ishmael circumcised? Dr. Murray says that in regard to Ishmael and Esau, "The covenant was established with neither."*

Quite so. Ishmael was never in the Covenant of Grace. "As for Ishmael, I have heard you . . . but my covenant I will establish with Isaac" (Gen. 17:20-21). Ishmael never had union and communion with Jehovah. Why did God command Abraham to circumcise him? Since he was never in the Covenant of Grace circumcision was not a sign and seal to him of the Covenant of Grace. Abraham cried, " 'Oh, that Ishmael might live before you!' Then God said, 'No' " (Gen. 17:18-19). Yet he received a sign of the covenant. Circumcision is a sign of the covenant. "You shall be circumcised in the flesh of your foreskins, and it shall be a sign of the covenant between me and you" (Gen. 17:11). What covenant was it a sign of for Ishmael?

Ishmael, as all unbelievers, was in the Covenant of Law. Circumcision was a sign of the Covenant of Law to Ishmael. He could not receive it as a sign of the Covenant of Grace. What did circumcision signify in regard to Ishmael? It was not a seal of the righteousness of faith since he had no faith. It signified that he was an Israelite belonging to the family of Abraham. To

---

* Murray, 60.

Ishmael it was simply a sign of an external relationship or of a merely racial and national identity. God promised Ishmael to multiply him and make him a great nation (see Gen. 17:20), but he never made spiritual promises to him. The spiritual promises were only attached to the Covenant of Grace.

> "The promise that Abraham should be the heir, possessor of Canaan, was to him and to his seed according to the law of circumcision; but the higher promise, 'that he should be the heir of the world' was 'through the righteousness of faith.' "*

Dr. Murray gives a meaning of the sign of circumcision,

> "These three notions—union and communion with God, the removal of defilement, and the righteousness of faith—are obviously, not antithetical. They are mutually complementary, and taken together, they indicate the deep soteric richness of the blessing that circumcision signifies and seals."†

That is true in Abraham's case but not in Ishmael's case. Ishmael died an unbeliever without God. He had never been united with God nor been in communion with God nor had his sins been cleansed nor was he righteous by faith. His circumcision never signified those things. What did it signify in regard to Ishmael? It was a sign of his national identity. Paedobaptists take the definition and significance of circumcision as it is defined in relation to Abraham, who was a believer before he received circumcision, and then apply this definition and significance to everyone including infants. This reasoning is not valid.

This type of reasoning led Dr. Murray to write, "Circumcision is the sign of this covenant in the highest reaches of its meaning and in its deepest spiritual significance"‡

Contrary to Dr. Murray, who eulogized circumcision with high praise,

---

* Brown, *Analytical Exposition of the Epistle of Paul to the Romans*, 53.
† Murray, 51.
‡ *Ibid.*, 49.

the apostle Paul does quite the opposite and denigrates circumcision. He wrote, "Circumcision is nothing . . ." (1 Cor. 7:19). It would be impossible to write that if "circumcision is the sign of this covenant in the highest reaches of its meaning and in its deepest spiritual significance." Circumcision is nothing! It is nothing according to the infallible scriptures. In Galatians the apostle says not once but twice: "neither circumcision nor uncircumcision avails anything" (Gal. 5:6; 6:15). Circumcision avails nothing regardless of who honors it. It avails nothing!

In the quote of Dr. Murray that is given above from page 51 he wrote that circumcision signifies and seals the, "deep soteric (saving) richness of the blessing." Paul says, "if you become circumcised Christ will profit you nothing" (Gal. 5:2). Paul is talking about circumcision as it is the sign of the Covenant of Law. Thus he utterly denied that he still preached circumcision although he had as an unsaved Pharisee (Gal. 5:11). In Philippians Paul speaks derogatorily of those who trust in and exalt circumcision as the "concision" that is the "mutilators." He called circumcision mutilation (Phil. 3:2).

Circumcision belonged to two covenants and its significance was both spiritual and natural. If this is not so the question that remains is: What was God's purpose in commanding males who were not in the Covenant of Grace to be circumcised? If it is a seal of the Covenant of Grace why did God command all Jewish males to be circumcised since the overwhelming majority were not true Jews and so outside the covenant?

> "For he is not a Jew who is one outwardly, nor is that circumcision which is outward in the flesh; but he is a Jew who is one inwardly, and circumcision is that of the heart, in the Spirit, and not in the letter; whose praise is not from men but from God" (Rom. 2:28-29).

Circumcision was a sign and seal of the physical nation the Jews. The Jews had two distinguishing traits. Their distinguishing physical trait was circumcision. Their distinguishing spiritual trait was uncircumcision. Stephen, just before being stoned, indicted them as, "You stiff-necked and uncircumcised in heart and ears! You always resist the Holy Spirit; as your fathers did, so do you" (Acts 7:51). The phrase, "the circumcised or the circumcision," means Jews in a physical sense in the New Testament. The "uncircumcised" signifies Gentiles. In the context of Romans 4 we find these phrases referring to Jews and Gentiles. Because of this facet of circumcision it was proper for unbelievers to be circumcised in the Old Testament. They were circumcised as Jews eight days after birth. They were not circumcised because they were God's spiritual children nor because they were children of believers. They were circumcised because they were the natural sons of Abraham.

This was vital because the spiritual promise was to come through Abraham's natural seed,

> "Who are Israelites, to whom pertain the adoption, the glory, the covenants, the giving of the law, the service of God, and the promises; of whom are the fathers and from whom, according to the flesh, Christ came, who is over all, the eternally blessed God. Amen" (Rom. 9:4-5).

Abraham's hope was in his natural seed, Christ. (Note that to Israel pertain the covenants, not covenant). The Jewish nation was to be kept separate from all nations to preserve them to be the family, the race, the nation of Abraham from which the Messiah, our glorious Lord, was to come. How well circumcision separated the Jews from other nations is seen in the reproof given to Peter for going and eating with Cornelius and his relatives, "You went in to uncircumcised men and ate with them" (Acts 11:3). This was unheard of.

Thus we see that two covenants were made with Abraham: the Covenant of Law and the Covenant of Grace.

> "It is to be remembered that there were two covenants made with Abraham. By the one, his natural descendants through Isaac were constituted a commonwealth—an external, visible community. By the other, his spiritual descendants were constituted a church. There cannot be a greater mistake than to confound the national covenant with the Covenant of Grace, and the commonwealth founded on the

one with the church founded on the other. When Christ came, the commonwealth was abolished, and there was nothing put in its place. The church remained . . . a spiritual society with spiritual promises, on the condition of faith in Christ."*

A further question is, why was circumcision discontinued in regard to believers in New Testament times? What made it inappropriate for the church? Because circumcision was a sign of being a Jew—it had tribal overtones. The "church", so called, included all the Jews. Circumcision was bound to a race, to a people. Every Jew was entitled to circumcision. This was a sacral society, "bound together by a common religious loyalty." The church and state were equal. This is Old Testament and pre-Christian and circumcision sustains such. Thus circumcision was dropped and baptism, a brand new ordinance, was commanded by Christ.

Circumcision as a sign of a race and a nation was no longer suitable in the new situation of a church that broke through all boundaries of race and nation. "In Christ there is neither Jew nor Gentile." Family, race or nation have nothing to do with the new creation, the church brought into being at Pentecost. Thus, baptism was ordained by Christ and it does not carry a blood line. The role of the family is done away with. Now men and women should individually examine themselves as to whether they qualify for the sacraments as commanded in 1 Corinthians 11:28, "Let a man examine himself." The question asked by the Ethiopian eunuch, "What hinders me from being baptized?" is a good question. But this was never so with circumcision. All Jews were automatically circumcised.

Also, since the Savior is not to come through our natural seed baptism does not have a function in regard to our natural seed as circumcision had. Praise God, the Savior has come. Baptism has no natural significance as circumcision had. What is the New Testament parallel to infant circumcision? There is none. Infant circumcision was to Israelite infants who "were by nature the children of wrath." There is of course, no sacrament for such found in the New Testament. As B. B. Warfield wrote,

---

* Hodge, *Princeton Review*, October 1853, 684.

"It is true that there is no express command to baptize infants in the New Testament, no express record of the baptism of infants, and no passages so stringently implying it that we must infer from them that infants were baptized."[*]

Dr. Murray must agree,

"It is only too apparent that if we had an express command or even a proven case with apostolic sanction, then the controversy would not have arisen; or at least it would be of a very different sort."[†]

In regard to our Lord, "And when eight days were completed for the circumcision of the child, His name was called Jesus . . ." (Luke 2:21).

The Lord Jesus, being born a Jew and a son of a daughter of Abraham, was circumcised under the Law of Moses. He was circumcised in obedience to God's command to Abraham, "Every male child among you shall be circumcised" (Gen. 17:10). All Jewish male infants were to be circumcised without exception. The only qualification was their natural birth as Jews.

But the circumcision that Christ underwent has far greater significance for his people. Christ was circumcised because he was born under the law. "God sent forth His Son, born of a woman, born under the law, to redeem those who were under the law, that we might receive the adoption of sons" (Gal. 4:4-5).

Since Christ was born under the law he became a debtor to keep the whole law. He was to keep the whole law throughout his life. Thus he became "the Lord our righteousness." But since he bore the sins of God's people he also came under the curse and punishment of the law. For this reason Christ submitted to the whole of the ceremonial law which included circumcision.

"But especially he was thereby engaged to keep the whole law for us; for Abraham's seed were all to be circumcised, and he that was circumcised was a debtor to the whole law: Gal.5:3, 'For I testify

---

[*] Warfield, 399.
[†] Murray, 72.

again to every man that is circumcised, that he is debtor to do the whole law.' And so the law will take hold of him, and so hereby he was made under the law; and this was one reason why he was a male child also, for they only were circumcised. Thus you see Christ hereby engaged to keep the law for us, yea, to satisfy for sin; for the ceremonial law was a bond against us, which he must cancel and destroy."[*]

What was God's purpose in Christ being born under the law? It was "to redeem those who were under the law" (Gal. 4:5). All God's people are also born under the law. All are born in the Covenant of Law being debtors to God's law. No one is born naturally into the Covenant of Grace. All infants, regardless of their parentage, are born under the law.

IN REGARD TO INFANTS

Although Abraham's circumcision could be called Believers' circumcision, infants' circumcision was unbelievers' circumcision. There is no parallel to infant circumcision in the New Testament for the Church. This is clearly shown by infant circumcision's components which are as follows:

- It was given to infants.
- It was given to unbelievers.
- It was given to all Abraham's natural descendants.
- It was given to those under law and its covenant.
- It was a sign of the old covenant.
- It was involuntarily received.
- It was unconsciously received.
- It carried only natural promises.
- It was given corporately.
- The qualification was birth as a Jew.

---

[*] Goodwin, 62.

Circumcision had both spiritual and natural significance. To the unbeliever it signified his natural birth as a Jew. To Abraham, a believer, it signified "the righteousness of faith" which he had before being circumcised. This helps us to meet an objection made by Paedobaptists, "*any argument against infant baptism is necessarily an argument against infant circumcision.*"* (italics retained).

This objection is raised because it is falsely assumed that God had the same purpose for circumcision in regard to Abraham that he had in regard to Ishmael and all Jewish infants. I have sought to prove above that that is not so. Calvin, likewise seems to overlook the different functions circumcision had,

> "For it is very clear from many testimonies of Scripture that circumcision was also a sign of repentance (Jer. 4:4; 9:25; cf. Deut. 10:16: 30:6). Then Paul calls it the seal of the righteousness of faith (Rom. 4:11). Therefore, let reason be required of God himself why he commanded it to be impressed on the bodies of infants. For since baptism and circumcision are in the same case, our opponents cannot give anything to one without conceding it to the other . . . since God communicated circumcision to infants as a sacrament of repentance and of faith, it does not seem absurd if they are now made participants in baptism unless men choose to rage openly at God's institution. But as in all God's acts, so in this very act also there shines enough wisdom and righteousness to repel the detractions of the impious."†

Without, I trust, being "impious" it should be noted that baptism and circumcision are not in the same case. He assumed the very point that is in controversy. Also, the verses that Calvin uses to support circumcision being a sign of repentance in reality say the opposite. In all the verses the physically circumcised Jews are spoken of as needing circumcision since they were uncircumcised, that is they were impenitent and had never been circumcised

---

* Booth, 109.
† Calvin, 2:1342-43.

in the heart.

> "Circumcise yourselves to the Lord, and take away the foreskin of your hearts, you men of Judah and inhabitants of Jerusalem, lest My fury come forth like fire, and burn so that no one can quench it, because of the evil of your doings" (Jer. 4:4).

> "Therefore circumcise the foreskin of your heart, and be stiff-necked no longer" (Deut. 10:16).

Obviously, circumcision was not a sign of repentance to such who had not repented. Their circumcision only marked them as the physical seed of Abraham. Physical circumcision was the sign of the physical nation the Jews. Spiritual or heart circumcision is the sign of the new nation, a spiritual nation, the Church. Another important distinction that Calvin overlooked is that circumcision of infants belongs to the Covenant of Law, a natural and necessary covenant. It was not by choice that infants received circumcision. Baptism of believers belongs to the Covenant of Grace, a free and voluntary covenant. Circumcision only is a sign of repentance if given to a believer (like Abraham) who had repented. God, of course, would never command a man to receive the sign of something he does not have. That would be a deception. How could an unbeliever receive "the seal of the righteousness of the faith" that he does not have? No unbeliever should be given baptism, whether an adult or infant, lest he hold a lie in his right hand.

All Jewish infants were born under the law and so received the sign of the covenant of law or works. Paul in Romans tells us that everyone is under the law for the law speaks to everyone who are under the law that every mouth may be stopped and all the world may become guilty before God. "Now we know that whatever the law says, it says to those who are under law, that every mouth may be stopped, and all the world may become guilty before God" (Rom. 3:19).

There are no exceptions. Everyone is under the curse of the law. The whole world is guilty. Every mouth is to be stopped. Why? Because all are guilty being under the law. All infants when circumcised were under the law not grace. As all are born physically uncircumcised whether born of circumcised fathers or not so all are born spiritually uncircumcised whether born of believers or not. It seems that David's mother was a child of God. In the eighty sixth psalm that is called "a Psalm of David" he speaks of his mother as being God's handmaid, "save the son of thy handmaid" (86:16). As Spurgeon wrote on this Psalm, "he gloried in being the son of a woman who herself belonged to the Lord." Yet David wrote, "Behold, I was brought forth in iniquity, and in sin my mother conceived me" (Psa. 51:5). David was born under law not the Covenant of Grace. Physical birth gets no one into the Covenant of Grace. Only those born of the Spirit are spirit (*i.e.*, spiritual) and so in the Covenant of Grace. To say that infants born of believers are born under the Covenant of Grace is to deny and reject the foundational doctrine that all are born, as David, in original sin. All are born children of wrath not children of grace. To say that the whole Jewish nation was in the Covenant of Grace because they were circumcised is to ignore Jewish history and clear scriptural statements.

If the whole nation was in the Covenant of Grace why does Jeremiah say, "All the house of Israel are uncircumcised in the heart" (Jer. 9:26)? For as R. R. Booth rightly wrote (in his defense of infant baptism), "to have an uncircumcised heart is to be unconverted and ungodly. By implication a regenerate and converted heart is a circumcised heart ...'" By this definition all the circumcised infants were unconverted and ungodly since they all had uncircumcised hearts according to Jeremiah 9:26.

A further question is: If the whole nation, being circumcised, was in the Covenant of Grace how could they be rejected and cast away? For they have been "cast away" (Rom. 11:15), "broken off" (vs. 17), "not spared" (vs. 21), and "all been committed to disobedience" (vs. 32). John Reisinger wrote,

> "If Israel was under the same covenant as the Church, then how can
> we be sure that God will not cast off the Church? Why is the Church's
> eternal security guaranteed when Israel's was not if both the Church
> and Israel are under the same covenant? The Biblical answer to these

---

* Booth, 101.

questions is simple. The Body of Christ can never be disowned by God because she is under a new and better covenant than the old covenant that Israel was under."*

It must be admitted that those who were circumcised were not in the Covenant of Grace or that they fell out of it. To choose the second alternative is to deny the perseverance of the saints. Indeed it is to deny the doctrines of grace and to take an Arminian stand. If the first alternative is chosen then the whole argument for infant baptism falls. However, that is the case; those circumcised were not in the Covenant of Grace and circumcision was not a sign of the Covenant of Grace to those unbelievers but a sign of the Covenant of Law.

Can anyone be in the Covenant of Grace and be eternally lost like our Paedobaptist brethren say? A couple of weeks ago I was translating Psalm 89 into the language of the people among whom we work. I was greatly struck by the change of person from "they" to "him" in verses 32 and 33.

> "If his sons forsake my law and do not walk in my judgments, if they break my statutes and do not keep my commandments, then will I visit their transgression with the rod, and their iniquity with stripes. Nevertheless my lovingkindness I will not utterly take from him, nor allow my faithfulness to fail. My covenant I will not break, nor alter the word that has gone out of my lips. Once I have sworn by my holiness; I will not lie to David" (Psa. 89:30-35).

Since it is a Psalm of the mercies of our Covenant God we would expect verse 31-33 to read, "If his sons forsake my law and do not walk in my judgments, if they break my statutes and do not keep my commandments, then will I visit their transgression with the rod, and their iniquity with stripes. Nevertheless my lovingkindness I will not utterly take *from them*." Yet it reads "*from him*." The covenant is made with our David, even our own Lord Jesus. It is not with the literal David for his throne has long ceased while the true David's throne "shall be established forever like the moon . . ." (vs.

---

* Reisinger, 17.

36-37). So then David's seed, that is the Lord Jesus Christ's seed "shall endure forever" since the "covenant shall stand firm with Him." Verses that speak of Christ's seed are Isaiah 53:10, "He shall see his seed" and Isaiah 8:18 (and Hebrews 2:13), "I and the children whom the Lord has given me." None of Christ's seed can be lost. I give two glorious quotations from Thomas Goodwin on Psalm 89,

> "Consider that all this is founded upon Christ, though the mercies are in the heart of God. It is a mighty expression when He says, 'If his children forsake my law, I will visit their transgressions.' He speaks to them, If they do so and so; but when he comes to make his promise, 'Notwithstanding my loving-kindness shall not be void from him.' From him, verse 28, *i.e.*, from Christ. What, does Jesus Christ need any mercy? Ay, it is well for us he doth not for himself. But thus, as he is the head of all the saints, and he and they make one body, the Covenant of Grace and mercy was made with him, and so they are called 'the sure mercies of David,' Isa. 55:3. All the mercies God bestows are for his sake; and it is well now that God hath sworn, that he will not take his mercies from Christ in relation to us; and that Jesus Christ can go to God and plead, Lord, I have no need of mercy; but thou hast given me all thy mercies for those who are mine; Lord, fulfil them to them.'"[*]

And again,

> "But you will say, will not men's sins break this covenant, though God will not? I answer, They would infallibly break between God and us, if God should not take order to keep us from such ways of sinning as would bring ever-lasting wrath upon us. He will have a watchful eye and a powerful hand to prevent such sinnings. As upon occasion of his like oath to the perpetuity of his Covenant of Grace, he declares to David, in Ps. 89:30- 32, 'If his sons forsake my law and do not walk in my judgments, if they break my statutes and do not keep my commandments, then will I visit their transgression with the rod, and

---

[*] Goodwin, 73.

their iniquity with stripes.' And by these chastisements I will reduce them again. But, as verse 34, 'My covenant I will not break, nor alter the word that has gone out of my lips.' And that God had all our sins before him, and well considered what they would be, when he takes this deliberate oath, the very parallel instance of what is inserted by God in Noah's covenant, may inform us. The words in Gen. 8:21 are, 'God said in his heart, I will not curse the ground any more for man's sake; for the imagination of man's heart is evil from his youth: neither will I again smite any more every living thing, as I have done.' "[*]

Thus we see how wrong it is to talk about "covenant breakers" in regard to the Covenant of Grace and those in that covenant losing their privileges through unfaithfulness. This shows a great lack of understanding of the Covenant of Grace and its stability and perpetuity. Allen C. Guelzo writes in his book *Who Should be Baptized? A Case for the Baptism of Infants*, "If we leave our children unbaptized . . . we are forcing them to break God's covenant."[†] Does he believe we can put our children out of the Covenant of Grace? R. R. Booth wrote, "Inclusion in the covenant has never automatically conferred personal salvation on any individual."[‡] If a person is in the Covenant of Grace it means that God has covenanted with him through Christ to be his God. Is faith a condition of the covenant or one of the blessings of the covenant? Certainly the latter. If being in the Covenant of Grace doesn't confer salvation what does? Mr. Booth talks about our faithfulness. This sounds very much to me like the Arminian teaching that after all it all depends on us and not on God's covenant. This greatly dishonors God's covenant faithfulness and his covenant promises.

"No one 'under grace' ever perished! To be under a Covenant of Grace and to be secure forever in Christ are one and the same thing in the Scriptures. The Word of God knows nothing of people perishing in hell who were under the Covenant of Grace."[§]

---

[*] *Ibid.*

[†] Guelzo, *Who Should Be Baptized?*, 6-7.

[‡] Booth, 150.

[§] Reisinger, 83.

The Paedobaptists often talk of "covenant breakers" who are cut off from the covenant. They say their unfaithfulness will bring "covenant curses." R. R. Booth writes, "The children of believers who are faithful to God's covenant will know the individual blessing of personal salvation. Covenant breakers will be cut off and receive the curses of the covenant."[*]

Why do they talk like this? Infants that are baptized often grow up and evidence their unregenerate state to everyone by their words and deeds. Even J. Murray admits this,

> "It may appear to be an argument of some weight to appeal to the sad record of so many who have been baptized in infancy—they have grown up to be indifferent to the baptismal engagements and have often lived lives of infidelity and godlessness. This record is not denied."[†]

Yet they were baptized as being in the Covenant of Grace. Here the Paedobaptist is in trouble. If the Paedobaptist says they were never in the Covenant of Grace this overthrows their whole argument which is that all believers' children are in the covenant so therefore they should be baptized. Rather than say that, the Paedobaptist chooses to say that such children are covenant breakers and cut themselves off from the covenant and are cursed with covenant curses. However, the reformed faith teaches the Biblical doctrine of the perseverance of the saints. Christ said, "And this is the Father's will which hath sent me, that of all which he hath given me (in the everlasting covenant) I should lose nothing, but should raise it up again at the last day" (John 6:39). How can this agree with their teaching that one in the covenant is cut off?

This talk of covenant breakers being cut off and receiving the curses of a broken covenant sounds to me like the law rather than the Covenant of Grace. The glory of the new covenant is that all in the covenant continue in faith and holiness for the law is written on their hearts.

---

[*] Booth, 46.
[†] Murray, 75.

> "Behold the days come, saith the Lord, that I will make a new covenant with the house of Israel, and with the house of Judah: not according to the covenant that I made with their fathers in the day that I took them by the hand to bring them out of the land of Egypt; which my covenant they brake, although I was an husband unto them, saith the Lord: but this shall be the covenant that I will make with the house of Israel; After those days, saith the Lord, I will put my law in their inward parts, and write it in their hearts; and will be their God, and they shall be my people" (Jer. 31:31-33).

Also, "And I will make an everlasting covenant with them, that I will not turn away from them, to do them good; but I will put my fear in their hearts, that they shall not depart from me" (Jer. 32:40). Note that God will not turn away from them and they shall not depart from him as they did in the old covenant. Surely it is a sure covenant to all of Abraham's seed.

What is this talk of curses on children of the covenant? Aren't all in the Covenant of Grace believing children of whom it is said, "Christ hath redeemed us from the curse of the law being made a curse for us . . . that the blessing of Abraham might come on the Gentiles through Jesus Christ" (Gal. 3:13-14)? This teaching of covenant children breaking the covenant and being cut off overthrows fundamental doctrine of all reformed evangelicals. How can they be willing to deny the glories of the new Covenant of Grace so they can hold on to infant baptism?

It seems the Paedobaptists are more willing to throw out vital gospel truths than to admit that children of believers are not in the covenant until they believe. Why not admit that godless men were never in the covenant and that children of believers are not born into the covenant but born in sin? As Christ plainly taught, "that which is born of the flesh is flesh." Who can deny that all children are born in sin, condemned in Adam and not subject to the law without denying total depravity and original sin? Paul writes of such children who are not born again, "so then they that are in the flesh cannot please God" (Rom. 8:7-8). Their only hope is not to be baptized but to be born of the Spirit.

All who have part in the Covenant of Grace have all the promises of God made sure to them, "for all the promises of God in Him are yea, and in

Him amen unto the glory of God by us" (2 Cor. 1:20). How then can they receive curses upon them from God their Father? Rather, "He establishes us in Christ, has anointed us, sealed us and given the earnest (pledge) of the Spirit in our hearts" (2 Cor. 1:21-22). The seal of the Spirit is a sure pledge! Surely God's pledge is dependable.

11

What Covenant Does Circumcision Belong To?

E xcept in the case of Abraham, circumcision belongs to the covenant of law called the old or first covenant in the New Testament. I give the following reasons:

1. Moses gave the law. "Did not Moses give you the law?" (John 7:19). For this reason it is often called the "law of Moses." With the law Moses gave circumcision. "Moses therefore gave you circumcision (not that it is from Moses but from the fathers)" (John 7:22). Another verse that identifies circumcision with the law is John 7:23, "A man receives circumcision so that the law of Moses should not be broken."

2. Part of the law is termed *ceremonial*. The book of Leviticus was written by Moses and contains the typical Jewish institutions and ceremonies that were committed to the care of the tribe of Levi. As we would expect Leviticus contains the law of circumcision. "On the eighth day the flesh of his foreskin shall be circumcised" (Lev. 12:3).

3. Leviticus contains ordinances that were types and shadows of the gospel realities. Physical circumcision was a shadow of spiritual or heart circumcision. Hebrews links these shadows with the law. "For the law, having a shadow of the good things to come . . ." (Heb. 10:1).

4. Disobedience to circumcision brought a curse, "And the un-circumcised male child, who is not circumcised . . . Shall be cut off from his people" (Gen. 17:14). Curses go with the law. However, those under grace have been redeemed from the curse of the law. "Christ has redeemed us from the curse of the law" (Gal. 3:13). For what reason? "That the blessing of

Abraham might come upon the Gentiles in Christ Jesus" (Gal. 3:14). Grace speaks blessing. Law speaks curses.

5. Circumcision was a major component of "the middle wall of division" between Jews and Gentiles, "who are called Uncircumcision by that which is called the Circumcision in the flesh made by hands" (Eph. 2:11, 14). The one thing King Saul dreaded more than death was death at the hands of the uncircumcised (1 Sam. 31:4). Circumcision was the root of the enmity. This wall and enmity that Christ abolished in His flesh is called the "law of commandments in ordinances" (Eph. 2:14-15). God gave the Jews special laws to separate them from all peoples. These laws of commandments in ordinances are the ceremonial law that made the division between Jews and Gentiles.

6. Circumcision has been abolished with the rest of the law of commandments contained in ordinances. "Having abolished in His flesh the enmity, that is, the law of commandments contained in ordinances" (Eph. 2:15). It is the old covenant that has been replaced. The Covenant of Grace is eternal (Heb. 13:20). Circumcision belongs to this old covenant such that now "circumcision is nothing" (1 Cor. 7:19).

7. Circumcision is a "fleshly (or carnal) commandment" (Heb. 7:16; 9:10). It had to do with the flesh and natural descent. The fleshly and carnal commandments are linked with the old covenant in Hebrews. Circumcision did not signify the spiritual state of the recipient. Both saved and unsaved are designated "the circumcision."

> "My fellow workers for the kingdom of God who are of the circumcision" (Col. 4:11).

> "There are many insubordinate, both idle talkers and deceivers, especially those of the circumcision" (Titus 1:10).

In the above verses, and there are many more, circumcision means Jews and nothing more. It does not signify those who had repented or those in the church or those in the Covenant of Grace as Paedobaptists say it signifies. The word Jews can be substituted for the word circumcision but not words such as the repentant or believers, etc. Its meaning is born a Jew. In most contexts it has no spiritual meaning.

May the above seven reasons be sufficient to prove that circumcision is a sign of the Covenant of Law or the old covenant, not the new covenant or Covenant of Grace (except in the case of Abraham, a believer). The New Testament epistles firmly link circumcision and law (Gal. 5:1-4; Rom. 2:25-29; Phil. 3:2-5).

Many Paedobaptist writers join circumcision and law (except when they are writing on the subject of infant baptism). Here are a few examples:

"Circumcision and the law belong together in God's covenant . . ."[*]

"Circumcision, which, as you know, was one of the sacraments of the old covenant."[†]

I think a person needs to have a previous bias to teach that circumcision (of infants) is a sign of the Covenant of Grace. It is not. Infant circumcision is a sign of the Covenant of Law. It belongs to Abraham's natural seed. No children are born under the Covenant of Grace whether their parents are believers or not. Since all infants are born "under the law" those receiving circumcision received it as a sign of the law and a commitment to obey the law. "I testify again to every man who becomes circumcised that he is a debtor to keep the whole law" (Gal. 5:3). This is one of the reasons Christ was circumcised.

Thus, the argument that infants of believers were circumcised as being in the Covenant of Grace so that infants of believers should be baptized since they are in the Covenant of Grace falls to the ground. The sign of circumcision is a sign of the Covenant of Law. Thus, it was given to Ishmael and Esau.

---

[*] Stott, *Romans*, 93.
[†] Daille, *Colossians*, 314.

12

Signs and Seals

The impress of a seal or signet signified possession and was used to secure valuables, books, rooms and documents.

A seal also authenticated letters, weights, contents of bags, etc. Strong defines seal as a mark of privacy or genuineness. The verb he defines as to stamp for security or preservation. A sign he defines as a miracle, sign, token, wonder. The verb he defines as to distinguish, mark.

Pierre Marcel wrote,

"Seals are distinct from signs in that they not only remind us of invisible things, but also authenticate these things to our religious consciousness by making them more certain and sure to us. During our daily practical life we constantly make use of seals, tokens for combating fraud, falsehood, and counterfeits. It is, in fact, necessary to distinguish the true from the false, what is authentic from what is not, the original from the counterfeit. A trade mark serves to authenticate and guarantee the source and quality of a product. Hallmarks declare the standard of alloy, the exact value, and the nationality of gold or silver articles. On weights and measures they testify to the accuracy of the inscription by reference to the scientifically determined original which they represent. Stamps, seals, and signatures guarantee the perfect authenticity of an important document—and so on. Scripture attests the usage of seals when there is a concern to prove that something is really authentic and when it is of importance to guarantee it against all falsification."[*]

Thus we see that a sign points to something or someone. It distinguishes or marks something or someone. A seal likewise guarantees or authenticates a person or thing. Paedobaptist writers call circumcision a sign and a seal. They call it a sign and seal of the Covenant of Grace. However, circumcision belongs to the Covenant of works not the Covenant of Grace. Circumcision was to Abraham's physical seed. Abraham's spiritual seed are in the Covenant of Grace. As is true of the legal covenant; breakers of the covenant of circumcision were under the curse. But all those in the Covenant of Grace have been redeemed from the curse.

What did circumcision signify? What did it seal? What did it guarantee and authenticate? Hodge wrote, "It signifies the cleansing from sin."[†] However, many, in fact most of the Israelites who were circumcised were not cleansed from sin. To say it signifies cleansing is to make circumcision to be a false sign. R. C. Sproul wrote, "God ordered that a sign of faith be given before faith was present."[‡] This is to make circumcision a sign of that which doesn't exist.

But William Cunningham shows the fallacy of that by writing, "Signifying and sealing naturally suggest the idea, that the things signified and sealed not only exist, but are actually possessed by those to whom they are signified and sealed."[§]

Calvin said, "Circumcision was also a sign of repentance."[**] Yet, none of the infants who received circumcision had repented. How could it be a sign of something that didn't exist? This is to make it a sham. Calvin went further,

> "For God's sign communicated to a child as by an impressed seal, confirms the promise given to the pious parent, and declares it to be ratified that the Lord will be God not only to him but to his seed and

---

[*] Marcel, *The Biblical Doctrine of Infant Baptism*, 30.

[†] Hodge, 3:554-555.

[‡] Sproul, *Essential Truths of the Christian Faith*, 228.

[§] Cunningham, *The Reformers and the Theology of the Reformation*, 278.

[**] Calvin, 2:1342-44.

that he wills to manifest his goodness and grace not only to him but to his descendants even to the thousandth generation.'"[*]

To confirm means to establish the truth, verify, to make firm. Yet, God does not manifest his grace and goodness to all the descendants of all believers. To say that God confirms such a promise is to put falsehood in God's mouth. God does not promise to anyone what He does not carry through. Anyone to whom God promises to be God to him in the sense of the New Covenant will be saved for eternity and cannot be anything but saved for eternity. Have any descendants of believers come short of faith and not received the eternal inheritance? There have been many. Obviously God did not promise to them to be God to them. How we should tremble to say that God promises what he doesn't fulfill. Such speech is most upsetting. R. R. Booth writes, "Circumcision signified the work of God's grace in the heart, as does baptism."[†] Did it signify the work of God's grace in Ishmael's heart? Did it signify the work of God's grace in Esau's heart? Did it signify the work of grace in the heart of the generation who perished in the wilderness? Likewise, does baptism "signify the work of God's grace in the heart"? It signifies no such thing or how could there be millions of baptized unregenerate.

Dr. Murray has also made extravagant statements about baptism. He, after stating that baptism signifies union with Christ goes on to say, "Of this union baptism is the sign and seal."[‡] Going back to the definitions of sign and seal we would ask, does baptism distinguish and infallibly mark the baptized person as one united with Christ? Does baptism attest to his genuineness and guarantee he is the Lord's? That's preposterous!

Suppose we use one of the examples of Marcel, whom we quoted above, such as a trademark which authenticates and guarantees the source and quality of a product. If a person opened a sealed carton with its seal or trademark on the package and discovered a cheap counterfeit he would never again trust that seal or trademark. Millions of men and women have

---

[*] *Ibid.*, 1332.
[†] Booth, 103.
[‡] Murray, 6.

been baptized but know nothing of the power of godliness.

They are counterfeits. If baptism is God's sign and seal how can we trust Him? Neither circumcision nor baptism are signs and seals for they do not authenticate or guarantee anything. A seal distinguishes such as when the 144,000 were sealed. Does baptism distinguish Christians from others? No, since many who are not Christians have been baptized. Therefore baptism is not a seal!

The godly men, yes, good godly men, who call circumcision and baptism signs and seals, err greatly. If someone stated that you had made a promise and signed and sealed it but you had not made any such promise you would be greatly upset. To protect your reputation and truthfulness you would adamantly oppose that person, denying you had made such a promise. A person like that would be putting a lie in your mouth and causing you to be esteemed as a liar. The men I have quoted are doing just that but not to another human being but to God, the judge of all. "Let God be true but every man a liar." Circumcision or baptism does not guarantee the person circumcised or baptized that they are in the Covenant of Grace, or are justified, forgiven, etc., nor did God ever make such promises to them.

Because Abraham believed God he was given circumcision as a seal. This seal was not to authenticate the righteousness of faith as authentic and so to encourage Abraham to believe. He had believed. That is, it was not to make it sure in itself but to make Abraham sure of it. It was to assure Abraham that he had been justified. Abraham could look on his circumcision as God's seal of his acceptance by faith, take assurance and rejoice.

In this sense baptism is to follow faith. It does not begin or work grace but it follows grace which produces faith. "They believed and were baptized," is the teaching of all of Acts. The baptism of a believer because it confirms his faith brings joy in the Spirit. The eunuch was baptized and "he went away rejoicing" (Acts 8:38). The jailor was baptized (Acts 16:33), and he rejoiced (verse 34). Does this happen in the case of infants? Sealing does not authenticate and assure a person of the truth of salvation in order to lead a person to believe. Rather sealing of the Spirit follows faith. The end of this sealing is to work assurance in the one that is sealed.

In Ephesians 1:13-14 we read, "In whom also, after that ye believed, ye were sealed with that Holy Spirit of promise, which is the earnest of our inheritance until the redemption of the purchased possession, unto the praise of his glory." Here we see that it isn't the inheritance that is sealed. It is persons, believers, that are sealed, sealed after believing. Thus the Holy Spirit persuades the hearts of believers that the inheritance is theirs.

Therefore, whether baptism is such a seal to infants let everyone judge.

Now it is true that to Abraham circumcision was "a seal of the righteousness of faith which he had yet being uncircumcised . . ." (Rom. 4:11). But it was only a seal to him because "he had the righteousness of faith" before he was circumcised. All his seed after him were circumcised before they had the righteousness of faith so that circumcision was not "a seal of the righteousness of faith" to them for when they were circumcised they had neither faith nor the righteousness that comes through faith. Yes, it is true that circumcision was a sign and a seal to Abraham because of the righteousness that he had by faith before circumcision. But it was not a seal to his posterity for they were circumcised as unbelieving infants and so had neither faith nor the righteousness that comes through faith. William Cunningham's statement is appropriate,

> "The sacraments are not seals of spiritual blessings in any such sense as implies, that they are attestations to the personal character or spiritual condition of those who receive them, or, that the mere reception of the sacraments is to be held as of itself furnishing a proof, or even a presumption, that those receiving them are true believers, and may be assured that they have reached a condition of safety. This is a point about which much ignorance and confusion prevail, and which it may be proper to explain somewhat fully.
>
> It is the almost universal practice of divines to apply the word 'seal' to the sacraments, and to call them 'sealing ordinances'. But what they usually mean by the application of this term to the sacraments, it is not so easy to determine. Indeed, we can scarcely resist the impression, that many divines, in professing to explain the function or influence of the sacraments as seals, have recourse to what is little better than an intentional ambiguity of language, as if they were anxious to insinuate, that there is something very

important and mysterious in this sealing, while yet they carefully avoid giving any clear and definite explanation of what it means, as if from a lurking apprehension that the attempt to do so would make the whole mystery evaporate in their hands.["]

Circumcision was only the sign of being an Israelite according to the flesh. It did not signify cleansing or forgiveness or any spiritual blessing. It was given promiscuously to all Israelites. Jewish Christians, who had been circumcised, were also baptized. No circumcised Israelite infant had the seal of anything spiritual for as John Murray rightly observes, "a seal or authentication presupposes the existence of the thing sealed . . ." If the thing sealed is absent the seal is not only worthless but worse still it will deceive. Thus all baptized infants, not having faith, do not have a seal or an authentication of the righteousness of faith but a counterfeit. How many has it deceived into a false hope? Don't all who baptize infants foster this deception by supplying that which the carnal will tend to trust in to their eternal loss? Surely millions have been so deceived.

What is it that guarantees to the person who has it eternal salvation? What is it that distinguishes Christians from others? What is it that authenticates the true child of God from the hypocrite? It is not circumcision! It is not baptism! A mere ordinance administered by men cannot "give assurance to those who receive it" that they shall be the recipients of the blessings of the Covenant of Grace. Evangelical religion is not sealed by physical signs. How can a ceremony which is an outward form seal that which is spiritual? Impossible! A physical knife or material water cannot do a spiritual work. That is superstition.

Dr. John Murray writes,

> "Though circumcision and baptism are the signs and seals of covenant union and communion, it does not follow that every one who bears this sign and seal is an actual partaker of the grace signified and sealed and is therefore an heir of eternal life. It frequently happens that the sign is administered to those who, from the

---

[*] Cunningham, *British and Foreign Evangelical Review*, 932.

standpoint of good government and discipline, ought not to be baptised. The church too often fails to maintain the proper oversight and discrimination in this matter as in all others. But apart from the question of looseness and carelessness in administering this rite, it does not even follow that all those who, from the viewpoint of administration, properly bear the sign and seal are possessors of the actual grace signified. That is to say, even when the church exercises the proper oversight and discipline, even when all the safeguards of divine institution are applied, it does not follow that the administration of this rite insures for the recipient the possession of the grace signified. It must be admitted that this appears very anomalous, and it presents us with great difficulty."*

Dr. Murray is quite right, it is a great difficulty for he says that "circumcision and baptism are signs and seals" that evidently are to distinguish, prove, evidence, confirm, attest, authenticate or place beyond doubt. He then goes on to say that "it does not follow that the administration of this rite insures for the recipient the possession of the grace signified." In other words these signs and seals of circumcision and baptism that evidence, prove, distinguish, guarantee and authenticate do not evidence, prove, distinguish or authenticate. This is a great difficulty. Surely these are strange signs and seals that do not sign and seal.

Greg Bahnsen says, "We must note well that the signs of the covenant, whether circumcision or baptism, being God's signs and ordained by Him— are God's testimony to God's gracious work of salvation."[†] No doubt God's testimony is dependable but where has Mr. Bahnsen heard this testimony of God?

John Murray rather says,

"God has not given us any assurance (or testimony I would add) that the operations of His saving grace are invariably present where the divine institution is observed . . . with respect to infants the sign is properly dispensed in many cases where the recipients do not possess

---

* Murray, 54.

† Bahnsen, *Baptism: Its Meaning and Purpose*, 3.

and may never possess the inward grace signified."[*]

Clearly circumcision *was not* and baptism *is not* a sign and seal. It is not the acts or the effects of the acts by the Holy Spirit that is the seal. The Holy Spirit does not seal us. He is the seal. We are sealed with him not by him. The one who seals is God the Father, "He who hath sealed us is God" (2 Cor. 1:21-22).

> "And herein consists the greatest testimony that God doth give, and the only seal that he doth set, unto any in this world. That this is God's testimony and seal, the apostle Peter proveth, Acts 15:8,9; for on the debate of that question, whether God approved and accepted of the humble believers, although they observed not the rites of Moses, he confirmeth that he did with this argument: 'God,' saith he, 'which knoweth the hearts, bare them witness.' How did he do it? how did he set his seal to them as his? Saith he, 'By giving them the Holy Ghost, even as he did unto us.' Hereby God gives testimony unto them."[†]

The only seal of true religion is God's seal—the Holy Spirit. Sealing is exclusively the work of God by the Holy Spirit. God alone guarantees eternal life to those whom His Spirit indwells. It is not water, even the water of baptism, that seals the Covenant of Grace but the blessed Holy Spirit. He is the seal that bears true witness, "The Spirit Himself bears witness with our spirit that we are the children of God" (Rom. 8:16). He is called a seal, "having believed, you were sealed with the Holy Spirit of promise who is the guarantee of our inheritance . . ." (Eph. 1:13-14). He is our guarantee. Baptism is neither our seal nor our guarantee. Away with the pernicious teaching of signs and seals.

Those who say that circumcision and baptism are God's testimony of His work of salvation bring God's name and testimony into disrepute. Such talk confuses and perplexes God's people. It is not by baptism we know we

---

[*] Murray, 56.
[†] Owen, 404-05.

are of God. Can we be assured that we are God's people because we have been baptized? No! How do we know? "By this we know . . . by the Spirit whom He has given us" (1 John 3:24). For "if anyone does not have the Spirit of Christ, he is not His" (Rom. 8:9). "By this we know that we abide in him, and He in us, because He has given us of His Spirit" (1 John 4:13). Here is assurance!

Part 3

BAPTISM

13

The Purpose of Baptism

What is the purpose of baptism? What is its design? What is it meant to do? There is no more important point to consider in regard to baptism. Yet, this is not even considered by many Paedobaptist writers on baptism. But if some ignore this the Church of Rome and others who believe in the sacramental principle emphasize the purpose of baptism and speak glowingly of what baptism does.

All men in a state of nature are enemies to the grace of God and seek to "set aside the grace of God" (Gal. 2:21), by either trusting in their good works or in the ceremonies and rites of the church. Men have a tendency to rely on what they can do to obtain God's favor and forgiveness or to rely on what the church or others can do for them. There have always been men who have had exaggerated and unscriptural views of the ordinances and particularly is this prevalent when sound doctrine is lost and living religion declines.

During the Middle Ages when the power of godliness had been lost Christianity was made up of outward ceremonies and ritual observances. Faith in the power and efficacy of the ordinances are leading features of false religion. Their belief is that the ordinances confer grace by some power or virtue given to them and operating through them. As an instance the Church of Rome teaches that baptism is the instrumental cause of justification and that sin is forgiven through it.

William Cunningham clearly exposes this false teaching,

"The essential idea of this Popish and Tractarian doctrine of the sacraments is this: that God has established an invariable connection between these external ordinances, and the communication of Himself,—the possession by men of spiritual blessings, pardon, and holiness; with this further notion, which naturally results from it, that He has endowed these outward ordinances with some sort of power or capacity of conveying or conferring the blessings with which they are respectively connected. The Protestant doctrine, upon the other hand, is, that the only thing on which the possession by men individually of spiritual blessings,—of justification and sanctification,—is made necessarily and invariably dependent, is union to Christ; and that the only thing on which union to Christ may be said to be dependent, is faith in Him: so that it holds true, absolutely and universally, that wherever there is faith in Christ, or union to Christ by faith, there pardon and holiness,—all necessary spiritual blessings,—are communicated by God and received by men, even though they have not actually partaken in any sacrament or external ordinance whatever."[*]

However some of the statements made by Paedobaptists imply baptismal regeneration. As an example we give the words of the Church of England Prayer Book for the Public Baptism of Infants: "Seeing now, dearly beloved brethren, that this child is regenerate" and later, "We yield thee hearty thanks, most merciful Father, that it hath pleased thee to regenerate this infant with thy Holy Spirit, to receive him for thine own child by adoption, and to incorporate him into thy holy church."

Also, Pierre Marcel, a leading Reformed writer, says, "Baptism given to little children is the witness and attestation of their salvation, the seal and confirmation of the Covenant of Grace which God contracts with them."[†]

He says baptism attests their salvation. Attest is defined by Webster's Third New International Dictionary as authenticate, establish, verify, prove, witness. Does baptism *authenticate* all infants salvation? Does it establish it? Does it verify it? Does it prove it? Does it witness it? Nothing of the kind!

---

[*] Cunningham, *Historical Theology*, 124.
[†] Marcel, 213.

God witnesses to no one that they are saved until they believe. And then the witness is not through baptism but through His Spirit.

Negatively: Baptism is not designed to confer grace and its purpose is not to be a channel of spiritual life. It exerts no influence whatever apart from the faith of the one baptized.

> "Protestants, as I have said, maintain that it is a scriptural doctrine, that the only thing on which the possession of spiritual blessing absolutely and invariably depends, is union to Christ; and that the only thing on which union to Christ depends, is faith in Him. As soon as, and in every instance in which, men are united to Christ by faith, they receive justification and regeneration; while without, or apart from, personal union to Christ by faith, these blessings are never conferred or received . . . If there be nothing in Scripture adequate to establish the doctrine of an invariable connection between baptism and the spiritual blessings of forgiveness and regeneration,—but, on the contrary, much to disprove it,—it is still more clear and certain that the Popish doctrine, that the sacraments confer grace *ex opere operato*, is destitute of any authority, and ought to be decidedly rejected."[*]

Positively: Baptism is designed to be a confession of faith.

Along with faith, a confession of that faith is required for salvation. Romans 10:9-10 makes that clear.

> "That if you confess with your mouth the Lord Jesus and believe in your heart that God has raised Him from the dead, you will be saved. For with the heart one believes to righteousness, and with the mouth confession is made to salvation."

In these verses confession with the mouth goes along with belief in the heart. A man is righteous by faith alone but the evidence of his faith will be confession. When a man believes he is then justified but confession manifests it. Indeed, faith causes the confession and the confession will be an evidence

---

[*] Cunningham, 131, 138.

of salvation even at the day of judgment. Yet if a man refuses to confess Christ at the hazard of his life or possessions he does not have faith, the faith that overcomes the world. Confession is not to be understood as merely a subscription to a creed but as a confessing the Lord Jesus and all that that means.

Christ himself pointed out the necessity of confession more than once.

> "Therefore whoever confesses Me before men, him I will also confess before My Father who is in heaven. But whoever denies Me before men, him I will also deny before My Father who is in heaven" (Matt. 10:32-33).

We must confess Christ upon earth or He will not own us as His people to His Father in heaven. This confession is to be made in one way and another before the world. It is also to be made publicly by baptism.

> "The profession of renouncing the world, and devoting ourselves to Christ, might have been required to be made in mere words addressed to the ears of those who hear; but infinite wisdom has judged it better that it should be made in a formal and significant act, appointed for the specific purpose. That act is baptism. The immersion of the body, as Paul has explained, signifies our burial with Christ; and in emerging from the water, we enter, according to the import of the figure, on a new life. We put off the old man, and put on the new man: 'As many of you as have been baptized into Christ, have put on Christ.' "*

Paul, in Romans 6, uses the design of baptism and its significance as an argument that Christians do not live in sin. Hodge comments on verse 3,

> "Baptism was the appointed mode of professing faith in Christ, of avowing allegiance, to him as the Son of God, and acquiescence in his gospel. Those, therefore, who were baptized, are assumed to believe what they professed, and to be what they declared themselves

---

* Dagg, *Manual of Church Order*, 71.

to be. They are consequently addressed as believers, as having embraced the gospel, as having put on Christ, and as being, in virtue of their baptism as an act of faith, the children of God. When a man was baptized unto Christ, he was baptized unto his death, he professed to regard himself as being united to Christ, as dying when he died, as bearing in him the penalty of sin, in order that he might be reconciled to God, and live unto holiness. How could a man who was sincere in receiving baptism, such being its design and import, live in sin? The thing is impossible. The act of faith implied and expressed in baptism, is receiving Christ as our sanctification as well as our righteousness."[*]

It is obvious that there must be some way of confessing Christ before men after conversion. Obviously infant baptism is not a means of confessing faith in Christ. If baptism is not used as the way of confessing Christ then another way has to be found. This has forced Paedobaptists to use Confirmation as a confessing ceremony but it has no scriptural basis.

I know of a Catholic man who was converted and wanted to join an evangelical Paedobaptist church. He desired to confess his faith by baptism but since he was baptized as an infant the church refused to baptize him again. He had no way of publicly professing his faith in God's appointed way.

According to the great commission, baptism accompanies the proclamation of the gospel in making disciples. When people are baptized they become disciples in a full sense. The Jews and Muslims of today do not regard a person as a Christian if they have not been baptized. But when a person is baptized they then regard him as a Christian. Baptism is often called a badge of discipleship. Hodge writes,

> "When Christ commanded the apostles to make disciples, baptizing them, etc., he obviously intended that baptism should be a badge of discipleship, or that by that rite his followers should acknowledge their relation to him."[†]

---

[*] Hodge, *Romans*, 194.
[†] Hodge, *The Way of Life*, 179.

Some Paedobaptist churches have confederate membership for those baptized as infants and communicant membership for those who have also professed faith but this has no scriptural authority and brings the real danger of a formal confession without meaning. This is particularly so since Paedobaptist churches make the parents confession of faith a condition for having their children baptized. (A further concept without scriptural support). This puts tremendous pressure on parents to make some sort of approved profession.

A. A. Hodge in speaking of the importance of confirmation writes,

> "Then they who have been members of the Church from their birth are admitted to full communion, and are confirmed in their church standing, upon their voluntarily taking upon themselves the vows originally imposed upon them by their parents in baptism. This is the CONFIRMATION, separated from the abortive mask of the so-called sacrament, that John Calvin declared was an ancient and beneficial custom, which he earnestly wished might be continued in the Church (*Institutes*, bk. 4, ch. 19:12,13.), and which Dr. Charles Hodge declared to be 'retained in some form or other in all Protestant churches' (*Princeton Review*, 1855, p. 445). As far as we misunderstand or ignore this beautiful ordinance of confirmation we abandon to the mercies of our Baptist brethren the whole rational ground and reason of infant baptism.'"*

That he calls confirmation, "this beautiful ordinance" although it has no scriptural authority show the straits they are brought to and reveals the need they have of having some formal way of confessing Christ before men. Confirmation is a substitute for a believer's confession by baptism but it is not God's way. Surely believers' baptism is the right way and the best way. Although it is an outward ceremony it is important as a profession of faith, as an act of obedience and as a pledge of the believer to walk in newness of life.

An objection to this is that it is said that baptism is God's act not man's. Dr. Saarnivaara writes,

---

* A. Hodge, *Evangelical Theology*, 337-38.

"The person who is baptized only receives it. He does not primarily confess the name of the triune God, even when he is an adult person. He is baptized into the name of the triune God. The very act of baptism is therefore in conflict with your doctrine. Or do you otherwise confess the name of Christ before men while doing nothing but only receiving something from others, or being acted upon by them? Don't you confess Christ and your faith only when you do or speak something?"[*]

Of course, it is true that a person does not baptize himself but does this mean he is only being "acted upon" rather than he himself acting? No, the person being baptized is not being baptized unwillingly or unconsciously. He chooses to be baptized and so is actively confessing Christ. Baptism is his act.

This is the same as for the death of Christ. Although He didn't put himself to death and was crucified by others, the crucifixion was His willing act. "He gave himself." Just so is believers' baptism. They willingly give themselves to be baptized. Of course, this is not true for infant baptism since the infant is not acting consciously or willingly in his baptism. He is only being acted upon. But to those who were baptized as believers it is written, "For all of you who were baptized into Christ have clothed yourselves with Christ" (Gal. 3:27). Note that such baptized persons actively "clothe themselves with Christ." This is not true of infant baptism.

Just as infants need to be dressed and cannot dress themselves, they are unable "to put on Christ" consciously and willingly. If Galatians 3:27 included infants it would have to be changed to "all of you who were baptized into Christ were clothed with Christ or had Christ put on you" rather than "you have put on Christ." The verb is *enedusasthe* in the middle voice not the passive voice and so means you (plural) have put on (yourselves) Christ or you have clothed yourselves with Christ. It is an action the believer does, not an action done to him or for him. This thus excludes infants from baptism.

The Paedobaptists further object to baptism being a profession of faith (since it excludes infants) by saying,

---

[*] Saarnivaara, *Scriptural Baptism*, 33.

"The difference between Baptists and Reformed paedobaptists has been the baptistic notion that baptism is the subjective testimony of the individual believer—his profession of faith—'the Christian man's badge of profession.' The Scriptures indicate that the covenant is sovereignly initiated by God, not by man, and therefore that the covenant sign and seal is God's, not the believer's.'"[*]

Mr. Booth is not being fair to Baptists to say, "The baptistic notion that baptism is the subjective testimony of the individual believer." His words "notion" and "subjective" both have negative connotations since subjective can be defined as: "peculiar to a particular individual modified by individual bias and limitations."[†] This is not the Baptists' "notion." We would rather say baptism is a confession of faith. It is true that God is the initiator of the covenant as Mr. Booth says. However, does this mean that man has no active part in accepting the covenant? Mr. Booth has likened the Covenant of Grace to the marriage covenant. Isn't marriage a mutual covenant? What is man's part but to enter into the covenant by faith and to acknowledge this by his confession at baptism. If God proposes man answers. "Baptism . . . the answer of a good conscience toward God" (1 Pet. 3:21).

He further quotes B.B. Warfield on the same page,

"Baptism, as circumcision, is a gift of God to his people, not of his people to God. Abraham did not bring circumcision to God; he 'received' it from God. God gave it to him as a 'sign' and a 'seal' not to others but to himself. It is inadequate, therefore, to speak of baptism as 'the badge of a Christian man's profession.' . . . The witness of baptism is not to others but to ourselves; and it is not by us but by God that the witness is borne."[‡]

My objection to Warfield's statement is that baptism is not God's witness to the one baptized. What does God witness? Certainly He does not witness to them that they are His people or His witness would oftentimes be

---

[*] Booth, 112.

[†] See *Webster's Third New International Dictionary*.

[‡] Warfield, *Selected Shorter Writings*, 1:327.

untrue, for multitudes of unregenerate are baptized. In fact all infants are unregenerate when sprinkled. However, the believer who is baptized does witness and confess his faith. This confession of faith is made to God before others. When the Jews cried out to Peter and the other apostles, "Brothers what shall we do?" the answer was, "Repent and be baptized." Baptism is a *doing*, an act of the one being baptized. It is not an act of God.

Because it is a conscious act it is often an unforgettable, emotional act that is a high point of a believer's experience. Some are greatly humbled and are solemnly baptized. Others are baptized with joy unspeakable. It is a motive for godly living as the apostle writes, "Therefore we were buried with Him through baptism into death, that just as Christ was raised from the dead by the glory of the Father, even so we also should walk in newness of life" (Rom. 6:4).

Leonard Verduin writing about the "stepchildren" of the Reformers, the Baptists, who considered "the moment of their baptism a high point in their total religious experience," has this to say,

> "Anyone who has read in the New Testament will know that in this the Stepchildren were on good New Testament ground. Baptism does indeed signify a dying unto sin and a rising again unto newness of life. But, strange though this may sound, the Reformers disliked what the Stepchildren said in this matter. So long had baptism and the language of baptism dealt with things that lie far removed from conscious experience, that when the Anabaptists contended that in the moment of baptism they experienced great refreshing of soul, their opponents called this claim old wives tales and the prattle of fools. For good measure Zwingli added, 'If they hold to this then they had better have themselves baptized not just once but over and over again, a thousand times. For if the baptism with water renewed and strengthened and comforted the soul then no one would withhold it from himself but would have himself baptized again and again, as often as he was assailed. Then the repeated lustrations or baptisms of the Old Testament would be re-introduced.'"*

---

* Verduin, *The Reformers and their Stepchildren*, 216-17.

14

Anabaptism or Rebaptism

Rebaptism is anathema to Paedobaptists. The Westminster Confession of Faith proclaims, "The sacrament of Baptism is but once to be administered unto any person." * And the Belgic Confession of Faith similarly states,

> "We believe, therefore, that every man who is earnestly studious of obtaining life eternal ought to be baptized but once with this only baptism, without ever repeating the same, since we cannot be born twice. Neither does this baptism avail us only at the time when the water is poured upon us, but also through the whole course of our life. Therefore we detest the error of the Anabaptists, who are not content with the one only baptism they have once received, and moreover condemn the baptism of the infants of believers, who we believe ought to be baptized and sealed with the sign of the covenant, as the children of Israel formerly were circumcised upon the same promises which are made unto our children."†

During the Reformation a name that was one of great reproach was *Weidertaufer,* meaning "Anabaptists" or "Rebaptizers." This name was given to those who rebaptized converts from the Roman Catholic and other inclusivist churches that embraced everyone by baptizing all at birth.

Rebaptizing did not begin with the Reformation. In fact, we find traces

---

* WCF 28.7.
† BCF 34.

of as early as the fourth century. According to Verduin,

> "There were Anabaptists, called by that name, in the fourth century. The Codes of Theodosius already prescribed very severe penalty, capital punishment, for anyone who was convicted of having rebaptized."[*]

He gives as verification *Codex Theodosianus*, XVI, 6:1.

The point of contention was whether all baptism was valid. For those who restricted the church to believers the "baptism" of infants and unbelievers was invalid. Those who rebaptized such after conversion and upon their confession of faith did not consider that as a rebaptism. They did not use the word rebaptism. Although called Anabaptist no Anabaptist was happy with that title. To them the baptism of unbelievers was no baptism at all. Pierre de Bruys, who lived in the twelfth century, taught that no one should be baptized before the age of understanding or if an unbeliever. He rejected the "christening" of the Roman Church.

> "The Petrobrusians, as Pierre's followers were called, declared, 'We wait until the proper time has come, after a man is ready to know his God and believe in Him; we do not, as they accuse us, rebaptize him who may be said never to have been baptized before.'"[†]

If baptism saves, as those who hold to baptismal regeneration believe, it should never be repeated. If all believers' children are in the Covenant of Grace and are baptized on that ground then they should never need to be baptized again. Likewise, if there is no such thing as invalid baptism then all baptisms have efficacy and nothing more is required. If baptism infallibly incorporates the one baptized into the church then rebaptism seems quite unnecessary. However, all the above hypothetical statements are false. Paedobaptists strongly object to "rebaptism." Yet if it accomplishes nothing apart from faith why shouldn't an unbeliever be baptized when he comes to

---

[*] Verduin, 190.
[†] *Ibid.*, 194.

faith regardless of whether he was baptized or christened before? This opposition to rebaptism seems to show that Paedobaptists have a secret trust in baptism regardless of who receives it.

Are all baptisms valid? It seems quite obvious that multitudes that have been baptized never should have been. Their ungodly lives testify to this. Their baptisms are invalid. Is it needless to talk about qualifications for baptism or do all qualify to be baptized? Is there any such thing as a person not being a proper subject for baptism? Most people believe there are qualifications for baptism and that is certainly true. Those who do not qualify and are baptized have received invalid baptism. What is invalid baptism?

In 1845 the Presbyterian General Assembly voted that Roman Catholic baptism was invalid. Charles Hodge argued against this position saying, "The great body of people constituting the Roman Catholic church do profess the essentials of the true Christian religion, whereby many of them bear the image of Christ, and are participants of His salvation." I put this in to show that *some* Paedobaptists do not accept all baptisms as valid. However, I think the Presbyterians ruled that Roman Catholic baptisms were invalid on the wrong principle and that Charles Hodge, too, argued on the wrong principle, nor do I believe his statement in regard to Roman Catholicism. They rejected Roman Catholic baptism on the basis of who did the baptizing. This reasoning is that the efficacy of baptism is given to it by those who baptize.

This is why many denominations may allow "laymen" to preach but would never allow them to baptize. Protestant seminaries may allow their students to preach but not to administer the Lord's Supper. Students may preach but they cannot lift up their hands and give the formal blessing to the congregation. All of this is sacramentalism and falls into the errors of the Popish priesthood and apostolic succession. Often sacramentalists depreciate preaching and exalt and idolize the sacraments.

> "The logic of salvation by sacramental manipulation leads straight to the idea of *ex opere operato*, the name given to the view that the transaction to which the Sacrament points is 'done in the doing.' It is the innate power of the Sacrament as the conveyor of grace that

assures the mediation of salvation, this rather than the state or the attitude of the dispenser—or of the recipient, for that matter. Small wonder that with those who resisted the Constantinian formula, the attitude of the recipient remained the one thing that mattered."[*]

No, it is not who gives baptism that makes it valid or invalid. It is who receive baptism that makes it valid or invalid. If baptism is a confession of faith then the baptism of unbelievers is invalid. If a believer is baptized on his credible profession of faith his baptism is valid.

A. A. Hodge, writing on who are to be baptized wrote,

> "Baptism is a sacramental action representing an inward invisible grace. Consequently, the outward action ought never consciously and intentionally to be applied where the inward invisible grace is absent. There could be no farce more profane, no empty show more ghastly, than that sealing the form of a covenant where there was no real promise, of applying an outward symbol of spiritual life and grace where all spiritual life and grace are absent. Such mockery would transform the sacred pledges of God's truth into a lie."[†]

Although Mr. Hodge would disagree it is clear to me that his assertion should exclude all infants from baptism. Without the inward grace their baptism is profane and an empty show. "There could be no farce more profane, no empty show more ghastly, than that sealing the form of a covenant where there was no real promise, of applying an outward symbol of spiritual life and grace where all spiritual life and grace are absent," as in their baptism. Doesn't "such mockery transform the sacred pledges of God's truth into a lie" time and time again? Since baptism symbolizes our identification with Christ in His death, burial and resurrection it is just an empty rite if it is given to those not in union with Christ by faith. Since it is a confession of faith it is a sham if given to anyone who does not make a confession of faith. The church is a company of believers and since baptism

---

[*] *Ibid.*, 140.
[†] A. Hodge, 326.

is the entrance into the church by confession of faith it should be limited to believers. The bond of communion in the New Testament was a common faith in Christ. Admission into the fellowship of the believers was baptism. Dr. Murray speaks of this confession of faith,

> "But it is the prerogative of man to judge in reference to public confession or profession. This, therefore, is the criterion in accord with which human administration is exercised. And what needs to be emphasized here is that this is so by divine institution. It is not the expedient of proven experience. And it is not simply a necessity arising from the limitations inherent in human nature. It is by divine institution that the church, as a visible entity administered by men in accordance with Christ's appointment, must admit to its fellowship those who make a credible profession of faith in Christ and promise of obedience to him."[*]

He continues and comments on Peter's confession,

> "There can be no question but that the church confession is the kind of confession made by Peter. And this means that the confession requisite for membership in the church is the confession of Jesus as the Christ, as the Son of God, as Saviour, and as Lord. It is a profession of true and saving faith."[†]

Without this confession of faith baptism is not valid. Acts 19:1-7 gives an account of rebaptism done by the apostle Paul. Paul was a rebaptizer or as they were called "Anabaptists." Calvin denied that it was water baptism. "I deny that the baptism of water was repeated because the words of Luke impart no other thing, save only that they were baptized with the Spirit."[‡]

However, they were "baptized in the name of the Lord Jesus" which is not speaking of spirit baptism but of water baptism as in the baptism of the people of Samaria who were baptized "in the name of the Lord Jesus" (Acts

---

[*] Murray, 39.
[†] *Ibid.*, 41.
[‡] Calvin, *Acts*, 1244.

8:16) and the baptism of Cornelius and his relatives and friends who were baptized "in the name of the Lord" (Acts 10:48).

So for whatever reason, this portion is an account of a water rebaptism. Although rebaptism is abhorrent to all Paedobaptists because it means some baptisms are invalid and it brings into question particularly infant baptism we do see that rebaptism is scriptural. Matthew Henry in his *Commentary on the Whole Bible*, commented on this portion,

> "It concerns us all who profess the Christian faith seriously to enquire whether we have received the Holy Ghost or not. Have we received the Holy Ghost since we believed? The tree will be known by its fruits. Do we bring forth the fruit of the Spirit? Are we led by the Spirit? Do we walk in the Spirit? Are we under the government of the Spirit? Surely your baptism was a nullity, if you know nothing of the Holy Ghost; for it is the receiving of the Holy Ghost that is signified and sealed by the washing of regeneration. Ignorance of the Holy Ghost is as inconsistent with a sincere profession of Christianity as ignorance of Christ is. Applying it to ourselves, it intimates that those are baptized to no real purpose, and have received the grace of God therein in vain, that do not receive and submit to the Holy Ghost."[*]

Those who believe that men should not be rebaptized even if their baptism was done in unbelief put faith in the bare rite of baptism. This clearly shows that they superstitiously regard the ordinance as if it had significance and power of itself. They put baptism in the place of Christ. They believe in baptism itself rather than in baptism as only a symbol. Baptism by and of itself can effect nothing. Salvation can only be ascribed to the reality of that which baptism is the figure, not to the baptism itself. Baptism does not confer grace on its own and has no invariable connection to forgiveness and regeneration. The Westminster Confession declares this, "grace and salvation are not so inseparably annexed into baptism as that no person can be regenerated or saved without it, or that all that are baptized are undoubtedly regenerated." Evangelical Paedobaptists will sometimes

---

[*] Henry, Volume 6, 244.

acknowledge that baptism is only a symbol,

> "operating beneficially only in those in whom faith already exists, and producing the beneficial effect of confirming and sealing the truths and blessings of the gospel to the individual only through the medium of the faith which participation in them expresses."*

Why then do they refuse to rebaptize those who were baptized when unbelievers, in whom baptism had no beneficial effect? Why refuse them the beneficial effect of baptism when they become believers? I fear the Paedobaptists have a secret trust in baptism and believe it works mysteriously somehow, some way in unbelievers and in unconscious infants.

Matthew Henry makes it very plain that baptism received apart from the Holy Spirit is "a nullity." It is null and void. He said such are baptized "to no real purpose." Without faith none are united with Christ and receive neither the Holy Spirit or God's grace which comes through Him. Such baptism is invalid. Why shouldn't it be replaced by a baptism of faith that is valid? Why refuse a believer the opportunity to profess his faith the way God has ordained? Why withhold from the believer the precious experience that obedience to God in baptism brings?

> "The obligation to make a baptismal profession of faith, binds every disciple of Christ. Some have converted the Eucharist into a ceremony of profession; but this is not the law of Christ. Baptism was designed, and ought to be used, for this purpose. If infant baptism be obligatory, the duty is parental; and if it be a ceremony in which children are dedicated by their parents to the Lord, it is a different institution from that in which faith is professed. He who has been baptized in infancy, is not thereby released from the obligation to make a baptismal profession of faith in Christ. If it be granted, that his parents did their duty in dedicating him to God, he has, nevertheless, a personal duty to perform. The parental act of which he has no consciousness, cannot be to him the answer of a good

---

* Cunningham, 134.

conscience toward God. Had it left an abiding mark in the flesh, an argument of some plausibility might be urged against the repetition of the ceremony. But the supposed seal of God's covenant is neither in his flesh, nor in his memory, and his conscience has no Scriptural release from the personal obligation of a baptismal profession."[*]

I am a missionary working in a third world country with a small Mission group. We have work in four different language groups. In all of these language groups a large Mission that is sacramentalist preceded us into the areas. They baptized by the hundreds, and even thousands, both infants and adults, although those baptized were unbelievers. The native people sought baptism because they believed the baptismal water would take away their sins. This Mission also gave the people new names out of the Bible and wrote them "in the book." To naive, uneducated tribal people this meant that they were God's people with their name in God's book. The overwhelming majority of these illiterate tribal people were baptized. Everyone followed that Mission. Following the Mission also brought many practical and material benefits.

When we went into those areas we received much opposition from that Mission. We went in and preached the law and the gospel. It was necessary to teach what saves but it was also necessary to teach what doesn't save. We had to emphasize again and again the negative aspects of the gospel by preaching that salvation is not by works nor any ceremony but only through faith in another, even the Son of God, the Lord of glory. We had to show what baptism couldn't do. We declared their foolishness and idolatry of trusting in physical water to spiritually produce new hearts. We explained that names on paper written by man is not the same as having your name written by God before the foundation of the world. We taught that no one is saved by baptism and rather men must be saved before being baptized. The light of the gospel began to dispel the darkness of their superstition. It dispelled not only their primitive fear of evil spirits but also their superstitious belief in baptismal regeneration. Some were convicted of sin

---

[*] Dagg, 73.

and their misery and were converted. They became believers through the regenerating work of the Spirit. What were we to do?

We taught that baptism was to follow faith with baptism as a profession of that faith. Could we allow the false teaching that had been propagated to rob these new believers of the right use of baptism? No! Our commission was to disciple all nations baptizing them in the name of the Father and of the Son and of the Holy Spirit.

In a highly emotional time of confrontation, after having been threatened, some of the believers returned their baptismal papers with their "new names" to the Mission leaders. This stand and their open declaration of their faith when baptized were victories that greatly helped to establish them in the faith. Some, being delivered from bondage and fear of their Mission, went out declaring their salvation. God's work could not be hidden. Baptism, restored to its rightful place, bore powerful testimony to the Savior's death, burial and resurrection. He was lifted up and He drew to Himself. If we had tacitly approved the old ritual washings by not baptizing the new believers a great opportunity to declare the gospel would have been lost and their Christian lives would have suffered. The Christians often speak about those early days of warfare with joy and satisfaction.

15

Household Baptism

C harles Hodge wrote, "In all cases, therefore, where parents enter into covenant with God they bring their children with them."* R. R. Booth wrote, "The individuals within households were baptized not because they necessarily believed (though some may well have) but rather, because they were members of the households of believers."†

These two quotations make it clear that Paedobaptists believe that children are in the covenant by their parents' faith and not their own faith and so should be baptized as members of the households of believers. Therefore, when household baptisms are described in the Bible they are claimed to be according to Paedobaptist principles. Their principle is that as all Abraham's household was circumcised due to his faith the household of believers should be baptized on their parents' faith.

A household, as Paedobaptists agree, include the servants in the household and also all the children regardless of age. What is household baptism? Household baptism is a whole household being baptized at one time. It would include all in the household such as children of all ages, servants and their children, married children living at home, grandparents, etc. However, no Paedobaptists practice household baptism. To baptize ungodly servants, youths and children living worldly lives and then bring them into church membership is so contrary to the spirit and teaching of the Word, that it is not advocated by anyone. Some households include more

---

* Hodge, 3:555.
† Booth, 143.

than one family, some include divorced children, some include grandparents, etc. If Paedobaptists followed their professed beliefs the end would be confusion and absurdity. Please reread the two quotations above to see the contradiction of household baptism with Paedobaptist practice.

I do believe in household baptism, however only under certain conditions. The conditions are that all in that household are believers and that they all have been saved at the same time. These conditions were met in the case of the jailor's household and Cornelius' household.

Mr. Booth reasons thus,

> "Of the nine cases mentioned (in Acts) as having been baptized, two probably did not have immediate families—Saul and the Ethiopian eunuch. We are not informed about any family of two others, Simon Magus and Gaius. In the remaining five cases, the entire household was baptized. We may conclude, then, that in every case where the apostles administered baptism to the known head of a family, they also administered it to his entire household."*

In 1 Corinthians 1:16, Paul wrote, "I baptized the household of Stephanas." He did not baptize Stephanas. In verse 14 Paul wrote, "I baptized none of you except Crispus and Gaius." Paul did not baptize either Crispus's household or Gaius's household. Why not? Possibly Gaius was single and had no children. Yet this seems unlikely since he was the host of Paul and even of the whole church according to Romans 16:23. Be that as it may Crispus had a household that believed according to Acts 18:8. Yet Paul baptized Crispus but not his household. Probably he was saved before his household and since Paul only baptized the first fruits and then left it to the Church in each place to baptize the later believers Paul did not baptize Crispus' household. For whatever reason it remains that Crispus together with his household were not baptized by Paul. Thus it is incorrect to say that households are baptized on the faith and baptism of the head. This was not true of the household of Stephanas either. He is mentioned in 1 Corinthians 16:17, but Paul did not baptize him with his household. They were not

---

* *Ibid.*

baptized on Stephanas's faith and baptism but upon their own faith.

THE PHILIPPIAN JAILOR

The Philippian jailor's household, Acts 16:30-34 supports the principle that households are baptized upon their individual faith not because of descent from believers nor upon the faith of the parents. The promise that was given to the jailor, "Believe on the Lord Jesus Christ, and you will be saved, you and your household," was fulfilled and his household was saved. They were baptized together as saved individuals who were saved at the same time. Paul and Silas, "spoke the Word of the Lord to him and to all who were in his house." This would exclude infants since we do not preach to infants. Further we read, "he rejoiced, having believed in God with all his household." It is true that a possible translation is, "and rejoiced with all his house, he having believed in God." Both verbs are in the singular with the Greek word translated "with all his house" between the two verbs. Many translations translate the verse, "rejoiced and believed in God with all his house" (see KJV, NKJV, NIV, and NASB). It seems most likely to tie the words "with all his house" to both verbs. The verses in this portion point to a saved household who having heard the Word rejoiced, believing in God. Any other interpretation would make the promise to the jailor untrue.

CORNELIUS

"And he told us how he had seen an angel standing in his house, who said to him, 'Send men to Joppa, and call for Simon whose surname is Peter, who will tell you words by which you and all your household will be saved.' And as I began to speak, the Holy Spirit fell upon them as upon us at the beginning. Then I remembered the word of the Lord, how He said, 'John indeed baptized with water, but you shall be baptized with the Holy Spirit.' If therefore God gave them the same gift as He gave us when we believed on the Lord Jesus Christ, who was I that I could withstand God? When they heard these things they became silent; and they glorified God, Saying, "Then God has also granted to the Gentiles repentance to life'" (Acts 11:13-18).

121

Here we again have the promise given of the salvation of his household to the head, Cornelius. This promise was fulfilled when "the Holy Spirit fell on all who heard the word." Everyone was converted simultaneously. None were baptized on the faith of another. Through the preaching of Peter, Cornelius and his household were saved. This was evidenced by the Holy Spirit falling upon them causing them to "speak with tongues and magnify God." This convinced all the apostles that they had believed on the Lord Jesus Christ just as they had. All the apostles and brethren who heard Peter's report, "became silent; and they glorified God saying, 'Then has God also granted to the Gentiles repentance to life'" (Acts 11:18). They were saved believers who had repented unto life having received the Holy Spirit. This, of course, excluded all infants. But with such evidences, and no one should be baptized without some evidence of conversion, we can confidently ask with Peter, "Can anyone forbid water, that these should not be baptized who have received the Holy Spirit just as we have?" (Acts 10:47).

THE HOUSEHOLD OF CRISPUS

"Then Crispus, the ruler of the synagogue, believed on the Lord with all his household. And many of the Corinthians hearing, believed and were baptized" (Acts 18:8).

Surely this passage is perfectly clear that Crispus and his whole household believed and were baptized, and in that order. However, R. R. Booth commenting on this portion says,

"The New Testament culture arose from the Old Testament culture, and therefore it is not surprising to find whole households believing because the head of the household believes."*

He wants to make the baptism of the household be in virtue of the faith of the head of the household. True faith in the New Testament (and Old

---

* Booth, 148.

Testament) is never because of the faith of someone else. True faith is in virtue of, or "according to the working of His mighty power" (Eph. 1:19). The source of faith is in God not in the faith of the head of a household. Faith is a gift from God. Those who believe because others believe are false believers and will fall away. To say that faith is based on another's faith is surely a grave doctrinal error.

Mr. Booth also writes under the heading "The Household of Crispus,"

> "Moreover, we must keep in mind that missionaries have seen entire families or tribes make professions of faith because the head of the family or tribe did so. We should expect that a first century Jewish family would similarly have followed the lead of its conventional head."[*]

It is true that there are such professions but speaking as a missionary of 40 years' experience professions that are made to follow someone else are false professions. If someone would say that they desired baptism because someone else was being baptized surely they should be rejected. We always reject such. Such "converts" continue living in the world and are a disgrace to the Lord. Faith that is based on men is false faith. True faith is a mighty work of God and occurs through the omnipotent power of the Spirit of God. Is following the lead of a man faith? Can true faith be produced by man? Never! Faith is only produced by the grace of God. As Paul wrote of his faith, "The grace of our Lord was exceeding abundant with faith" (1 Tim. 1:14).

It should also be noted that Paul, although he baptized Crispus, did not baptize Crispus's household (see 1 Cor. 1:14). If "the baptism of all household members (not just infants)" is "by virtue of the faith of household heads" as Mr. Booth says (p. 143), then Paul would have baptized Crispus and his household.

---

[*] *Ibid.*, 147-48.

THE HOUSEHOLD OF LYDIA

"Now a certain woman named Lydia heard us, She was a seller of purple from the city of Thyatira, who worshiped God. The Lord opened her heart to heed the things spoken by Paul. And when she and her household were baptized, she begged us, saying, 'If you have judged me to be faithful to the Lord, come to my house and stay.' And she constrained us" (Acts 16:14-15).

This is the final account of household baptisms that we will look at in the book of Acts. Although we do not have Lydia's household described as saved or believers or receiving the Spirit or repenting as we find in all the other accounts of household baptisms there is nothing in the account to lead anyone to think the account is an exception to the other accounts. Since the Word of God is consistent all the households who were baptized should be consistently looked at as believing households, having been regenerated by the Spirit.

There are certain things said that would lead to the probability that Lydia was either unmarried or a widow without children. It is seen that she was the head of the household. The house is called "Lydia's house" (Acts 16:40). If she had a husband who was alive it would have been called his house. Lydia also was a business woman described as a dealer in purple cloth. Such purple cloth was bought by the wealthy. She was the one who "persuaded" the apostles, single men, to stay in her house. This would point to her being an older woman able to persuade or constrain younger men and not make it questionable for such to stay in her home. The probability is very strong that there were no infants in the household so that no infants were baptized. This is the point in dispute.

STEPHANAS' HOUSEHOLD

"I baptized the household of Stephanas" (1 Cor. 1:16.)

Here we see that the household was baptized by Paul but not the head of the household, Stephanas. It does not say I baptized Stephanas and his household. Thus, Mr. Booth's statement on p. 143, that household members are baptized by virtue of the faith of household heads is false. "The household of Stephanas were the first converts in Achaia" (1 Cor. 16:15). They were baptized upon conversion not because they belonged to a "covenant family." Their faith was evidenced by their works, "they devoted themselves to the service of the saints" (1 Cor. 16:15). Stephanas, the father, was not a "first convert" and was not saved until later, possibly after Paul had left Corinth such that he was not baptized by Paul (see 1 Cor. 1:16; 16:15, 17).

Dr. Murray wrote, "We cannot prove conclusively that there were infants in these households."[*] And, "We do not have an overt and proven instance of infant baptism."[†]

Very true. However, we can prove conclusively that those baptized were believers and not infants in every case except Lydia's household. Yet even there the probability that there were no infants baptized is strong. In short household baptisms give no support to infant baptism. We would expect that household baptisms would occur during times of revival when whole households are saved simultaneously but not in other times. The book of Acts portrays such a dynamic time when thousands were added to the church very quickly and the gospel was spreading everywhere. Today household baptisms are infrequent for sadly we do not see multitudes being added to the Church by conversion.

---

[*] Murray, 68.
[†] *Ibid.*, 69.

16

Repentance: Baptism, The Baptism of John

John the Baptist was born miraculously to Zacharias and Elizabeth, who "was barren and they were both well advanced in years" (Luke 1:7). The angel Gabriel was sent to Zacharias to tell him of the birth of John and to describe this son to be born as one who would be, "great in the sight of the Lord," a Nazarite, consecrated to God for life and, "filled with the Holy Spirit even from his mother's womb" (Luke 1:15). Gabriel prophesied that "he will turn many of the children of Israel to the Lord their God" (vs. 16). He was to be an extraordinary man for a great and extraordinary task. He was to have the "spirit and power of Elijah." He was prophesied by Isaiah and Malachi and was to be the one who prepared the way for the Lord Jesus Christ. He was none other than Christ's herald and forerunner.

John was hidden in the desert until his manifestation to Israel. At the appointed time "the word of God came to John" (Luke 3:2). Then was the fulfillment of, "The voice of one crying in the wilderness; 'Prepare the way of the Lord.'" His ministry is called "a baptism of repentance for the remission of sins" (Luke 3:3). Thus the first mention of baptism, a New Testament ordinance, is in regard to John's baptism. As Goodwin wrote, "The first of every kind is the measure of the rest of that kind that do after follow."*

Thus, all following baptisms were to follow John's baptism. His was the pattern. It was, "a baptism . . . from heaven" (Mark 11:30), and given on the authority of God. Thus, John's baptism is of great significance as to the meaning of baptism and the lawful recipients of baptism.

---

* Goodwin, 45.

Being a baptism of repentance John only baptized those who evidenced repentance and "they were baptized by him in the Jordan, confessing their sins" (Matt. 3:6). All commentators that I have read agree that this excludes all infants. One example is Francis Turretin, "John admitted none to baptism but those who confessed their sins; because his business was to baptize adults."[*] Turretin was a highly regarded Paedobaptist who ably defended "the strictest orthodoxy of the Canons of Dort."

What do Paedobaptists say about this? Some say very little. Others, such as Dr. Murray seek to nullify John's baptism as a pattern by saying,

> "We may no more identify the baptism of John with the ordinance instituted by Christ than we may identify the ministry and mission of John with the ministry and mission of Christ. Hence we cannot derive from the nature of John's baptism the precise import of the ordinance of Christian baptism."[†]

However, Dr. Murray gives no scripture for his assertion. Surely it would be strange if the baptism instituted by Christ would differ in any significant way from John's baptism since John was his forerunner and John's baptism was "from heaven" (see Matt. 21:25). Christ made it clear that John's authority was from God. Also, John baptized Christ "to fulfill all righteousness," since Christ vicariously bore His people's sin and identified Himself with them. John's baptism of the people, his baptism of Christ and Christ's baptism of others through his disciples had a common thread that bound all together. If John's baptism was not Christian baptism then the baptism that Christ received was not Christian baptism. John's baptism, which is clearly believers' baptism, is an embarrassment to Paedobaptists so A. A. Hodge likewise seeks to nullify John's baptism as a pattern for later baptism by writing,

> "John, the forerunner of Jesus, came baptizing also. But this was not Christian Baptism, because—(1) John was the last Old Testament

---

[*] Turretin, *Institutes of Elenctic Theology*, section 4, question 22.
[†] Murray, 5.

prophet, and not a New Testament apostle (Luke 1:17); (2) He did not baptize in the name of the Father, and of the Son, and of the Holy Ghost; (3) His baptism was unto repentance, not into the faith of Christ; (4) He did not by baptism introduce men into the fellowship of the Christian Church, as the apostles did at Pentecost (Acts 2:41, 47); (5) Those baptized by John were baptized over again by the apostles when they were admitted to the Christian Church (Acts 18:24-28; 19:1-5)."[*]

Let us look at Hodge's reasons: He wrote, "John was the last Old Testament prophet, and not a New Testament apostle." His proof verse is Luke 1:17. I don't see the pertinence of this verse to the discussion so I will ignore it. John was not an Old Testament prophet. The last Old Testament prophet was Malachi. Calvin wrote,

> "Malachi, distinguishing the two conditions of the Church, places the one under the Law, and commences the other with the preaching of John. He unquestionably describes the Baptist, when he says, 'Behold, I send my messenger' (Mal. 3:1), for, as we have already said, that passage lays down an express distinction between the Law and the new order and condition of the Church. Hence we infer, that the abrogation of the Law, and the beginning of the Gospel, strictly speaking, took place when John began to preach."[†]

Matthew 11:13, "For all the prophets and the law prophesied until John," supports Calvin as does John 1:17.

"*He did not baptize in the name of the Father, and of the Son, and of the Holy Ghost.*" None of the baptisms in Acts were in the name of the Father, and of the Son, and of the Holy Ghost. Does this mean that they were not Christian baptism?

"*His baptism was unto repentance, not into the faith of Christ.*" This is false. John the Baptist preached the necessity of faith. He preached, "He who believes in the Son has everlasting life; and he who does not believe the Son

---

[*] A. Hodge, *Confession of Faith*, 339.
[†] Calvin, *The Gospels*, 76.

shall not see life, but the wrath of God abides on him" (John 3:36). Note Acts 19:4, "Then Paul said, 'John indeed baptized with a baptism of repentance, saying to the people that they should believe on Him who would come after him, that is on Christ.'"

It is written of John, "He will turn many of the children of Israel to the Lord their God" (Luke 1:19). That is he truly converted them through the Gospel. Since John's baptism was unto repentance it of necessity was also unto faith since repentance and faith always go together. As a theologian, Dr. A. A. Hodge knew this even as Dr. Murray, who wrote,

> "The faith that is unto salvation is a penitent faith and the repentance that is unto life is a believing repentance . . . Turning to God implies faith in the mercy of God as revealed in Christ. It is impossible to disentangle faith and repentance. Saving faith is permeated with repentance and repentance is permeated with faith."[*]

"He did not by baptism introduce men into the fellowship of the Christian Church, as the apostles did at Pentecost" (Acts 2:41, 47). Since the Church did not begin until Pentecost the Church was not manifested by believers gathering in local churches during the time John baptized. Therefore, those John baptized did not join local churches immediately since there were none at that time. Does this then mean John's baptism was not Christian as Hodge says. No, Philip baptized the Ethiopian eunuch but the eunuch did not immediately join a local church since there was none in Ethiopia. Obviously, that doesn't mean that Philip's baptism of the eunuch was not Christian baptism. Apollos was probably baptized by John since we read he knew only the baptism of John. Yet he was part of the church and was mightily used to such an extent that the brethren of a local church wrote exhorting the disciples of the churches of Achaia to receive him. See Acts 18:24-28. Can we not say that Apollos' baptism introduced him into the fellowship of the church? Undoubtedly!

---

[*] Murray, *Redemption Accomplished and Applied*, 113.

"Those baptized by John were baptized over again by the apostles when they were admitted to the Christian church" (Acts 18:24-28; 19:1-5). Hodge uses Acts 18:24-28 and 19:5 as his proof verses. Acts 18 says nothing about the rebaptism of anyone. Although Apollos was not rebaptized he was in fellowship at Ephesus with the believers and accepted as a brother. They wrote to Achaia commending him. It is true that a few disciples at Ephesus were rebaptized. Since they had not received the Spirit it seems evident that they were not believers so they were baptized after hearing the message explained more accurately and believing the message. The issue was not the baptism of John as Hodge falsely assumes. The issue was their failure to "believe on Him who would come after him, that is, on Christ Jesus" (Acts 19:4). Some of the twelve were first disciples of John and were probably baptized by John but they were not rebaptized by Christ.

Dr. Murray and A. A. Hodge seek to emphasize the difference between John's ministry and Christ's. Yet the Bible teaches that John's ministry began the gospel era and that his message and mission were not diverse from Christ's but in complete agreement with it. Note the beginning of the gospel of Jesus Christ as written in Mark,

> "The beginning of the gospel of Jesus Christ, the Son of God. As it is written in the Prophets: Behold, I send My messenger before Your face, who will prepare Your way before You. The voice of one crying in the wilderness: 'Prepare the way of the Lord, make His paths straight' " (Mark 1:1-4).

The beginning of the gospel of Jesus Christ is John's ministry. The first event is John's ministry. John is not in some transition period. He is in the gospel age. "The law and the prophets were until John. Since that time the kingdom of God has been preached, and everyone is pressing into it" (Luke 16:16). What did he preach? "Repent, for the kingdom of heaven is at hand!" (Matt. 3:2). What did Christ preach? "Repent, for the kingdom is at hand" (Matt. 4:17).

As we listen to John preach, "He who believes in the Son has everlasting life; and he who does not believe the Son shall not see life, but the wrath of

God abides on him," (John 3:36) we hear the same message that Christ preached,

> "For God did not send His Son into the world to condemn the world, but that the world through Him might be saved. He who believes in Him is not condemned; but he who does not believe is condemned already, because he has not believed in the name of the only begotten Son of God" (John 3:17-18).

Whom did John baptize? He baptized repentant believers. Whom did Christ baptize? The same. He baptized those He made disciples (John 4:1).

An objection has been made that John's baptism and Christ's baptism are not the same but contrasted by John and by Christ. "John truly baptized with water, but you shall be baptized with the Holy Spirit" (Acts 1:5). However, this contrast is not between John's water baptism and Christ's water baptism but between John's water baptism and Christ's baptism with the Holy Spirit. To this B. H. Carrol wrote,

> "The answer is obvious. John instituted no manner of comparison between his baptism in water and Christ's baptism in water, but he does contrast his baptism in water with Christ's baptizing in the Holy Spirit and in fire, proving Christ's superiority of power and position to John, but in no way discriminating between the water baptism of the two, as has already been shown."*

John Owen wrote of John the Baptist,

> "God calls a man in a marvelous and miraculous manner; gives him a ministry from heaven, commands him to go and baptize all those who, confessing their sins, and professing repentance of them, should come to him."†

---

* Carrol, *The Four Gospels*, 133.
† Owen, 465.

This is a powerful testimony. If baptism was first given only to those who repented and this by the authority of God where is the scripture that changes baptism to include infants? To do so would drastically change baptism so that it would lose its outstanding characteristic which is repentance. Its meaning would be lost.

Dr. John Murray asks some questions of those who oppose infant baptism. I have sought to answer his questions later under the section, Dr. Murray's Questions. I would now like to take his questions and accommodate them to make them applicable to John's baptism. If infants are included now, it cannot be too strongly emphasized that this change implies a complete reversal of John's divinely instituted practice. So we must ask: do we find any hint or intimation of such reversal later in the New Testament? More pointedly, does the New Testament revoke or does it provide any intimation of revoking so expressly authorized a principle as that of the exclusion of infants from baptism?

The great change the New Covenant brought about in distinction to the Old Covenant was that national Israel was to be replaced by spiritual Israel, the church. This had been intimated in the story of Ishmael and Isaac and the story of Jacob and Esau. Yet the nation as a whole completely misunderstood the phrase: "to you and your seed." That all the natural seed of Abraham were rejected was so shocking and radical as to be thought blasphemous. Although Jeremiah had written, "Behold, the days are coming," says the Lord, "that I will punish all those who are circumcised with the uncircumcised—Egypt, Judah, Edom, the people of Ammon, Moab, and all who are in the farthest corners, who dwell in the wilderness. For all these nations are uncircumcised, and all the house of Israel are uncircumcised in the heart" (Jer. 9:25-26). Few Israelites did not believe all Abraham's children were better than the uncircumcised. That salvation was an individual matter and had to be sought rather than coming automatically through birth was so revolutionary to the Jews that it was unimaginable.

It fell to John the Baptist to start the revolution. He was Elijah who would come and "restore all things" (Matt. 17:11). John's teaching was that the people of God were not coextensive with Abraham's children; with him arises the format of the New Testament church. As Verduin wrote, "With

John begins the idea of a composite society. He was indeed great."[*]

John's teaching was that sacralism (everyone in a unit of society having the same religion) was finished and society was composite, or as Paul phrases it, "not all Israel is Israel." John made this clear, "and do not think to say to yourselves, 'We have Abraham for our father.' For I say to you that God is able to raise up children to Abraham from these stones" (Matt. 3:9). He went on to say, "And even now the ax is laid to the root of the trees. Therefore every tree which does not bear good fruit is cut down and thrown into the fire" (Matt. 3:10). He was speaking not of the heathen nations but of Israel, the tree of Abraham. And he said that the threshing floor was to be purged and the chaff (Abraham's natural seed) was to be burned up. He was speaking of the fig tree that Christ would later curse.

Paul further developed this theme of the natural branches being cut off through unbelief in Romans 11. Human descent would no longer join to the tree. Likewise Christ plainly taught this in the words, "That which is born of the flesh is flesh. You must be born again" (John 3:6-7). An Israelite, a covenant child, hearing this gasped in amazement, "How can these things be?" (In passing, I should say that the phrase, "covenant child" is not scriptural and is confusing at best).

Further, John insisted on conversion, and a conversion evidenced by works. He thoroughly examined all those who desired baptism. Verduin wrote,

> "With the band of the forerunner's followers a peculiar and distinguishing life-style comes to expression as the necessary feature for all who would belong. For 'fruits worthy of repentance' is the equivalent of manifest metanoia, a change of heart that comes to expression in a contrasting way of life. One's being converted is expressed when a man who has two coats imparts one of them to a person who has none, when a publican 'exacts no more than is appointed,' when a soldier 'does no violence to any man nor accuses any falsely,' and considers his legitimate wage to be enough, etc." (Lk.

---

[*] Verduin, *The Anatomy of a Hybrid*, 54.

3:10- 14).*

All this was revolutionary to the extreme. Under the Old Covenant all who were born Jews were circumcised. This was automatic. Who ever heard of further qualifications? Who ever heard of being examined? Why, everyone belonged to the Jewish church. "We are Abraham's seed" was the cry but John the Baptist rejected them. The Baptist would have nothing to do with a "people movement" or a mass movement without conversion. As Verduin wrote, "Gone was the old ethnic idea of a 'church' embracing a total society."[†] The Baptist's conception of the church runs through the whole New Testament and is found in the apostles' writings.

Objection: An objection is made to only believers receiving God's ordinances.

> "Bahnsen (Baptism: Its meaning and Purpose) has pointed out, God Himself commanded that circumcision be applied to those whom He perfectly well knew would not have saving faith in Him (e.g., Ishmael in Gen. 17:18-27). Likewise, in plenty of instances hypocrites who are not true believers have been baptized (cf. Heb. 6:2-6; e.g., Simon Magus in Acts 8:13, 20-23). Some might object that, while God knowingly applied a sign of the Old Covenant to unbelievers (like Ishmael or Esau), this would be inappropriate in the New Covenant. They say New Covenant signs are only for those we have reason to think are believers (by their profession of faith). Such reasoning is well meaning, but nonetheless unbiblical. God the Son knowingly applied the sign of even the New Covenant to the unbelieving 'son of perdition,' Judas Iscariot (Luke 22: 20-21; Matt. 26:23-29)."[‡]

The Paedobaptists fail to see that God commanded all Israel, who were mostly unbelievers, to be circumcised as a sign of being Jews, his outward people. It carried no spiritual significance for such. Indeed if it did it would

---

* Verduin, 55.

† *Ibid.*, 57.

‡ Booth, 118.

be a deceptive, deceitful sign given by God. We abhor the thought that God gave a sign to unbelievers that, "was a sign of regeneration and sanctification,"* "a sign of God's calling,"† "God's testimony to God's gracious work of salvation" (quoted from Bahnsen), "signs (that) unite the recipient with God's promised Redeemer, Jesus Christ."‡ God did not give such signs or testimonies. To do so would be false. Something God could never do.

Mr. Booth says that those who say New Covenant signs are only for those we have reason to think are believers (by their profession of faith) are well meaning but nonetheless unbiblical. His reason is because, he says, Judas received the Lord's supper at Christ's hand. Did he? Let us consider.

Christ and his disciples first ate the Passover and then Christ instituted His supper in remembrance of Himself.

The sop, the dipped bread, that Christ gave to Judas belonged to the Passover meal, not the Lord's supper.

John tells us that Judas having received the sop, "went out immediately" (John 13:30). Note the whole context 13:21-30.

Thus, Judas partook of the Passover but not of the Lord's supper. Luke did not write chronologically so that Luke 22:21-22 is not written in the sequence that things happened. Matthew and Mark, who wrote more chronologically, tell us that Christ's announcement of the betrayer came before the institution of the Lord's supper, cf. Matthew 26:26-29 with 26:20-25 and Mark 14:22-25 with 14:17-21.§

We can note from this argument that Paedobaptists not only baptize unbelievers but argue for the ordinances to be given to unbelievers. It is bad doctrine to argue to include God's enemies in his holy ordinances. The reason they argue thus is because they baptize infants who are unbelievers. But such arguing contradicts their own standards as given in the Shorter

---

* *Ibid.*, 113.
† *Ibid.*, 114.
‡ *Ibid.*, 116.
§ For those who want to look into this further see Edwards, *Works*, Volume 1, 468 or Hendriksen, *Luke*, 964, Lenski, op. cit., 1001. A. T. Robertson, H. N. Ridderbos, Van Mastricht, and Dr. Dodderidge all take the same stand.

Catechism question 92, which says that the sacraments were designed to represent, seal, and apply the benefits of Christ and the new covenant to believers.

17

Disciple Baptism

J esus made and baptized disciples." This is a clear, concise statement. We see that Christ's baptism followed John's and was in complete harmony with it in regards to its significance and recipients. John's baptism was Christian baptism. Please note the order: Christ made disciples and then baptized them. Baptism did not make them disciples. Whom did Christ baptize? He baptized disciples and only disciples. Here is the practice of excluding infants. In the great commission we have the precept. B. B. Warfield agrees, "Nobody supposes that Jesus and his disciples were in the habit of baptizing infants."[*]

Paedobaptists find difficulty in explaining disciple baptism. R. R. Booth writes of an imaginary conversation,

> STEVE: Another thing that has bothered me is that I've been told that Baptists believe in "disciple baptism" but that paedobaptists don't.
>
> RANDY: We have to be careful about how terms like that are used. What do you mean by "disciple baptism"?
>
> STEVE: Well, I've always assumed that a disciple is someone who has decided to follow Jesus.
>
> RANDY: More accurately, a disciple is a student, or one who learns. As believing parents, we make our infant children disciples from the

---

[*] Warfield, 399.

time they're born, instructing them in many things concerning the Christian faith. Every time we teach them, and every time we bring them to church to be instructed, we are making them disciples or students.

STEVE: But all the children of the church don't grow up to be faithful Christians.

RANDY: Unfortunately, that's true, and neither do all the people who make professions of faith turn out to be faithful Christians.

STEVE: So, how can we really call them disciples?

RANDY: If I asked a school teacher how many students he had in his history class, what would he say?

STEVE: I suppose he would tell you the total number that were enrolled in the class.

RANDY: That's right. But suppose I asked that teacher about a student in his class named John, and the teacher replied, "Yes, John is in my class but he's not a student." And suppose I asked the same teacher about another student in his class named Kimberly, and he replied, "Oh, now Kimberly is a student!" Are John and Kimberly both students?

STEVE: I see. You're using the word "student" in different ways and with different meanings.

RANDY: Yes, and likewise we may think of disciples in different ways. We may not be able to tell in kindergarten who is going to turn out to be a good or bad student, but in time it will become evident. In the meantime, they are all treated the same and taught the same material. So too, the children of believers are made into disciples or students and taught God's Word. In time, if parents and the church are faithful in their duties toward these children, most will become disciples indeed—true followers of Jesus Christ.:

STEVE: So, Reformed paedobaptists do believe in "disciple baptism."

RANDY: Sure.[*]

Please note that Mr. Booth writes of making infants disciples after they are baptized. This is to invert the scriptural order since our Lord made disciples before He baptized them. He only baptized disciples. This completely rules out infant baptism.

Of course, many baptized infants never become disciples of Christ. Mr. Booth tries to use different meanings of the word disciple to dilute its meaning but this will not do. We must use a scriptural definition. What is a disciple? He is one who has faith in the Son of God and rests upon him alone for salvation. A disciple is a believer, that is a Christian. Thus, "the disciples were called Christians" (Acts 11:26).

"A disciple, absolutely taken, signifies in the New Testament, a believer, a Christian, a scholar, a follower of Christ or his apostles."[†]

To describe a disciple as a student or learner is inadequate and not according to the Word of God. No one who is not a believer is a disciple. Since all disciples are regenerate they deny themselves and follow Christ. To be seen to be a disciple of Christ a man must deny himself and follow and imitate Christ. Those who do not follow and imitate Christ are not his disciples and should not be baptized. As Christ taught, "Whoever of you does not forsake all that he has cannot be my disciple" (Luke 14:33). I think it is obvious that no infants are disciples. They should not be baptized. Paedobaptists do not believe in or practice "disciple baptism," even though Mr. Booth says they do.

Children may be brought to church and instructed but such a school in which people learn of Christ is not the church. As Jonathan Edwards wrote concerning many who go to "church,"

"I grant, that no other qualifications are necessary in order to being members of that school of Christ which is his visible church, than

---

[*] Booth, 161-62.
[†] Cruden, *A Complete Concordance to the Old and New Testament*, 134.

such as are requisite in order to their subjecting themselves to Christ as their Master and Teacher, and subjecting themselves to the laws and orders of his school: nevertheless I deny, that a common faith and moral sincerity are sufficient for this; because none do truly subject themselves to Christ as their Master, but such as having their heart purified by faith, are delivered from the reigning power of sin: for we cannot subject ourselves to obey two contrary masters at the same time. None submit to Christ as their Teacher, but those who truly receive him as their Prophet, to teach them by his word and Spirit; giving up themselves to his teachings, sitting with Mary at Jesus' feet to hear his word; and hearkening more to his dictates, than those of their blind and deceitful lusts, and relying on his wisdom more than their own. The Scripture knows nothing of an ecclesiastical school constituted of enemies of the cross of Christ, and appointed to bring such to be reconciled to him and submit to him as their Master.

Whatever ways of constituting the church may to us seem fit, proper, and reasonable, the question is, not what constitution of Christ's church seems convenient to human wisdom, but what constitution is actually established by Christ's infinite wisdom."*

Not only did Christ not baptize infants but He commanded that only disciples should be baptized.

> "Go ye therefore and teach all nations, baptizing them in the name of the Father and of the Son and of the Holy Spirit, teaching them to observe all things that I have commanded you; and lo, I am with you always, even to the end of the age" (Matt. 28:19-20).

The verb to teach, *matheteusate,* is literally, "make disciples," from the word *mathetes,* "a disciple."

Richard Baxter, the Puritan, wrote,

> "This is not like some occasional historical mention of baptism, but

---

* Edwards, *Works*, Volume 1, 461.

it is the very commission of Christ to his apostles for preaching and baptism, and purposely expresseth their several works in their several places and order. Their first task is by teaching to make disciples, which are by Mark called believers. The second work is to baptize them . . . The third work is to teach them all other things, which are afterwards to be learned in the school of Christ. To contemn this order is to renounce all rules of order; for where can we expect to find it if not here?"[*]

The order is clear. As Calvin, the great reformer, wrote on this portion:

"Christ enjoins that those who have submitted to the gospel, and professed to be disciples, shall be baptized; partly that their baptism may be a pledge of eternal life before God, and partly that it may be an outward sign of faith before men."[†]

And again,

"But as Christ enjoins them to teach before baptizing, and desires that none but believers shall be admitted to baptism, it would appear that baptism is not properly administered unless when it is preceded by faith."[‡]

Commenting on Acts 8:36,

"Whereas the eunuch is not admitted to baptism, until he have made confession of his faith, we must fetch a general rule hence, That those ought (not) to be received into the Church, who were estranged from the same before, until they have testified that they believe in Christ. For baptism is, as it were, an appurtenance of faith, and therefore it is later in order. Secondly, if it be given without faith

---

[*] Baxter, *Disputations of Right to Sacrament*, 149.

[†] Calvin *The Gospels*, 588.

[‡] *Ibid.*, 589.

whose seal it is, it is both a wicked and also too gross a profaning.'"

To sum up then Christ only baptized disciples. We ignore his example if we do otherwise. In Christ's only command to baptize he excluded infants. His command is to baptize disciples. Both his command and his practice make it clear that baptism is of disciples.

Not only do Paedobaptists not believe in disciple-baptism in regard to infants they vigorously oppose it. If a person who had been sprinkled as an infant was converted and desired baptism as a disciple of Christ what would the Paedobaptists say? They would dogmatically oppose such disciple-baptism and refuse to baptize such a new believer. They baptize infants who are not disciples but refuse to baptize adults who are disciples if they were sprinkled as infants.

Objection: An objection is made against baptizing the children of believers upon their profession of faith rather than as infants.

Robert Shaw wrote in 1845,

> "We have no record of the baptism of a single individual born of Christian parents. From this silence we justly infer that they must have been baptized in their infancy; and we defy the advocates of adult baptism to adduce a single scriptural example of their practice."[†]

On the day of Pentecost about three thousand Jews believed and were baptized. These three thousand had been circumcised and are called by Paedobaptists, "children born of the faithful." See for example Dr. Murray, "Children born of the faithful were given the sign and seal of the covenant." This is their usual way to describe those circumcised. The Paedobaptist position is that they were circumcised because they were Abraham's seed, born of believers in the "church." Thus, according to them, all the three thousand being Abraham's seed were born of Christian parents. If not they would not have been circumcised according to the paedobaptist belief.

---

[*] Calvin, *John–Acts*, 1075.
[†] Shaw, *The Reformed Faith*, 290.

These three thousand, who were covenant children, were baptized as adults upon believing contrary to Mr. Shaw. After Pentecost other Jews became Christians and were baptized so that the number came to 5,000. All these, according to Paedobaptists, were children born of the faithful. Robert Shaw defies us to adduce a single scriptural example. Unless I am mistaken here are 5,000. The disciples of our Lord all fall into this category. Timothy, whose mother was a believer, was doubtless baptized.

According to the Paedobaptist position salvation principally runs in family lines so we would expect that many of the early Jewish converts would be from believing families. There was always a remnant in Israel who were godly. No doubt many of the early believers came from this godly remnant. Were they baptized on their confession of faith? Assuredly. We have no record of any believer not being baptized because he had been circumcised although we do have record of thousands who were circumcised and then baptized when they became believers. And, if circumcision is the equivalent of baptism, as our Paedobaptist brethren say, then all who were baptized as infants should be baptized if they become believers, even as the circumcised infants who later believed were baptized as adults in the record of Acts.

Another example of one born of believers who was baptized as an adult is our Lord Jesus Christ. The reason he gave for his baptism was, "to fulfill all righteousness" (Matt. 3:15). He was baptized in obedience to the ordinance. That he did it to be an example to all believers cannot be doubted. Believers follow the Lord in baptism. Christ, by his baptism, sanctioned John's baptism as an ordinance of God. It was indeed from heaven (Luke 20:4).

> " '. . . to fulfill all righteousness.' If this be rendered, with Scrivener, 'every ordinance' or with Campbell, 'every institution', the meaning is obvious enough; and the same sense is brought out by 'all righteousness' or compliance with everything enjoined, baptism included."[*]

---

[*] Jamieson, Fausset, & Brown commentary on Matthew 3:15.

An objection has been made that because of Jesus' uniqueness it is not appropriate to give Jesus as an example of one born of believers baptized as an adult. However, if it is contrary to God's ordinances and inappropriate for the children of believers to be baptized as adults how much more would it have been inappropriate for Christ to have been baptized as an adult. No, he is our supreme example that the baptism of believers children when adults is not only appropriate but according to God's will and command. True, Christ was not baptized for the remission of sins but he was to fulfill all righteousness in obeying the Father's will. He is the head so his act was an example to be followed by the rest of the body. The phrase to fulfill all righteousness is translated by various translations as follows:

- *The New English Bible*: "to conform in this way with all that God requires."
- *Today's English Version*: "for in this way we shall do all that God requires."
- *Philip's*: "to meet all the Law's demands."
- *Jerusalem Bible*: "do all that righteousness demands."

Christ was baptized in obedience to God's will and it was the willing obedience of an adult to God's ordinance. If he had been baptized as an infant the Paedobaptists would have used it to support infant baptism but it could not be since Christ came to fulfill all the active righteousness of the Law and it had to be voluntary obedience. Our obedience to baptism must be the same.

> " 'I came not to destroy the law, but to fulfill it.' Even every iota of it. For (says he, Mat. 3:15), speaking of the necessity of being baptised, which was a branch of righteousness, 'Suffer it to be so, for it becomes us thus to fulfill all righteousness.' "*

But not only was our Lord an adult at baptism he was also the son of

---

* Goodwin, 5:508.

believers. Paedobaptists call such, children of the Covenant. They believe such should be baptized as infants in obedience to God. However, Christ was not baptized as an infant and saw his baptism as an adult to be to fulfill all righteousness in obedience to God.

I give one more example. Paul went to Corinth and "continued there a year and six months, teaching the Word of God among them" (Acts 18:11). "Crispus, the ruler of the synagogue, believed on the Lord with all his household. And many of the Corinthians, hearing, believed and were baptized" (Acts 18:8). This is a summary of the results of Paul's preaching during that year and a half. Crispus and his household would have been baptized since "the Corinthians, hearing, believed and were baptized." However, Paul wrote, "I baptized none of you except Crispus and Gaius" (1 Cor. 1:14). Later, he remembered that he had also baptized the household of Stephanas (vs. 16). He did *not* baptize Crispus' household—but only Crispus, although he baptized Stephanas' household—but not Stephanas.

Why? The household of Stephanas were the first ones saved. "You know the household of Stephanas, that it is the firstfruits of Achaia" (1 Cor. 16:15). Stephanas himself was not mentioned as the firstfruits. However he was saved later as Paul wrote of him as a believer, "I am glad about the coming of Stephanas" (1 Cor. 16:17). He was no doubt baptized by others after his conversion. Probably Crispus' family were not saved with him but rather were saved after him.

Paul only baptized the first fruits and left it to the church to baptize later converts to encourage spiritual leadership among them. The church decides who are to be accepted into fellowship with them. This means that the children coming from a believing father, Crispus, must have been baptized later by others since Acts tells us they believed. They were not baptized by virtue of the head of the household's faith, but by virtue of their own faith and profession. They were not baptized by Paul although they had a believing father. They were baptized later on their own profession of faith.

Part 4

THE COVENANTS

18

Definition, Number, and Headship

DEFINITION OF A COVENANT

"An absolutely complete covenant is a voluntary convention, pact, or agreement, between distinct persons, about the ordering and disposal of things in their power, unto their mutual concern and advantage."[*]

This is broken up into four points by Owen starting on the same page. I will reword in more modern language but the points are Owen's.

- Distinct persons are required for a covenant. Galatians 3:20, "a mediator does not mediate for one only . . ." so if a mediator is used in a covenant the covenant is not made by one person alone.

- This agreement must be voluntary and the terms of the covenant made by the parties of their free choice. Coercion would make an imperfect covenant.

- The terms of the covenant must be within the power of the ones who enter into the covenant.

---

[*] Owen, *Hebrews*, Volume 2, 82.

- The end of a covenant is made to the mutual advantage and profit of the persons concerned in it.

He then states: "Such covenants have three things in them: (1) A proposal of service; (1) A promise of reward; (3) An acceptance of the proposal. The one who proposes the covenant with its duties and promises a reward is superior to the one who accepts the proposal."

THERE ARE TWO COVENANTS

Romans 11:6 tells us that there are two great principles that are incompatible such that if it is of the one it is not of the other. They are mutually exclusive. "And if by grace, then it is no longer of works; otherwise grace is no longer grace. But if it is of works, it is no longer grace, otherwise work is no longer work." Thus there are only two covenants but there are two covenants. All the covenants then are either covenants of works or of grace.

> "There were never absolutely any more than two covenants. The first was the covenant of works, made with Adam, and with all in him...The other is that of grace, made originally with Christ, and through him with all the elect."*

TWO FEDERAL HEADS

Likewise, there are only two federal heads that are the heads of covenants. Adam is the head of the covenant of works and is called "the first man." It is true, he was the first man but he is designated the first man because he was the first to act as a legal representative for the whole race. Christ is called "the second man" even though many lived in the time after Adam and before Christ. He is called the second man because he was the second man to act as the federal head of his people who are considered by God to be in him. Christ is also called "the last Adam" because he, as Adam,

---

* Owen, *Hebrews*, Volume 5, 391.

is a covenant head but since there are no more covenant heads after him he is the last Adam. Thus there are two covenants but only two covenants. The verses we have been considering are 1 Corinthians 15:45, 47. "And so it is written, "the first man Adam became a living being." The last Adam became a life-giving spirit. The first man was of the earth, made of the dust; the second man is the Lord from heaven."

This reinforces Owen's statement that there are only two covenants but that there are two covenants called the covenant of works and the Covenant of Grace.

Since Adam and Christ are the only heads of their respective people they are the only ones from whom sin and righteousness are conveyed. "For as by one man's disobedience many were made sinners, so also by one man's obedience many were made righteous" (Rom. 5:18). This portion in Romans 5 is talking about two men as the fountains, Adam of sin, Christ of righteousness. As Goodwin says, "Adam and Christ are the only common roots of all sin and grace."[*]

Objection: A reader of this paper wrote to me after reading the above paragraphs, "I don't think there really is a biblical justification for the accepted idea that there was a 'covenant' of works between God and Adam. The only covenant I see is the one God gave to Israel through Moses." I will seek to defend my view that Adam is the head of the Covenant of Works. I've divided my answer to the objection into six points.

(1.) "Adam, who is a type of Him who was to come" (Rom 5:14b).

Adam is a type of Christ. Romans 5:12-21 reveals what the resemblance was between Adam and Christ. They were both covenant heads and representatives of their people. Did Christ act for his people? So Adam acted for all united with him in covenant.

(2.) The promise, condition and penalty that God gave to Adam in Gen. 2:16-17 imply a covenant.

The definition of a covenant as given in the previous chapter is fully met in the covenant made with Adam in Genesis 2:16-17.

---

[*] Goodwin, 10:62.

- There are the contracting parties, the Lord God and man.
- The condition, "thou shall not eat of it."
- The penalty, "thou shall surely die."
- By clear implication a promise, "do this, and thou shall live."

Adam, being holy and sinless, heartily consented to the covenant proposal.

James Buchanan wrote,

> "And yet it was more than a mere law; it was a law in the form of a covenant. In the words of Bishop Hopkins, 'If God had only said, "Do this," without adding, "Thou shalt live," this had not been a covenant, but a law; and if He had only said, "Thou shalt live," without commanding "Do this," it had not been a covenant, but a promise. Remove the condition, and you make it a simple promise; remove the promise, and you make it an absolute law: but, both these being found in it, it is both a law and a covenant.' "[*]

(3.) Imputation is only through a covenant.

For those who do not believe Adam was in a covenant I would ask, "How then was his act reckoned to the whole race?" Adam's act was imputed to all as their own act. And as Owen says,

> "And this makes way for the solution of the general question, How one may be said to do anything in another which shall be reckoned unto him as his own act? And this may be by virtue of a covenant, and no otherwise."[†]

All are joined to Adam since he is the covenant head of all mankind. The imputation of his sin is grounded on the unity of all men with their covenant head.

(4.) God dealt with Adam as the head of the race.

---

[*] Buchanan, *The Doctrine of Justification*, 287.
[†] Owen, 5:387.

The command God gave to Adam to multiply and fill the earth was meant for the whole race as was the dominion he was given over all creatures. Likewise the curse against the ground effected all mankind as it was meant to do. The sentence that he would return to the dust included all Adam's descendants. Since all are included we are led to the federal headship of Adam. All are included because all are in covenant.

(5.) "But they like Adam transgressed the covenant" (Hos. 6:7a).

This clearly teaches that a covenant was made with Adam as well as the Jews. Some, however, translate Adam as man since it is the same word in Hebrew. But if we translate it as man it adds no information for we would expect a man to act like a man. Others translate it "at Adam" rather than "like Adam". It is true that there is a town named Adam in Joshua 3:16 but it is an obscure, unimportant town. It is also true that the prefix b or *beth* (at) is easily confused with k *kaph* (like). These letters may be seen in some Bibles that write the Hebrew alphabet in Psalm 119. *Beth* is written before the section of verses 9-16 while *kaph* is written before the section 81-88. However, no texts support this translation using *beth*, 'at' as the prefix instead of *kaph* 'like' Adam. Writing about this change made by some Derek Kidner writes, "There is no textual basis for this change."[*]

Such a translation is a modern emendation, that is, it is a conjecture or supposition with no textual support. Such emendations should be rejected.

(6.) Since all mankind are born under the Covenant of Works and Adam is their covenant head, as stated under the above heading "Two Federal Heads," Adam necessarily was under a covenant of works.

THE PAEDOBAPTIST UNDERSTANDING OF THE COVENANTS

Paedobaptists base their belief on the covenants. They make much of the unity of the covenants. O. Palmer Robertson writes, ". . . the covenants of God are one."[†] Likewise, Robert Booth states,

---

[*] Kidner, *The Message of Hosea*, 69.
[†] Robertson, *The Christ of the Covenants*, 28.

"The terms 'historic covenants', 'covenantal administrations' or 'covenants of promise' refer to the particular covenants that God made with Adam, Noah, Abraham, Moses and David and sometimes to the new covenant. These particular covenants are but the individual parts, or the unfolding of the one 'Covenant of Grace'."[*]

That the Word of God is a unit and is all, both Old and New Testaments, to be received as the infallible Word of God I have no doubt. That God's redemptive plan was progressively revealed is also clear. However, are the covenants of God one as Robertson says and are all the covenants parts of the unfolding of the one "Covenant of Grace" as Booth says?

That all the covenants are one is plainly refuted by Paul when he writes about Abraham and his two sons and says, "Which things are an allegory; for these are the two covenants" (Gal. 4:24). Paul then goes on to show that although the Jews were "children of the covenant" as they proudly claimed, they are children of the covenant made on Mount Sinai and not the children of the promise belonging to the new Covenant of Grace. Much of Galatians contrasts the two covenants. It is the diversity of the covenants not their unity that is declared. Paedobaptists emphasize the unity of the covenants but not their diversity however Paul in the scriptures emphasizes their diversity.

Likewise, the book of Hebrews was written to show the differences of the two covenants. The priesthood is contrasted, the sacrifices are contrasted, indeed, there is contrast throughout Hebrews. Note,

"But now hath he (the Lord Jesus Christ) obtained a more excellent ministry, by how much also he is the mediator of a better covenant which was established upon better promises. For if that first covenant had been faultless then should no place have been sought for the second" (Heb. 8:6-7).

There, of course, cannot be a "better covenant" if there is only one covenant

---

[*] Booth, 47.

as the Paedobaptists teach.

THE OLD AND NEW COVENANTS

The two covenants are called the New Covenant and the Old Covenant. Covenant Theology does not accept a New Covenant that is really new. They want to call it a new administration of the Old Covenant. The Paedobaptist struggles with this word "new." Some Paedobaptists much prefer to say the "newer" covenant rather than the New Covenant. Thus, R. R. Booth writes,

> "The Hebrew word for 'new,' *hadash,* used in reference to the new covenant in Jeremiah 31:31, is not the word meaning 'brand new'; rather, it means 'renewed' or 'fresh.' The new covenant, like previous covenantal administrations, added to and expanded the redemptive revelation of God. It renewed the previous covenants, rather than replacing them."[*]

A cursory look at the word "new" in a Concordance such as Strong's or Young's will show that R. R. Booth's definition is wrong. The Hebrew word "*hadash*" is used for a brand new house (Deut. 20:5); a brand new wife (Deut. 24:5); brand new ropes (Jdgs. 15:3); a brand new cart (1 Chron. 13:7); a brand new song (Ps. 33:3); brand new heavens and brand new earth (Isa. 65:17); brand new hearts and brand new spirits (Ezek. 18:31). In fact there is not another Hebrew word which is used in the Old Testament meaning brand new. *Hadash* is the word used for new and fresh and is so defined by Strong.

When Jeremiah 31:31 is quoted in the New Testament in Hebrews 8:8-13 the Greek word used by the Holy Spirit for new was "*kaimos*" which is defined as "new, fresh, recent, newly made" by Young. The other Greek word for new, "*neos*", is also used for the New Covenant in Hebrews 12:24. This tells us that the New Covenant is new in every sense of the word. The same word as used in Hebrews 8:8-13 for new in regards to the covenant is used

---

[*] Booth, 51.

in 2 Corinthians 5:17 for "a new creation," and in Revelation 21:1, "a new heaven and a new earth."

In language as it is commonly spoken and understood old and new refer to two objects distinct from one another. The Old and New Covenants are two Covenants, diverse and distinct from one another. The New Covenant is not the Old modified or remodeled. It is not the old renewed, as Mr. Booth wrote, but brand new.

The two covenants are also referred to as the first and second, Hebrews 8:7, "For if that first covenant had been faultless, then no place would have been sought for a second," which clearly shows that the writer of Hebrews is writing about two separate and distinct covenants. They have a reason for strongly asserting the unity of the covenants, rather than the diversity of the first and second. This allows them to use the following type of argument for infant baptism.

- Children of Israelites (God's people) were included in the covenant and received the covenant sign of circumcision.
- All the covenants are one.
- Therefore all children of believers (God's people) are included in the Covenant of Grace and receive baptism as the covenant sign.

If the covenants of law and grace are quite distinct then their argument falls to the ground. Taking this distinction seriously Abraham Booth argues quite differently to the Paedobaptist. He said,

> "The different state of things under the old and new economy, and the apostle's distinction between the carnal and the spiritual seed of Abraham, being duly considered, the argument from analogy will run thus: As, under the old covenant, circumcision belongs to all the natural male descendants of Abraham so under the new covenant, baptism belongs to all the spiritual seed of Abraham, who are known to be such only by a credible profession of repentance and faith."[*]

---

[*] A. Booth, *Paedobaptism Examined*, 55.

His argument depends on the interpretation of Paul's that the old covenant had children of the flesh while the new covenant has children of the promise. Thus circumcision is to all Abraham's natural or fleshly descendants while baptism is for Abraham's spiritual seed, the spiritual seed being believers alone. "For ye are all the children of God by faith in Christ Jesus. And if ye be Christ's then are ye Abraham's seed, and heirs according to the promise" (Gal. 3:26, 29).

Paedobaptists largely ignore or contest the truth that the new covenant has replaced the old as Hebrews 8:7 says, "For if that first covenant had been faultless then should no place have been sought for the second" and again, "In that he saith, new covenant, he hath made the first old. Now that which decayeth and waxeth old is ready to vanish away" (Heb. 8:13). Ignoring this, R. Booth, a Paedobaptist, asks, "Does he end one covenant and then replace it with a new one?" and then goes on to argue strongly against that position. Yet 2 Corinthians 3 speaks of "that which is done away" as the "ministration of death written and engraven in stones" and contrasts it strongly with "the ministration of the Spirit" which remaineth.

This is the principle of interpreting the Old Testament from the added light of the New Testament. The Old Testament shadows are seen in the New Testament as the spiritual substance. The old was, "the shadow of heavenly things" (Heb. 8:5). Thus, "that was not first which is spiritual but that which is natural and afterward that which is spiritual" (1 Cor. 15:46). This is exemplified in Abraham's natural seed in the Old Testament being circumcised while the New Testament teaching is that the spiritual seed of Abraham are baptized being children of the promise by faith—"first . . . natural and afterward that which is spiritual." First there is the shadow then the substance, fleshly circumcision under the old covenant, spiritual circumcision under the new.

The Jewish nation was under the Mosaic covenant under which they received circumcision. Circumcision was received so that the Law of Moses should not be broken (see John 7:23). Therefore, a most vital question is whether the Mosaic covenant is a covenant of works or a Covenant of Grace.

19

The Mosaic Covenant—of Works or of Grace?

D r. Hodge wrote,

"The apostle often speaks of the Mosaic law as he does of the moral law considered as a covenant of works; that is representing the promise of life on the condition of perfect obedience. He represents it as saying, Do this and live; as requiring works and not faith, as the condition of acceptance. Rom. 10:5-10. Gal. 3:10-12. He calls it a ministration of death and condemnation. He denies that it can give life. Gal. 3:21 . . . The law of Moses was, in the first place, a re-enactment of the covenant of works."*

Thomas Goodwin reinforces this,

"He makes a covenant with the Jews, in outward appearance little better than a covenant of works (whereof it bears the name), then brings in that of grace, established upon better principles and promises."†

Owen concurs when he writes of the covenant at Sinai as reviving the covenant of works: It revived, declared, and expressed *all the commands of that covenant in the decalogue*; It revived the *sanction of the first covenant*, in the curse or sentence of death which it denounced against all trans-gressions.

---

* Commenting on 2 Corinthians 3:6 in his *Commentary*.
† Goodwin, 7:36.

It revived the promise of that covenant—*that of eternal life upon perfect obedience.* Now this is no other but the covenant of works revived.[*]

The above men are Paedobaptist so I add John Bunyan: [†] "The covenant of works or the law, here spoken of, is the law delivered upon Mount Sinai to Moses."

Having given the opinion of these mighty men I would like to give reasons why the Mosaic covenant is a covenant of works not grace. I am not denying that all covenants that God makes with man are gracious covenants since all covenants have gracious promises. Grace in that sense is found in all the covenants. Also, for the infinite, eternal God to enter into covenant with men who are but dust and soon carried away is amazing condescension. Yet, it remains that there are two covenants contrasted in scripture; the covenant of works and the Covenant of Grace.

In Hebrews the apostle writes of two covenants and compares and contrasts one with the other. He also declares that the one covenant he calls the first was done away by the introduction of the second or new covenant. These two covenants are the covenant made with Israel at Sinai called the first or Mosaic covenant and that made by God with His people through the death of Christ, usually termed the Covenant of Grace and called the second covenant in Hebrews. The difference concerning these two covenants are whether they are two distinct covenants as most Baptists hold or only different ways of administration of the same covenant. The latter is held by Paedobaptists to give support to infant baptism.

Our argument is not that Old Testament saints and New Testament saints are different people. I acknowledge that there is but one church and all believers are but one family of God. Also, our argument is not that Old Testament saints were saved in a different way from New Testament believers. No, there is only one way of salvation. Reconciliation is only through Christ, justification only through faith and redemption only through the Savior's precious blood. Old Testament believers had the promise of Christ even as New Testament believers. But having said this I

---

[*] Italics are Dr. Owen's *Hebrews,* 6:77-78.

[†] Bunyan, *Works,* 1:498.

believe the two testaments or covenants are dramatically different and two distinct covenants not a different administration of the same covenant.

> "The Scripture doth plainly and expressly make mention of two testaments, or covenants, and distinguish between them in such a way, as what is spoken can hardly be accommodated unto a twofold administration of the same covenant . . . And these two covenants, or testaments are compared one with the other and opposed one unto another, 2 Cor. 3:6-9; Gal. 4:24-26; Heb. 7:22, 9:15-20 . . . Wherefore we must grant two distinct covenants rather than a twofold administration of the same covenant merely to be intended."*

I also agree that the Old Testament saints were saved through the Covenant of Grace, there is no other way, so that the Covenant of Grace was in force under Old Testament times. None are saved except by being brought under the Covenant of Grace and the benefits of its mediator our Lord Jesus Christ. If they were saved by the virtue and promises of the Old Covenant then the Old Covenant could be seen to be but a different administration of the new but it is not so. Let us now consider scripture that tells us that the Old Covenant, the Mosaic, and the New Covenant are distinct and separate covenants. The following verses substantiate this: "The Lord our God made a covenant with us in Horeb. The Lord did not make this covenant with our fathers, but with us . . ." (Deut. 5:2-3).

Moses tells the Israelites that the covenant God made with them at Horeb (Sinai) God had not made with their fathers, Abraham, Isaac and Jacob. The Abrahamic covenant was the Covenant of Grace so the covenant made with Israel was a covenant of works.

"These are the words of the covenant which the Lord commanded Moses to make with the children of Israel in the land of Moab, besides the covenant which He made with them in Horeb" (Deut. 29:1).

After the children of Israel had wandered in the wilderness for forty years God made a covenant with them in the land of Moab. In Deuteronomy 29 and 30 the Lord is referring to this Covenant of Grace and it is called in

---

* Owen, 6:76.

29:1, "in addition to (or besides) the covenant he had made with them at Horeb." The word "besides" *bad* (Hebrew) comes from the root "to divide, to be solitary, alone" (see Strong's Concordance). It is used as follows, "beside the first famine" (Gen. 26:1); "men besides children" (Exod. 12:37), "besides the ram" (Num. 5:8); "besides the inhabitants of Gibeah" (Judg. 20:15). It speaks of another famine, other people, another offering, other inhabitants. It is not speaking of the renewal of the covenant made at Horeb but of another covenant; a covenant in addition to or besides that covenant. This other covenant was not made with them before but was entered into that day.

> "That you may enter into covenant with the Lord your God, and into His oath, which the Lord your God makes with you today, that He may establish you today as a people for Himself, and that He may be God to you, just as He has spoken to you, and just as He has sworn to your fathers, to Abraham, Isaac, and Jacob" (Deut. 29:12-13).

> "Yet the Lord has not given you a heart to perceive and eyes to see and ears to hear, to this very day" (Deut. 29:4).

The Israelites under the covenant made at Horeb did not have "a heart to perceive and eyes to see and ears to hear." They had not received the new heart that is promised in the new covenant. "I will give you a new heart" (Ezek. 36:26). They were under the old covenant, a different and distinct covenant. "And the Lord your God will circumcise your heart and the heart of your descendants, to love the Lord your God with all your heart and with all your soul, that you may live" (Deut. 30:6).

The promise, as given above, of the new covenant made in the land of Moab was to be given to the remnant whom "the Lord your God will bring back from captivity" (Deut. 30:3). Thus the old covenant that did not have this promise was not the Covenant of Grace.

When God gave the Ten Commandments the people said to Moses, "All that the Lord our God says to you we will hear and do it" (Deut. 5:27). God replied, "Oh, that they had such a heart in them that they would fear me and always keep all my commandments." Under the legal covenant the people did not have such a heart that they would fear God. They had not entered the Covenant of Grace that gives such a heart as Jeremiah 32:40 says, "I will make an everlasting covenant with them, that I will not turn away from doing them good; but I will put my fear in their hearts so that they will not depart from me."

A surety is one who is to pay the debts of the ones he is surety for and to do what they are required to do but are unable to. Christ is such surety for those in the new covenant (Heb. 7:22).

> "He undertook, as the surety of the covenant, to answer for all the sins of those who are to be and are made partakers of the benefits of it; - that is, to undergo the punishment due unto their sins; to make atonement for them, by offering himself a propitiatory sacrifice for their expiation; redeeming them by the price of his blood from their state of misery and bondage under the law and the curse of it, Isa. 53:4-6, 10; Matt. 20:28; 1 Tim. 2:6; 1 Cor. 6:20; Rom. 3:25-26; Heb. 10:5-10; Rom. 8:2-3; 2 Cor. 5:19-21; Gal. 3:13."[*]

However, he is not a surety for those in the Mosaic Covenant. They are on their own. The Mosaic Covenant is a covenant of works. "Though it is only a man's covenant, yet if it is confirmed, no one annuls or adds to it" (Gal. 3:15). "What purpose then does the law serve? It was added because of transgressions" (Gal. 3:19).

Galatians 3:15 says no one adds to a covenant. Covenants cannot be altered, annulled or added to without the consent of all parties concerned. Yet, the law was added to the Abrahamic covenant. But since a covenant cannot be added to this means that the law was a separate covenant. They are two distinct covenants.

"I will make a new covenant . . . not according to the covenant that I made with their fathers in the day when I took them by the hand to lead them out of Egypt" (Heb. 8:8-9). The new covenant was not according to the Mosaic covenant. It was a different covenant.

---

[*] Owen, 5:507.

"I will make a new covenant . . . because they did not continue in my covenant" (Heb. 8:9). So that that will not occur again the new covenant promise is that, "I will put My Spirit within you and cause you to walk in my statutes, and you will keep my judgments and do them" (Ezek. 36:27). The two covenants are drastically different. There are such great differences in the covenants that they are seen to be two different covenants. Some of these differences are:

THE COVENANTS DIFFER IN THEIR RESULTS

All under the Old Covenant of works are eternally lost. All under the New Covenant, a Covenant of Grace, are eternally saved. Believers in the Old Testament time were saved under the New Covenant which they entered by faith. David, as an example of this, was as an Israelite under the Mosaic law covenant but spiritually as a believer under the Covenant of Grace. As a believer under grace he wrote, "You do not desire sacrifice" (Psa. 51:14)—as under the Mosaic covenant—for he looked to the sacrifice of our Redeemer.

The heart of the Mosaic Covenant was the Ten Commandments. Indeed the Ten Commandments are called the covenant, "He wrote on the tablets the words of the covenant, the Ten Commandments" (Exod. 34:28). This Old Covenant, coming after the promise of Abraham was not a way or means of salvation. The apostle Paul time and again contended that there was no law that could give life.

> "There neither is, nor ever was, either righteousness, justification, life or salvation to be attained by any law, or the works of it, (for this covenant at Mount Sinai comprehended every law that God ever gave unto the church) but by Christ alone, and faith in him."[*]

As long as a man is under law he is under the curse (Gal. 3:10). As long as he is under law sin has dominion over him (Rom. 6:14). It is only when a

---

[*] Owen, 6:82.

man is united with Christ by faith that he is free from the law and found under the grace of the Covenant of Grace. Christ, having endured the curse of the law as found under the Mosaic Covenant (Deut. 27:26) is able to save to the uttermost those who come to God through him.

THE COVENANTS DIFFER IN THEIR ENDS

"The principal end of the first covenant was to discover sin, to condemn it, and to set bounds unto it. So saith the apostle, 'It was added because of transgression'."

"The end of the new Covenant is, to declare the love, grace, and mercy of God; and therewith to give repentance, remission of sin, and life eternal."*

THE COVENANTS DIFFER IN THEIR EFFECTS

The Covenant "written and engraved on stones" was called "the ministry of death" (2 Cor. 3:7). "For the letter (law) kills" (2 Cor. 3:6). It was "a ministry of condemnation." But the New Covenant which is of the Spirit "gives life" (2 Cor. 3:6) and is called the "ministry of righteousness." This righteousness ministered by the New Covenant is the opposite of the law's condemnation and so is a free and full justification.

THE COVENANTS DIFFER IN THEIR CONFIRMATION

The Mosaic covenant was not confirmed by an oath. If it had been it would have been absolute and unchangeable. The second covenant was confirmed with an oath as had been the Abrahamic covenant. Because the old covenant was made without an oath the priesthood and law were able to be changed and indeed were changed. "For the priesthood being changed, of necessity there is also a change of the law" (Heb. 7:12). However, Christ was made priest with an oath so he has an eternal unchanging priesthood. "For

---

* *Ibid.,* 6:91

they have become priests without an oath, but he with an oath" (Heb. 7:21). Nothing in the legal covenant of Moses was confirmed by an oath.

> "Nothing, therefore, in the whole legal administration being confirmed by the oath of God, it was always ready for removal at the appointed season."[*]

> "Although God never changeth any real internal acts of his will, or his purposes,—for "with him there is neither variableness nor shadow of turning,"—yet he often works an alteration in some things, which on some conditions, or for some time, he hath purposed and enjoined unto his church, unless they were confirmed by his oath; for this declares them to be absolutely immutable."[†]

The covenant referred to in Deuteronomy 29 and 30 was made with an oath, as Deuteronomy 29:12 and repeated in verse 14 says. Thus it was the Covenant of Grace. All the covenants that typified and manifested the Covenant of Grace were made with an oath; the Noahic (Isa. 54:9); the Abrahamic (Heb. 6:13-14); the Davidic (Psa. 89:3); the Messianic (Heb. 7:20-22, 28). God's oath made such covenants absolutely immutable, not that they were many covenants, for they were all the Covenant of Grace.

THE COVENANTS DIFFER IN THE PROVISION OF THE FORGIVENESS OF SINS

There was no provision for forgiveness in the Mosaic covenant. It demanded perfect obedience and a continuance in it. Anything short of that brought a curse. "Cursed is everyone who does not continue in all things which are written in the book of the law, to do them" (Gal. 3:10b). Since there is no forgiveness under law the conclusion of that statement is: "as many as are of the works of the law are under the curse" (Gal. 3:10a).

Does the Mosaic Covenant have any promise of forgiveness? Is there a

---

[*] Owen, 5:491.
[†] Ibid., 488.

place for repentance in the Mosaic Covenant? Is there any grace found in it? The Mosaic Covenant promised blessings upon obedience and curses upon disobedience (Deut. 28:1-19). It is contrasted with the New Covenant in 2 Corinthians 3:6-11 and called "the ministration of death written and engraven in stones," and "the ministration of condemnation" (vs. 7, 9). It could not justify nor was there any provision in it for forgiveness since repentance under law avails nothing. It was meant to reveal sin and imprison and keep men locked up under law until faith (or the faith) should be revealed (Gal. 3:23). To live unto God a man must die to the law (Gal. 2:19). Life is "by faith in the Son of God" (Gal. 2:20). Grace only comes through him, not through the law.

THERE IS NO FORGIVENESS THROUGH THE LAW

John Flavel, in his reply to a Mr. Cary who denied the right of believers' infants to baptism, rejects this by saying that there was forgiveness in the law.

> "Either there was pardon or repentance in Moses' covenant, and the Sinai dispensation of the law, or there was none; if you say none, you directly contradict Lev. 26:40, 46. If there were, then it cannot be Adam's covenant of works.'"*

Flavel elsewhere wrote, "The law required perfect working, under the pain of a curse, Gal. 3:10, accepted of no short endeavours; admitted of no repentance."†

Yet he says above that "there was pardon or repentance in Moses' covenant." He seems to contradict himself since the curse that he mentions was for disobedience to the law given on Sinai, the Mosaic covenant. Paul quotes Deuteronomy 27:26 in Galatians 3:10 to prove that those under the Mosaic covenant were under the works of the law. Such must "continue in all things which are written in the book of the law" (Gal. 3:10). This is

---

* Flavel, *Works*, Volume 6, 332.
† *Ibid.*, Volume 2, "Method of Grace," 272-73.

speaking of the law given by Moses. All the unsaved Israelites were under this law and so perished. That the Law of Moses is the covenant of works is evident by Acts 13:38-39,

> "Therefore let it be known to you, brethren, that through this man is preached to you the forgiveness of sins; and by him everyone who believes is justified from all things from which you could not be justified by the law of Moses."

Mr. Flavel himself, declares that Galatians 3:18 in this same context tells us, "The apostle . . . directly opposes the covenant of works as such to the Covenant of Grace, Gal. 3:18."[*]

Mr. Flavel continues,

> "That this text, Lev. 26:40 hath the nature of a gracious promise in it, no man will deny, except he that will deny that God's remembering of his covenant, for the relief of poor broken-hearted sinners, is no gospel promise pertaining to the Covenant of Grace: That it was made to the penitent Israelites upon mount Sinai, and there delivered them by the hand of Moses for their relief, is as visible and plain as the words and syllables of the 46th verse are to him that reads them."[†]

However, I believe Mr. Flavel erred since the covenant spoken of in Leviticus 26 that God would remember so that he would not "cast them away" nor "abhor them" (vs. 44), is not the Mosaic covenant but the "covenant of their ancestors" (vs. 45), the "covenant with Jacob, and also my covenant with Isaac, and also my covenant with Abraham" (v. 42). He is speaking of the Covenant of Grace not the covenant of works made later at Sinai. Deuteronomy 5:2-3 tells us that the covenant made at Horeb was not the same covenant made with the fathers. They were two different covenants. "The Lord our God made a covenant with us in Horeb. The Lord

---

[*] *Ibid.*, 335.
[†] *Ibid.*, Volume 6, 333.

did not make this covenant with our fathers, but with us, those who are here today, all of us who are alive" (Deut. 5:2-3). The gracious phrase, "I will remember my covenant" always refers to the Covenant of Grace. Leviticus 26:39-46 is a promise of forgiveness and mercy through that covenant to the remnant who would "confess their iniquity," humble themselves and accept their punishment. Notice it is to "those of you who are left . . ." (vs. 39). The promise is to the remnant. Thus God would not utterly destroy them but be merciful and gracious to them, that is "the remnant according to the election of grace" (Rom. 11:5). "But if it is by grace, it is no longer on the basis of works" (Rom. 11:6).

Why does Mr. Flavel in his controversy with Mr. Cary over infant baptism deny the Mosaic Covenant to be a covenant of works? Mr. Flavel agrees that circumcision belongs to the ceremonial law which is part of the Mosaic covenant. So if the Mosaic covenant is a covenant of works then circumcision belongs to the covenant of works and not the Covenant of Grace and is not the sign of the Covenant of Grace at all. Thus the analogy that all believers' natural seed are in the Covenant of Grace as were all Abraham's natural seed falls to the ground. Abraham's natural seed were not in the Covenant of Grace and only received the sign of the covenant of works and the conditional promises that went with that covenant. That is why they could be cut off from that covenant.

No one in the Covenant of Grace is ever cut off nor does it threaten curses to the disobedient. Abraham's spiritual seed are in the Covenant of Grace and to them only are the spiritual promises. No spiritual promises ever come apart from faith which alone unites to Christ. "And if you are Christ's, then you are Abraham's seed, and heirs according to the promise" (Gal. 3:29). Thus John the Baptist called the circumcised seed of Abraham "brood of vipers" and warned them not to say, "We have Abraham as our father." Natural descent carries no promise to either Abraham's descendants or believers' children. God's true children "were born, not of blood, nor of the will of the flesh, nor of the will of man, but of God" (John 1:13). Is this the birth you glory in?

THE COVENANTS DIFFER IN THEIR DAY OF REST

The day of rest or the Sabbath was the seventh day of the week under the old covenant. It is the Lord's day or the first day of the week under the new covenant. From Christ's resurrection a new day has been observed by the church. As the old creation had its day of rest and worship so the new creation has its day of rest and worship. As the Old Covenant Sabbath was founded on God's work of creation the New Covenant Sabbath is founded on Christ's work of redemption (see Heb. 4:3-10). Two different days of rest prove two different covenants.

> "The renovation and change of the covenant must and did introduce a change in the rest annexed unto it; for a Sabbath, or a holy rest, belongs unto every covenant between God and man . . . When that covenant was absolutely, and in all respects as a covenant, taken away and disannulled, and that not only as to its formal efficacy, but also as to the manner of the administration of God's covenant with men, as it is under the gospel, there was a necessity that the day of rest should also be changed, as I have more fully showed elsewhere. I say, then, that the precise observation of the seventh day enjoined unto the Israelites had respect unto the covenant of works, wherein the foundation of it was laid, as hath been demonstrated. And the whole controversy about what day is to be observed now as a day of holy rest unto the Lord, is resolved fully into this inquiry, namely, what covenant we do walk before God in."*

THE COVENANTS DIFFER IN THEIR RESULTS

"For the law made nothing perfect; but the bringing in of a better hope (did), whereby we draw nigh unto God" (Heb. 7:19).

When God gave the law at Sinai he was at pains to show the people they could not come near to him.

---

* Owen, 391-92.

"You shall set bounds for the people all around, saying, 'Take heed to yourselves that you do not go up to the mountain or touch its base. Whoever touches the mountain shall surely be put to death.'" Exod. 19:12).

The law contained in the Mosaic Covenant could not bring a sinner nigh unto God. It made nothing perfect. It did not perfect the promises, the worship nor the people. But the bringing of a better hope through the new and better covenant did. "For by one offering He has perfected forever those who are being sanctified" (Heb. 10:14).

There was "a disanulling of the commandment going before for the weakness and unprofitableness thereof" (Heb. 7:18-19). What the new covenant does that the old covenant could not do is to make all things perfect. That is it saves all those within it in the fullest sense of the word "saves". All those in the New Covenant are saved eternally. They cannot fail of their eternal inheritance. The new covenant saves! The promise is "sure to all the seed" (Rom. 4:16).

THE COVENANTS DIFFER IN THEIR DURATION

The duration of the two covenants tells us that they are two separate contrasting covenants. These covenants differ in their duration. The Mosaic Covenant came to an end while the New Covenant has no end. "In that He says, 'A new covenant,' He has made the first obsolete. Now what is becoming obsolete and growing old is ready to vanish away" (Heb. 8:13). At the time of writing it was "ready to vanish away" or "near unto a disappearance." It had "waxed old."

"The introduction of the new covenant did actually take away and abolish the old, making it to disappear."[*]

"A particular temporary covenant it was, and not a mere dispensation of the Covenant of Grace."[†]

The old covenant was "abolished" (2 Cor. 3:11). Although Christ's

---

[*] Owen, 6:174.
[†] *Ibid.*, 6:86.

death established the New Covenant and did away with the old in fact the Jewish system under the Mosaic Covenant continued until the destruction of the temple and the doing away with the priesthood and sacrifices in A.D. 70. But it was the New Covenant that replaced the old. Can that which is done away and that which replaces it be the same covenant? Hardly.

This reason is given by the Lutherans to show that there were two covenants that were distinct and not a twofold administration of the same covenant.

> "Because the Covenant of Grace in Christ is eternal, immutable, always the same, obnoxious unto no alteration, no change or abrogation; neither can these things be spoken of it with respect unto any administration of it, as they are spoken of the old covenant."[*]

An Objection: An objection to the Old Covenant being replaced by the New Covenant is made by some Paedobaptists.

> "Some Baptists maintain that the moral law expressed in the Old Testament is still valid for New Testament believers. This arbitrary determination is inconsistent with the contention that the old covenant has been replaced by the new covenant."[†]

Pastor Walter Chantry, a Baptist, also disagrees that the old covenant was done away, "When God makes a covenant, it is here to stay!"[‡]

However, 2 Corinthians 3:11 tells us, "For if that which was done away was glorious, much more that which remaineth is glorious."

The word that is translated "done away" is the Greek word *katargoumenon*. It's root, *katargeo*, is defined as:

> "to render useless or unproductive, occupy unprofitably, Lu. 13:7; to render powerless, Ro. 6:6; to make empty and unmeaning, Ro. 4:14;

---

[*] This is quoted by Owen, 6:74.

[†] R. Booth, 29.

[‡] Chantry, *The Covenants*, 13.

to render null, to abrogate, cancel, Ro. 3:3,31; Ep. 2:15, et al., to bring to an end, 1 Cor. 2:6; 13:8; 15:24,26; 2 Cor. 3:7, et al, to destroy, annihilate, 2 Thess. 2:8; He. 2:14; to free from, dissever from, Ro. 7:2, 6; Gal. 5:4."[*]

Strong's Concordance defines it as follows:

"to be (render) entirely idle (useless), lit. or fig. abolish, cease, cumber, deliver, destroy, do away, become (make) of no (none, without) effect, fail, loose, bring (come) to nought, put away (down), vanish away, make void."

It is used in Ephesians 2:15, "having abolished in His flesh the enmity, that is, the law of commandments contained in ordinances." 2 Timothy 1:10, ". . . who has abolished death and brought life and immortality to light," and Romans 6:6, "that the body of sin might be done away with."

2 Corinthians 3:11 is stating that the old covenant was abolished or done away with while the new covenant (which took its place) remains. Charles Hodge writes on this verse,

"The old dispensation and its ministry were temporary, the new is permanent . . . That the binding authority of the law ceased on the introduction of the gospel, is a doctrine which the apostle had to sustain against the Judaizing tendency of the early Christians, on many occasions. To this point the epistles to the Galatians and to the Hebrews are principally directed. The gospel did away with the law, but is itself never to be superseded."[†]

God had revealed the abolition of the Mosaic Covenant but the Hebrews could not understand it nor accept it until God through the Roman army completely destroyed Judaism.

Mr. Booth stated as quoted above that to hold that "the moral law

---

[*] *The Analytical Greek Lexicon*, 219.

[†] Hodge, 2 Corinthians Commentary.

expressed in the Old Testament is still valid for New Testament believers . . . is inconsistent with the contention that the Old Covenant has been replaced by the New Covenant."

The argument of some is that the Ten Commandments and the rest of the Mosaic law is a unit. Dr. Philpot, in arguing that the law is not the believer's rule of life, wrote,

> "God does not leave us at liberty to take at will one part of the law and leave the other. It must be taken as a whole or left as a whole, for God has so revealed it."*

If that is true then the moral law as given in the Ten Commandments as well as the ceremonial law is done away. However, there are reasons for separating the Ten Commandments from the rest of the Mosaic law.

THE TEN COMMANDMENTS DIFFER FROM THE REST OF THE MOSAIC LAW

The Lord himself spoke them to the assembly in an audible voice but Moses spoke the other laws to the people. God's commands concerning the institutions that were to be later changed He spoke only to Moses (Deut. 5:22; 4:33; 33:2-3).

Only the Ten Commandments were written by the finger of God. The other laws were written by Moses (Deut. 31:24-26).

Only the Ten Commandments were written on stone signifying their permanence. The ceremonial were written in a book (Deut. 31:24-26).

Only the Ten Commandments were laid up in the ark for safe keeping (Deut. 10:5; Exod. 31:26). Other temporary laws were placed outside the ark as a sign of their later removal (Deut. 31:26).

God called them the ten words to distinguish them (Deut. 10:4).

The Ten Commandments are called "spiritual." "We know that the law is spiritual" (Rom 7:14). This is spoken of the ten since in the context the

---

* Philpot, Sermon #72 "On the Law and Gospel."

tenth commandment is quoted. However, the ceremonial laws are called "carnal." "The law of a carnal commandment" (Heb. 7:16). They were as the tabernacle "symbolic for the present time . . . concerned only with foods and drinks, various washings, and fleshly ordinances imposed until the time of reformation" (Heb. 9:9-10).

Theologians make a valid distinction between positive laws and moral laws. Some call laws positive laws and natural laws saying that the positive are founded just on God's will while natural laws or moral laws are founded on God's nature. These moral laws are inherently good or intrinsically good in themselves. As such they are unchangeable. They have always been and always will be. They are perpetual.

Spurgeon said in one of his sermons:

> "The law of God must be perpetual from its very nature, for does it not strike you the moment you think of it that right must always be right, truth must always be true, and purity must always be purity? Before the Ten Commandments were published at Sinai there was still that same law of right and wrong laid upon men by their necessity of their being God's creatures. Right was always right before a single command had been committed to words. When Adam was in the garden it was always right that he should love his Maker, and it would always have been wrong that he should have been at cross purposes with his God; and it does not matter what happens in this world, or what changes take place in the universe, it never can be right to lie, or to commit adultery, or murder, or theft, or to worship an idol God. I will not say that the principles of right and wrong are as absolutely self-existent as God, but I do say that I cannot grasp the idea of God himself as existing apart from his being always holy and always true; so that the very idea of right and wrong seems to me to be necessarily permanent, and cannot possibly be shifted. You cannot bring right down to a lower level; it must be where it always is: right is right eternally, and cannot be wrong. You cannot lift up wrong and make it somewhat right; it must be wrong while the world standeth. Heaven and earth may pass away, but not the smallest letter or accent

of the moral law can possibly change. In spirit the law is eternal."[*]

God's people delight in the moral law for it is "holy, just and good" (Rom. 7:12). However, positive laws are not good in themselves but only as commanded by God. Such were the ceremonial laws and the temporary laws to guide the Commonwealth of Israel. Such were called a heavy yoke by Peter (Acts 15:10). But God's moral laws are not a heavy yoke to God's people. "His commandments are not burdensome" (1 John 5:3).

Positive laws before they were given were not necessary. They came into being by God's authority. And by His authority they may be taken away or abolished even as the laws concerning sacrifices, food, etc. have been abolished. The middle wall of partition has been broken down. These laws were a shadow that faded away when Christ the substance came (Col. 2:16-17). "Having abolished in His flesh the enmity, that is, the law of commandments contained in ordinances" (Eph. 2:15).

This means that the Ten Commandments then are moral or natural law, perpetual and unchangeable. We do not look to Moses for the Ten Commandments are not his but God's. So, since Christ, the greater than Moses, has come as our lawgiver we must take heed to God's exhortation, "This is my beloved Son. Hear Him!" (Mark 9:7) and "when they had looked around, they saw no one anymore, but only Jesus with themselves." Moses had faded from view.

As Luther wrote speaking of Moses, "Thus where he gives Commandment, we are not to follow him except so far as he agrees with the natural (moral) law."[†]

Quite often a comparison is made between Moses and Christ as law givers and between the ten commandments and the law given by Christ to show the superiority of the law of Christ to the law of Moses. However, the Mosaic law is not Moses law but God's law just as much as Christ's law is God's law. Christ, not Moses, was the giver of the law at Sinai. He was the one who spoke on earth, "Whose voice then shook the earth" (Heb. 12:25-

---

[*] Spurgeon, Sermon #1660, "The Perpetuity of the Law of God."
[†] Backham, ed., *Luther's Works*, 35:173.

26). Goodwin wrote of these verses, "And this, as it is the clearest scripture in the New Testament, that it was Christ that gave the law."[*]

Stephen, speaking of Christ, said, "the Angel who spoke to him (Moses) on Mount Sinai." Christ is that angel that God spoke of,

> "Behold, I send an angel before you to keep you in the way and to bring you into the place which I have prepared. Beware of Him and obey His voice; do not provoke Him, for He will not pardon your transgressions; for My name is in Him" (Exod. 23:20-21).

Thus, Christ was the law giver on Sinai when he spoke the Ten Commandments just as much as He is the law giver today to His church. Christ was the prophet of His church in all ages.

My final point is to show that God makes a distinction between the Ten Commandments and the ceremonial law is that in many scriptures God opposes moral duties to ceremonial duties.

"Then Samuel said: 'Has the Lord as great delight in burnt offerings and sacrifices, as in obeying the voice of the Lord? Behold, to obey is better than sacrifice, and to heed than the fat of rams'" (1 Sam. 15:22).

God hates the doing of the ceremonial law when the righteousness and justice of the Ten Commandments are not followed and obeyed. This makes a strong distinction. Please read Isaiah 1:10:17: "Give ear to the law of our God . . . Bring no more vain sacrifices; incense is an abomination to me. . . . Cease to do evil, learn to do good, seek justice."

This teaching is also found in the New Testament. "For circumcision is indeed profitable if you keep the law; but if you are a breaker of the law, your circumcision has become uncircumcision" (Rom. 2:25). The breaking of God's moral law in the Ten Commandments nullifies circumcision while the keeping of the moral law nullifies the breaking of the law of circumcision (vs. 26).

---

[*] Goodwin, 5:441.

THE LAW DONE AWAY AND ABROGATED AS A COVENANT

In 2 Corinthians chapter three Paul is writing of "the ministry of condemnation" and "the ministry of righteousness," "the ministry of death," and "the ministry of the Spirit." The first is the Mosaic administration of the law under the Old Covenant. The second is the administration of the gospel under the New Covenant. This covenant aspect of the law has been brought to an end and so done away. The law has been abrogated as a covenant.

THE LAW NOT DONE AWAY OR ABROGATED AS A RULE

"Do we then make void the law through faith? Certainly not? On the contrary, we establish the law" (Rom. 3:31).

The word that is translated, "void" is the Greek word *katargoumen*. It's root is *katargeo*. I defined it to mean done away, make empty and void, abrogate, cancel, etc. above under the heading "An objection." It is the same word in 2 Corinthians 3:7, 11, 13 which tells us the law is abolished, done away and abrogated.

However, here in Romans 3:31 we have Paul's strong denial. The law is not abolished or done away. God forbid. In fact it is rather established and made to stand strong through faith. Is this a contradiction? No, surely not. The law is abolished in one sense but not abolished in another sense. It is done away as a covenant but continues as a rule of action, walk and conduct.

"But now, though the law is made void as a covenant of works, it still continues a rule of action, walk and conversation; though it is done away as to the form of the administration of it by Moses, the matter, the sum and substance of it remains firm, unalterable, and unchangeable in the hands of Christ; though it is destroyed as a yoke of bondage, it is in being as a perfect law of liberty; and though believers are delivered from the curse and condemnation of it, they are not exempted from obedience to it; and though they are not to seek for justification by it, they are under the greatest obligations, by the strongest ties of love, to have regard to all its commands."[*]

I am not contending for freedom from law for the believer nor for its abolition but for freedom from the curse of the law and abolition of the Mosaic Covenant. Although "we have been delivered from the law" (Rom. 7:6) we are "not without law" (1 Cor. 9:21). Christians are "not under law" (Rom. 6:14) but they are "under law to Christ" (1 Cor. 9:21). Paul wrote that he had been made "free from the law of sin and death" (Rom. 8:3) but he also wrote that "with the mind I myself serve the law of God" (Rom. 7:25). It is interesting to note that the word Paul uses for "serve" comes from the same root as the word for slave. A slave hates the bondage of the law but a freeman "delights in the law of God" (Rom. 7:22) and delights to call himself a slave of Christ. "Christ is the end of the law for righteousness" (Rom. 10:3) so God's people do not pursue the law of righteousness for justification (Rom. 9:30-31) but they do "pursue holiness without which no one will see the Lord" (Heb. 12:14). Those "who walk in the law of the Lord" are declared blessed (Psa. 119:1). Indeed, law guides the saints in their service. It is never wrong to obey God's law. It is required for all people for all time. It is only wrong if we trust in our law keeping in any sense. Some wrongfully object to God's law requiring obedience of believers.

Horatius Bonar wrote,

> "Some will tell us that it is not service they object to, but service regulated by law. But will they tell us what it is to regulate service, if not law? Love, they say. This is a pure fallacy. Love is not a rule, but a motive. Love does not tell me what to do; it tells me how to do it. Love constrains me to do the will of the Beloved One; but to know what the will is, I must go elsewhere. The law of our God is the will of the Beloved One, and were that expression of His will withdrawn, love would be utterly in the dark; it would not know what to do. It might say, I love my Master, and I love His service, and I want to do His bidding, but I must know the rules of His house, that I may know how to serve Him. Love without law to guide its impulses would be

---

[*] Gill, "The Law Established in the Gospel," 19-20.

the parent of will-worship and confusion, as surely as terror and self-righteousness, unless upon the supposition of an inward miraculous illumination, as an equivalent for law. Love goes to the law to learn the divine will, and love delights in the law, as the exponent of that will; and he who says that a believing man has nothing more to do with law, save to shun it as an old enemy, might as well say that he has nothing to do with the will of God. For the divine law and the divine will are substantially one, the former the outward manifestation of the latter. And it is 'the will of our Father which is in heaven' that we are to do (Matt. 7:21); so proving by loving obedience what is that 'good, and acceptable, and perfect will of God' (Rom. 12:2). Yes, it is 'he that doeth the will of God abideth forever' (1 John 2:17); it is to 'the will of God' that we are to live (1 Pet. 4:2); 'made perfect in every good work to do His will' (Heb. 13:21); and 'fruitfulness in every good work' springs from being 'filled with the knowledge of His will' " (Col. 1:9, 10).*

I would explain that believers are not under the law as a covenant but they are under it as a rule of life. They are not under it as a covenant because their surety, our blessed Lord, has endured the curse in their place, that is, the curse of a broken law. Also, believers are not under the legal covenant that demands perfect obedience and absolute conformity to be declared righteous and so justified and accepted by God. The reason is that they are declared righteous through the righteousness of their covenant head, which righteousness is imputed to them by faith. Rather than being under the law in that sense believers are under grace. They are not justified by law but by grace. They have been pardoned freely and forgiven fully for Christ's sake. This is declared forcefully, "Ye are not under law (the article is not in the original) but under grace" (Rom. 6:14). Believers are not under the law principle as found in the Mosaic Covenant. They are under a gracious covenant, even the New Covenant. To be under law as a legal principle is to be under the dominion of sin.

"Sin shall not have dominion over you: for ye are not under law but

---

* Bonar, *God's Way of Holiness*, 43.

under grace" (Rom. 6:14). This means that the Old Testament saints who were saved by faith were not under law in the sense of Romans 6:14. They were under grace. However, does this mean believers are not under law in any sense? Are they then free to sin? Surely not. Paul's argument is, "What then? shall we sin, because we are not under law, but under grace?" He answers with righteous indignation, "God forbid" (Rom. 6:15).

Manton writing on James 2:12,

> "1. It is a 'law:' 1 Cor. 9:21, 'I am not without the law, but under the law to Christ.' There is a yoke, though not an insupportable burden. Though there be not rigour, yet there is a rule still. It is directive: 'He hath showed thee, O man, what is good,' Micah 6:8. The acceptable will of God is discovered in the law of ten words, and the moral part of the scripture is but a commentary upon it. And it is also imperative. It is not arbitrary to us whether we will obey or no. Laws are obliging. The will of the creator being signified to us in the law, we are under the commanding power of it. Things moral and just are perpetually obliging: Rom. 7:12, 'The law is holy, and the commandment holy, just, and good.' It is holy, it discovereth true strictness. It is just or suitable to those common notices of right and equity which are impressed upon the creature; and it is good, that is, profitable, useful for man. All which things infer a perpetual obligation; and if the law were not obliging there could be no sin; for where there is no obligation, there is no transgression: 1 John 3:4, 'Whosoever committeth sin, transgresseth the law; for sin is the transgression of the law.' Now natural conscience would soon be offended at that doctrine that should make murder, incest, or adultery no sins; and therefore it is but the vain conceit of profane men in these times to think that the gospel freeth us from the obligation of the law because it freeth us from the curse of it, for then all duty would be will-worship, and sin but a fond conceit."*

The freedom we have from the moral law is not a freedom to sin but a freedom from God's just requirement to fulfill it in our own strength. It is a

---

* Manton, *Complete Works*, Volume 4, 219.

freedom from the condemnation of the law but this is not inconsistent with an obligation to keep the law as a rule of life out of love to so good a Savior and in thankfulness to a gracious, forgiving God. Are such at liberty to disregard God's good and holy law? Can they now sin without fear? All God's people utterly reject such thinking with detestation for the grace they have found teaches them to deny ungodliness and worldly lusts and to live soberly, righteously and godly in the present age (see Titus 2:11-12). They say with righteous David, "O how I love your law! It is my meditation all the day" (Psa. 119:97).

> "If law has been abrogated then all duty has been abolished along with it,—our duty to God, our duty to men, our duty to ourselves; sin has disappeared, and even the possibility of sin has been annihilated,—for where there is no law, there is no transgression."[*]

> "The law of God, which is the rule of man's duty, is also a revelation of God's eternal Justice and Holiness."[†]

> "It thus appears that the law, besides being an authoritative expression of God's will, is also a revelation of His eternal justice and holiness, - that it is the unchangeable rule of His moral government, - and that, however it may consist with a sovereign purpose of mercy toward sinners, it can never be abrogated, modified, or relaxed, but must be executed or fulfilled, in such a way as shall manifest, in their actual exercise, the same divine perfections which it was designed to reveal and secure the end of punishment itself - the glory of His great name."[‡]

John, an apostle, defined sin in the New Testament by reference to the law, "Sin is the transgression of the law" (1 John 3:4 KJV). A translation closer to the original is, "Sin is lawlessness" (NKJV). The word in the Greek text that is translated lawlessness is anomia. It is made up of 'a' and 'nomia.'

---

[*] Buchanan, Justification , p. 298
[†] ibid., p. 302.
[‡] ibid., p. 304.

Nomia is the word for law. The prefix 'a' in this context is a negative similar to 'un' in English in such words as unable, unforgiving, untidy, unknown, etc. Literally *anomia* means 'not law' or 'lawlessness' or 'without law.' We, who speak English, call those who disregard law or despise law 'lawless.' Since sin is the transgression of law if a person argues that the moral law as given in the Ten Commandments has been abrogated or believers have nothing to do with law then there is by consequence no sin. "Where there is no law there is no transgression" (Rom 4:15b). And if there is no sin there is no need of a Savior from sin since, "Sin is not imputed when there is no law" (Rom 5:13b). May our good Lord deliver us from such teaching.

Some say the law can only kill, it can only curse. If this is so it is hard for me to understand how David and Paul delighted in the law. Can a man delight in that which can only kill him and curse him with eternal damnation? A man who lived in the 1800's said, "If then I, as a believer, take the law as my rule of life, I take it with its curse . . . he, (the believer) by adopting the whole puts himself under the curse."*

He continues speaking to believers, "the law can only minister condemnation and death." He is saying that a believer who would take the law as a rule of life is cursed and condemned to death, yes, even eternal death. Now our dear brother, and I am persuaded by his overall testimony that he is a brother now in heaven, is trying to magnify the gospel of grace and the work of the Savior. However, he really nullified the gospel and made Christ's work to be ineffective for a believer. If the believer, who seeks to obey the law, is cursed then Christ's death has not redeemed believers from the curse of the law and the gospel is untrue. Then the atonement has failed of its end. I shudder to write such things. Is every believer that "serves the law" lost? If such a believer is condemned then what of the promise that multitudes of believers have found comfort in, "There is therefore now no condemnation to them that are in Christ Jesus" (Rom 8:1)?

I suppose all who follow our brother could extricate themselves from this dilemma by saying that those who use the law as a rule of life are not true believers so they are condemned. I would hope that they don't doubt the

---

* Philpot, Sermon #72 "On the Law and Gospel."

salvation of all who disagree with their view of the law for all the great confessions of faith teach the same as The Baptist Confession of Faith and I quote it,

> "5. The moral law doth for ever bind all, as well justified persons as others, to the obedience thereof, and that not only in regard of the matter contained in it, but also in respect of the authority of God the Creator, who gave it; neither doth Christ in the Gospel any way dissolve, but much strengthen this obligation.
>
> Although true believers be not under the law as a covenant of works, to be thereby justified or condemned, yet it is of great use to them as well as to others, in that as a rule of life, informing them of the will of God and their duty, it directs and binds them to walk accordingly; discovering also the sinful pollutions of their natures, hearts, and lives, so as examining themselves thereby, they may come to further conviction of, humiliation for, and hatred against, sin; together with a clearer sight of the need they have of Christ and the perfection of his obedience: it is likewise of use to the regenerate to restrain their corruptions, in that it forbids sin; and the threatenings of it serve to shew what even their sins deserve, and what afflictions in this life they may expect for them, although freed from the curse and unallayed rigour thereof. These promises of it likewise shew them God's approbation of obedience, and what blessings they may expect upon the performance thereof, though not as due to them by the law as a covenant of works; so as man's doing good and refraining from evil, because the law encourageth to the one and deterreth from the other, is no evidence of his being under the law and not under grace.
>
> Neither are the aforementioned uses of the law contrary to the grace of the Gospel, but do sweetly comply with it, the Spirit of Christ subduing and enabling the will of man to do that freely and cheerfully which the will of God, revealed in the law, requireth to be done.'"

---

* *Baptist Confession of Faith of 1689*, Chapter 19, 5-7.

THE UNBELIEVER'S RELATION TO LAW AND THE BELIEVER'S RELATION TO LAW

"Because the carnal mind is enmity against God; for it is not subject to the law of God, nor indeed can be. So then, those who are in the flesh cannot please God" (Rom. 8:7-8).

This verse tells us that the unbeliever is not subject to the law of God. "Subject" is the translation of the Greek word *hupotasso* (the word translated 'under' in Romans 6:14, in the phrase 'under law' is *hupo*). Strong defines it, "to subordinate, be under obedience, put under, subject to, submit self unto." Thus unbelievers are not under obedience to the law, are not subject to it and do not submit to it. They are rebellious and not under God's law. They are not under the law and do not obey it. Indeed they are unable to be subject to the law to obey it. However, they are under law as to its condemnation and its curse. They are under the law since they are obligated to obey it as a covenant of works. Yet in relation to obeying it they are not under the law. In one sense they are under the law; that is as a covenant; in another sense they are not under it as to obedience, and rebel against it.

What about a believer? In contrast to an unbeliever he is subject to the law. The spiritual mind is not at enmity against God but is subject to the law of God. Being regenerated by God's Holy Spirit the believer is not in the flesh and so able to please God as he subjects himself to God's law. However, in another sense he is not under law, "For sin shall not have dominion over you, for you are not under law but under grace" (Rom 6:14). In what sense is he not under law?

> "To be under the law is to be under the obligation to fulfill the law of God as a rule of duty, as the condition of salvation. Whosoever is under the law in this sense is under the curse . . . We are not under the law in this sense, but under grace: that is under a system of gratuitous justification."*

---

* Hodge, *Romans*, 205-06.

Some understand that a believer is in no sense "under law." In the *International Bible Commentary*, F. F. Bruce, general editor, it is written, "Calvin distinguishes between the directing capacity of the law and the penalty of the law. Its directing capacity remains, but grace frees us from the penalty."* This is a biblical distinction. We (believers) are not under law as to its penalty but we are as to its directing or commanding power. In the same book on page 1425, commenting on Galatians 5:2-12, it says,

> "It is not circumcision as an act which is in view (as v. 6 shows) but rather circumcision entered into as a deliberate commitment to the Jewish rite, or on relying on its efficacy for salvation."

This is a vital statement! I believe there is misunderstanding of the issue. Thus, many misunderstand "every man who becomes circumcised, Christ will profit nothing . . . he is debtor to keep the whole law...you have fallen from grace" (Gal. 5:3-5). They understand it to refer to all who would obey God's law as a rule. Not so! Circumcision as an act does not condemn. Circumcision as an "attempt to be justified by law does." Paul circumcised Timothy. This does not mean Timothy had fallen from grace or that Christ would profit him nothing.

Likewise, keeping the law does not condemn but the keeping of law to justify one's self does bring a curse. To make obedience to God's law a bad thing is a grave error.

Romans 6:14 is true of a believer for all of his life. Can he put himself under the law (in the sense of Romans 6:14) if he takes the law as a rule for his life? Impossible! God alone has power to put men under law and to put men under grace. We cannot overthrow grace. Praise God! Romans 6:14 is not talking about not being under law as a rule but not being under its curse or its demands for a perfect righteousness of our own to be justified. If a believer could put himself under law, in the sense of Romans 6:14, he would come under the curse but that of course is impossible since "Christ has redeemed us from the curse of the law, having become a curse for us." A

---

* Bruce, 1426.

believer does subject himself to God's law by obedience to it and he does put himself under it most willingly as a rule. Does this mean that a believer then is under law and not under grace? No, not in the sense of Romans 6:14. If so, he comes under condemnation. But a believer is justified so how can he be condemned? They are mutually exclusive. They can't be together in the same person.

Some speak quite disparagingly of God's law. However, "the law is holy, and the commandment holy and just and good" (Rom 7:12). They seem to imply the law is unholy and the commandment unjust and evil. Obedience to law is not an evil course of action. We see this in David's desires to keep the law.

> "Oh, that my ways were directed to keep your statutes! Then I would not be ashamed, when I look into all your commandments. I will praise You with uprightness of heart, when I learn Your righteous judgments. I will keep Your statutes" (Psa. 119:4-8).

This is not to say that the law does not produce death, condemnation and the curse to those who misuse the law to seek salvation by it. But it should be noted that these effects are only to the unregenerate who are enemies to God and his holy law. Indeed they hate the law of God. McCheyne in a sermon on "The Christian's Warfare" commenting on the phrase in Romans 7:22, "I delight in the law of God after the inward man," said, "1. Before a man comes to Christ, he hates the law of God; his whole soul rises up against it—'The carnal mind is enmity against God, and is not subject to the law of God.'" (Rom. 8:7).

First, unconverted men hate the law of God on account of its purity— "Thy Word is very pure, therefore Thy servant loveth it." For the same reason worldly men hate it. The law is the breathing of God's pure and holy mind. It is infinitely opposed to all impurity and sin. Every line of the law is against sin. But natural men love sin, and therefore they hate the law, because it opposes them in all they love. As bats hate the light, and fly against it, so unconverted men hate the pure light of God's law, and fly against it.

Second, they hate it for its breadth—"Thy commandment is exceeding broad (Psa. 119:96). It extends to all their outward actions, seen and unseen; it extends to every idle word that men shall speak; it extends to the looks of their eye; it dives into the deepest caves of their hearts; it condemns the most secret springs of sin and lust that nestle there. Unconverted men quarrel with the law of God because of its strictness. If it extended only to my outward actions, then I could bear with it; but it condemns my most secret thoughts and desires, which I cannot prevent. Therefore, ungodly men rise against the law.

Third, they hate it for its unchangeableness. Heaven and earth shall pass away, but one jot or one tittle of the law shall in no wise pass away. If the law would change, or let down its requirements, or die, then ungodly men would be well pleased. But it is as unchangeable as God; it is written on the heart of God, with whom is no variableness nor shadow of turning. It cannot change unless God change; it cannot die unless God die. Even in an eternal hell its demands and curses will be the same. It is an unchangeable law, for He is an unchangeable God. Therefore ungodly men have an unchangeable hatred to that holy law.

2. When a man comes to Christ, this is all changed. He can say, "I delight in the law of God after the inward man." He can say with David, "O how love I Thy law; it is my meditation all the day." He can say with the Lord Jesus in the 40th Psalm, "I delight to do Thy will, O God, yea, Thy law is within My heart."

> "For when Gentiles, who do not have the law, by nature do the things contained in the law, these, although not having the law, are a law to themselves, who show the work of the law written in their hearts, their conscience also bearing witness, and between themselves their thoughts accusing or else excusing them" (Rom. 2:14-15).

The above verses tell us that those without the written law have "the work of the law written in their hearts." Not written by them or of their own making or tradition but rather inscribed in their hearts by God. Since Adam was created in God's image (Gen. 1:27), he was created by God "in righteousness and holiness" (Eph. 4:24). This was no doubt done since all

God made was good and to enable God and man to have communication and fellowship. God made man to be a rational creature accountable to him and being fitted for government by God, he needed to be put under law.

The doctrine arising from these truths is that the rule which God at first revealed to man for his obedience was the moral law.

As Thomas Boston preached,

> "It is here supposed, that man always was and is under a law, for being a rational creature, capable of obeying the will of God, and owing obedience to his Creator by virtue of his natural dependence upon him, he behooved to be under law."*

Every man has the work of God's law written within him. It has been defaced by the fall but men still "show the work of the law written in their hearts, their conscience also bearing witness, and between themselves their thoughts accusing or else excusing them." All men have this law that differentiates between good and evil. This law, being lost and ruined by the fall, was revealed to the Israelites again at Sinai.

Owen, commenting on Hebrews 12:18-19, concerning this giving of the Ten Commandments, wrote,

> "This law, for the substance of it, was written in the hearts of mankind by God himself in their original creation but being much defaced, as to the efficacious notions of it by the entrance of sin and the corruption of our nature, and greatly affronted as unto the relics of it in the common practice of the world, God gave it in the church this becoming renovation with terror and majesty. And this he did, not only to renew it as the guide unto all righteousness and holiness, as the only rule and measure of obedience unto himself and of right and equity amongst men, and to give check, by its commands and sanction, unto sin; but principally to declare in the church the eternal establishment of it, that no change or alteration should be made in its commands or penalties, but that all must be fulfilled to the uttermost,

---

* Boston, "The Moral Law, the Rule of Man's Obedience."

or sinners would have no acceptance with God: for it being the original rule of obedience between him and mankind, and failing of its end through the entrance of sin, he would never have revived and proclaimed it, in this solemn, glorious manner, if it had been capable of any abrogation or alteration at any time. Therefore these words he spake himself immediately unto the people, and these only."[*]

Thus this "holy, just and good commandment" that God gave to man at creation continues without abrogation until today. That "original rule of obedience between him and mankind," still continues to teach and guide men in their relationship to their Creator and after conversion in their love relationship to their Lord and Savior and his people, and will do so until heaven and earth pass away.

"A creature can no more be morally independent of God in its actions and powers, that it can be naturally independent of Him. A creature, as a creature, must acknowledge the Creator's will as its supreme law; for as it cannot exist without Him, so it must not be but for Him, and according to His will; yet no law obliges, until it is revealed. And hence it follows, that there was a law which man, as a rational creature, was subjected to in his creation; and that this law was revealed to him.

'God made man upright.' This supposes a law to which he was conformed in his creation; as when any thing is made regular, or according to rule, of necessity the rule itself is presupposed. Whence we may gather that this law was no other than the eternal, indispensable law of righteousness, observed in all points by the second Adam, opposed by the carnal mind, and some notions of which remain yet among the Pagans, who, 'having not the law, are a law unto themselves,' (Rom. 2:14). In a word, this law is the very same which was afterwards summed up in the ten commandments, and promulgated, on mount Sinai, to the Israelites, called by us the moral law; and man's righteousness consisted in conformity to this

---

[*] Owen, 7:321.

law or rule."*

"Now all has been heard: here is the conclusion of the matter: Fear God and keep His commandments, for this is the whole duty of man" (Eccl. 12:13).

I would just note here that the will of God revealed is the law of God. Since God's law was in Christ's heart He delighted to do God's will. All the New Testament exhortations are God's will revealed in His law. Thus I have tried to meet the objection that the moral law is abrogated.

A SUMMATION

To get back to our main theme there are other points of difference that demonstrate that the Old covenant or Mosaic Covenant and the New Covenant of Grace are two separate and distinct covenants but may these suffice. I am indebted to John Owen for many of the above thoughts. For anyone who wants to look into this further or still has doubts I would recommend Owen's Hebrews for a complete and satisfying presentation.

All the above points are contrasting the Mosaic Covenant with the New Covenant, the Old Covenant of law with the New Covenant of Grace mediated by Christ. It is the differences between the covenants that are emphasized. In doing this we are only following the great apostle to the Gentiles. Paul, in his great doctrinal letters, contrasted these same covenants. This is particularly evident in passages such as Romans 4—5, 7 and 9; 2 Corinthians 3; Galatians 3—4; and Hebrews 7—10.

We cannot open up all these passages but I will just comment on 2 Corinthians chapter 3 and quote others as a sample of all to prove that the two covenants are contrasted in Scripture. It is their distinctness that puts the grace of the New Covenant in focus and reveals its glory and beauty.

"You are manifestly an epistle of Christ, ministered by us, written not with ink but by the Spirit of the living God, not on tablets of stone

---

* Boston, *Human Nature in its Fourfold State*, 39-40.

but on tablets of flesh, that is, of the heart" (2 Cor. 3:3).

Paul is contrasting the law given on Sinai and written on tablets of stone and the New Covenant promised in Jeremiah 31:31-33. At Sinai God wrote the law on tablets of stone which was external to sinful man. This revealed his sinfulness and inability to keep the law. However, Jeremiah promised that the law would be written internally on the heart by a spiritual work. This writing was accomplished through the ministry of Paul upon the Corinthians. It was a divine, supernatural work done at their conversion by the Spirit of God proving that Paul was indeed a minister of Christ.

> "Who also made us sufficient as ministers of the new covenant, not of the letter but of the Spirit; for the letter kills, but the Spirit gives life" (2 Cor. 3:6).

The words "letter" and "spirit" mean the law and gospel. Thus, the law kills but the spirit (gospel) gives life. Our apostle labels the Mosaic Covenant as a legal system. Its function as a Covenant of works is again and again presented and taught by Paul.

Hodge writes of this when commenting on 2 Corinthians 3:6,

> "The apostle often speaks of the Mosaic law as he does of the moral law considered as a covenant of works; that is, presenting the promise of life on the condition of perfect obedience. He represents it as saying, Do this and live; as requiring works, and not faith, as the condition of acceptance. Rom 10, 5-10. Gal. 3, 10-12. He calls it a ministration of death and condemnation. He denies that it can give life. Gal. 3, 21. He tells those who are of the law (that is, Judaizers) that they had fallen from grace; that is, had renounced the gratuitous method of salvation, and that Christ should profit them nothing. Gal. 5:2, 4. In short, when he uses the word law, and says that by the law is the knowledge of sin, that it can only condemn, that by its works no flesh can be justified, he includes the Mosaic law; and in the epistle to the Galatians all these things are said with specific reference to the

law of Moses."[*]

Dr. John Murray, however, does quite the opposite to the Apostle Paul. He rather than contrasting the two covenants to show their distinctness seeks to emphasize their similarities to prove their oneness. He does that in The New Bible Dictionary published by Inter Varsity Press in his article "Covenant" on p. 266. He seeks to prove their oneness by writing of the Mosaic Covenant as a Covenant of Grace, "Israel was sovereignly chosen. The covenant was made with a redeemed people. Israel had been adopted into a filial relation to God."[†]

Israel's election was election as a nation. Every Israelite belonged to this elected nation. However, most Israelites were not "chosen in Christ before the foundation of the world." God from the beginning did not choose them for salvation through sanctification by the Spirit, and belief in the truth. There is an analogy between Israel's national election to certain privileges and a person's personal election to salvation but it is only an analogy not an equivalence as Dr. Murray implied.

Yes, as Dr. Murray wrote, the covenant is made with a redeemed people but again this is very different from God's chosen people redeemed from sin and "justified freely by His grace through the redemption that is in Christ Jesus" (Rom 3:24). The nation of Israel was redeemed from the physical bondage of Egypt such that an unsaved Israelite could say he was redeemed in that sense but he was still spiritually in bondage and eternally lost.

Likewise, Israel's adoption was a type of the adoption of God's children in Christ Jesus but not the same thing. It should be noted that Romans 9:4, "who are Israelites, to whom pertain the adoption, the glory, the covenants, the giving of the law, the service of God, and the promises" is speaking of unsaved Israelites, Paul's kinsmen according to the flesh.[‡]

Dr. Murray, seeking to show the likeness of the Mosaic Covenant and

---

[*] Hodge, Commentary on 2 Corinthians.

[†] Murray, *The New Bible Dictionary*, 266.

[‡] I write later on Israel being a type and on their characteristics under the heading, "The Characteristics of the Nation of Israel."

the Abrahamic Covenant, continues,

> "of equal significance for the interpretation of the Mosaic Covenant is the fact that it was made with Israel in pursuance and fulfillment of the Abrahamic Covenant (Exod. 2:24; 3:16; 6:4-8; Psa. 105:8-12, 42, 45; 106:45).
>
> These facts conspire to show that the Mosaic Covenant is not to be construed in a way that would place it in sharp contrast with the Abrahamic and indicate that the same concept of sovereign administration of grace rules in this case as in earlier covenants."[*]

I don't think we can say the Mosaic Covenant is the fulfillment of the Abrahamic Covenant. Rather, the verses Dr. Murray gives tell us that God delivered Israel from Egypt and gave them the land of Canaan as fulfillment of a promise of the Abrahamic covenant. It was a promise of a physical deliverance to a carnal nation.

Again he wrote,

> "The spiritual relationship which is at the centre of the Abrahamic Covenant is also at the centre of the Mosaic. 'And I will take you to me for a people and I will be to you a God; and ye shall know that I am the Lord your God'" (Exod. 6:7: cf. Deut. 29:13).[†]

He left out the words, "who brings you out from under the burdens of the Egyptians" in Exodus 6:7. These words tell us that the promise was a natural promise to a carnal nation and not the spiritual promises of the New covenant to a regenerated people. Although the same words are used it is quite a different relationship to be a God to a rebellious and stiff-necked people who were cut off than to be a God to a spiritual nation that have been united for eternity with God's own dear Son. The verse that he used for comparison, Deuteronomy 29:13, is not talking about the Mosaic Covenant made at Sinai but with the covenant made that day in the land of Moab (see

---

[*] Murray, 266.
[†] Ibid.

Deut. 29:1). That covenant, in distinction from the Mosaic legal covenant, carried the promise to circumcise their hearts as found in the New Covenant. "And the Lord your God will circumcise your heart and the heart of your descendants, to love the Lord your God with all your heart and with all your soul, that you may live" (Deut. 30:6).

Dr. Murray wrote,

> "The demand for obedience and the keeping of the covenant does not place the Mosaic in a different category and does not make it a conditional covenant of works."[*]

Dr. Murray in his *Collected Writings* quoted Robert Rollock's treatise, *Quaestiones es Responsiones Aliquot de Foedere Dei* (Edinburgh, 1596) and William Perkins accordingly,

> "The Covenant of Works, also called the Covenant of Nature, Rollock defines as the covenant in which God promises to man eternal life on the condition of good works performed in the strength of nature, a condition which man in turn accepts . . . As regards repetition, the covenant is repeated again and again from the creation and fall of man to the coming of Christ but particularly in the promulgation from Mount Sinai by the hand of Moses (Ex. 19:5-8). The end of this repetition, however, was not that men might be justified and live by this covenant, but that, being convicted of sin and of the impossibility of good works in the strength of nature, they might take refuge in the Covenant of Grace."

> "William Perkins plainly speaks of the Covenant of Works as God's covenant made on the condition of perfect obedience and expressed in the moral law (*A Golden Chaine*, London, 1612, 32)."[†]

Please note that in these quotations, contrary to Dr. Murray, the Mosaic Covenant is called a covenant of works promising eternal life on condition

---

[*] *Ibid.*
[†] Murray, 220-221.

of perfect obedience. I don't know whether Dr. Murray had changed his position or whether he was just quoting them to give an historical overview but his quotations contradict his statements that I have quoted above. The demand for obedience of the Mosaic Covenant is a repetition of the Covenant of Works and is a demand for absolute and perfect obedience to the law of works! The Mosaic Covenant is certainly conditional since the condition is, "The man that doeth these things shall live in them" (Lev. 18:5 KJV). "You shall therefore keep My statutes and My judgments, which if a man does, he shall live by them" (Lev. 18:5 NKJV). The condition is "if a man does." The Mosaic Covenant revived the promise of the covenant of works—the promise of eternal life upon perfect obedience. The apostle quotes this verse in Romans 10:5 as the "righteousness of the law" contrasted with "the righteousness of faith" verse 6.

However, the Covenant of Grace is an unconditional covenant for man since Christ is the surety of the New Covenant and He has fulfilled all the conditions for His people. The covenant is not dependent on man's works or contributions. If it was it would not be "sure and steadfast." Does the Old Covenant still exist as a law? Yes, it still continues to demand perfect obedience and still threatens the curse for disobedience. As Owen wrote,

> "Hence, if any man believeth not, 'The wrath of God abideth on him.'
> For it commands and curses depending on the necessary relation
> between God and man, with the righteousness of God as the
> supreme governor of mankind, they must be answered and fulfilled.
> Wherefore it was never abrogated formally. But as all unbelievers are
> still obliged by it, and unto it must stand or fall, so it is perfectly
> fulfilled in all believers,—not in their own persons, but in the person
> of their surety."*

In the New Covenant, the Covenant of Grace, the promise of God is, "I will put My laws in their mind and write them on their hearts," etc. There is no condition to this promise to be done by man to make it good. Owen comments on this verse, Hebrews 8:10,

---

* Owen, 6:62.

"In the description of the covenant here annexed, there is no mention of any condition on the part of man, of any terms of obedience prescribed unto him, but the whole consists in free, gratuitous promises, as we shall see in the explication of it."*

Dr. Murray's zeal to make the Mosaic Covenant to be in the same category as the Abrahamic Covenant of Grace and not to allow it to be "in sharp contrast with the Abrahamic" has to either moderate the Mosaic Covenant of Works or take away the grace of the New Covenant or both. He wrote, "The demand for obedience in the Mosaic Covenant is identical in principle with the same demand in the New Covenant."[†]

For that to be so the Mosaic Covenant must be emptied of its legal principle or the New Covenant emptied of its grace. Either way, Dr. Murray is drastically changing the scriptural principles of the Mosaic and/or New Covenants. Can it really be that law and grace are after all just the same? I think the whole scriptures protest against such a thought. "And if by grace, then it is no longer of works; otherwise grace is no longer grace. But if it is of works, it is no longer grace; otherwise work is no longer work" (Rom. 11:6).

The end of the Mosaic Covenant was not to save. As Dr. Murray wrote concerning Rollock's views of the repetition of the covenant of works in the Mosaic Covenant that I quoted above,

"The end of this repetition, however, was not that men might be justified and live by this covenant, but that, being convicted of sin and of the impossibility of good works in the strength of nature, they might take refuge in the Covenant of Grace."

This is the end of the law as found in the Mosaic Covenant. It was given to reveal sin and the holiness of God. It was meant to show man's inability to do works acceptable to God and to bring man guilty before his judge. Dr. Murray puts grace into the Mosaic Covenant but there is no grace in the Mosaic Law. To put grace in the law is to dull the sharp edge of the law to cut

---

* *Ibid.*, 135.
[†] Murray, 266.

and wound and produce death and condemnation. The law is a mighty weapon to humble proud man and to crush self-righteousness but it can only do this since forgiveness and mercy are not found in it. It is pure justice which cuts off all hope for natural man. No relief, no escape from its curse is declared by the law. Here is its power. If this was not so one of our greatest weapons in evangelizing the unsaved would be lost.

What would we do on the mission field without this sword that causes men to flee for refuge to the Savior? This aspect of the Word of God is compared to one of the most destructive weapons existing during Bible times. "It is sharper than a two-edged sword." "It pierces" to the very core and produces death. This work of the law is set before us at Mount Sinai when the law was given.

> "For you have not come to the mountain that may be touched and that burned with fire, and to blackness and darkness and tempest, and the sound of a trumpet and the voice of words, so that those who heard it begged that the word should not be spoken to them anymore. (For they could not endure what was commanded: 'And if so much as a beast touches the mountain, it shall be stoned or thrust through with an arrow.' And so terrifying was the sight that Moses said, 'I am exceedingly afraid and trembling')" (Heb. 12:18-21).

Owen comments on these verses,

> "This communication was done in such a way of dread and terror as that sundry things are manifest therein; as, (1) That there was no evidence, in all that was done, of God's being reconciled unto them, in and by those things. The whole representation of him was as an absolute sovereign and a severe judge. Nothing declared him as a father, gracious and merciful. (2) There was no intimation of any condescension from the exact severity of what was required in the law; or of any relief or pardon in case of transgression. (3) There was no promise of grace, in a way of aid or assistance, for the performance of what was required. Thunders, voices, earthquakes, and fire, gave no signification of these things. (4) The whole was hereby nothing

but a glorious ministration of death and condemnation, as the apostle speaks, 2 Cor. 3:7; whence the consciences of sinners were forced to subscribe to their own condemnation as just and equal. (5) God was here represented in all the outward demonstrations of infinite holiness, justice, severity, and terrible majesty, on the one hand; and on the other, men in their lowest condition of sin, misery, guilt, and death."*

Is the Mosaic Covenant a Covenant of Grace? Hardly! The two covenants are sharply opposed. But when a man stands guilty before God with his mouth stopped by the law (Rom. 3:20), he is ready to hear the best news there is, "But now the righteousness of God apart from the law is revealed" (Rom 3:21; see Rom. 3:19-26). Thank God for the law.

---

* Owen, 7:307.

20

Circumcision—A Type of Spiritual Circumcision

The Paedobaptist believes that circumcision is the old covenant's counterpart to baptism. There is an analogy between the two but what corresponds to circumcision in the old is the reality in the new, that is the shadow to the substance, the symbol to the thing symbolized, the natural to the spiritual. Therefore, the spiritual interpretation of circumcision in the new would not be a physical rite as baptism. It is that which is spiritual corresponding with that which is natural or physical in the old covenant.

Colossians 2:11 is used by Paedobaptists to illustrate baptism as the new covenant parallel or analogy to physical circumcision. However, a careful reading of Colossians 2:11 rather leads to spiritual circumcision, the circumcision made without hands or the circumcision of Christ (Christian circumcision as J. O. Buswell translates it), as the thing symbolized by circumcision. There is no mention made of physical circumcision in Colossians 2:11. Rather believers are called the circumcised with the circumcision made without hands. What is the shadow of this in the old covenant but physical circumcision made with hands. If we accept that spiritual or inward circumcision is of the heart, "in the spirit and not in the letter," then we see that this is regeneration; a "putting off (of) the sins of the flesh" and a "putting on Christ."

Thus circumcision and baptism have a similar symbolic meaning but the true parallelism is physical circumcision to all the natural seed under the old covenant and spiritual circumcision to the spiritual seed or believers in the new. David Kingdon writes,

> "When Paul says in Eph. 2:11 that in their pre-Christian condition
> his readers were in a state of uncircumcision, he was not referring to
> their lack of the sign in their flesh. Rather he meant that in their
> unregenerate state they were, 'without Christ, being aliens from the
> commonwealth of Israel and strangers from the covenants of
> promise.'"*

Thus the type in the old covenant is circumcision, the antitype in the
new covenant is spiritual circumcision (regeneration).

Kingdon continues,

> "Paul's definition of spiritual circumcision allows no place
> whatsoever for the concept of believers and their infant seed. It is
> believers and believers only who are the circumcision, whereas in
> Israel every male according to the flesh received this sign."†

Only regenerate believers "have put off the old man with his deeds and
have put on the new man." Thus only the regenerate should be baptized as
symbolizing this new life, "Buried with him in baptism wherein also ye are
risen with him" (Col. 2:12).

The phrase, "circumcised with the circumcision made without hands"
in Colossians 2:10 and the phrase "buried with Him in baptism" in verse 11
have led many Paedobaptists to say that Paul is teaching that baptism
symbolizes spiritual circumcision and then by a roundabout argument say
that physical circumcision also symbolizes spiritual circumcision so then
circumcision and baptism are the same. Commenting on these two verses R.
Booth says,

> "In this passage, Paul clearly identifies the signs of circumcision and
> baptism with each other. As he writes to the church of the new

---

* Kingdon, 33.
† *Ibid.,* 34.

covenant, he explains that believers are circumcised in the spiritual sense of that word, and that this spiritual circumcision takes place as they are buried with Christ in baptism. This equating of the essential meaning of circumcision and baptism could not be any clearer. Just as physical circumcision indicated a circumcision of the heart, so now physical baptism indicates a circumcision of the heart."[*]

Of course, Mr. Booth should not have written that "spiritual circumcision takes place as a believer is buried with Christ in baptism" unless he believes that baptism regenerates. He was also incorrect to say "physical circumcision indicated a circumcision of the heart." No infant who was circumcised had the spiritual circumcision. They were all born spiritually uncircumcised even as they were born physically uncircumcised. Likewise, physical baptism does not indicate spiritual circumcision unless he is speaking of believers' baptism. Spiritual circumcision is of the heart. It is regeneration.

Mr. Booth says, "The Covenant sign was not an indication that those who received it were regenerated."[†] Quite right. But then how can he write as above, "Physical circumcision indicated a circumcision of the heart?" This is contradictory. He says circumcision does not indicate regeneration and then says it indicated circumcision of the heart, which is regeneration. However, let us get back to our text.

It seems unlikely that Paul is trying to identify physical circumcision, which he doesn't mention, with baptism. He is rather giving the order of a believer's experience; "circumcised with the circumcision made without hands" followed by baptism. Circumcised with the circumcision made without hands is regeneration which by God's appointment precedes baptism and both are part of a Christian's completeness. Paul is writing of this completeness. Notice the verse just previous to verse 10, "And you are complete in Him" (verse 9). He does not mention literal circumcision. Physical circumcision is no part of a believer's completeness and so should not be confounded with baptism. The identity of the two rites is not taught

---

[*] R. Booth, 107.
[†] *Ibid.*, 9.

in these two verses.

21

The Old Covenant and Circumcision

ircumcision was to all the carnal seed of Abraham without any regard to faith. Thus, Ishmael was circumcised. Nevertheless, not being of Abraham's spiritual seed he was cast out and "could not be heir with the son of the freewoman." As Paul so forcefully writes,

> "Neither because they are the seed of Abraham are they all children: but 'In Isaac shall thy seed be called'" (Rom. 9:7).

> "Nevertheless what saith the scripture? Cast out the bondwoman and her son: for the son of the bondwoman shall not be heir with the son of the freewoman. So then, brethren, we are not children of the bondwoman but of the free" (Gal. 4:30-31).

Spiritual qualifications had nothing to do with circumcision. The only qualification for circumcision was carnal and of the flesh. All Israelites were circumcised at birth. What qualified them? Just their physical birth as Israelites. The overwhelming number of them were ungodly men born of ungodly men.

Further proof of this is that if a man was damaged in his sexual organs he was "cut off from the congregation of the Lord" (Deut. 23:1). It made no difference if he was a believer. Likewise an illegitimate child was not circumcised nor able to enter into the congregation of the Lord. Even his children to the tenth generation were barred. Whether they were godly did not enter in. The qualifications were not spiritual. If they were illegitimate they were "cut off." Once again this is a purely fleshly disqualification having to do with physical birth (Deut. 23:2).

Thus circumcision is not parallel to baptism nor did baptism take the place of circumcision. Paul adamantly refused to circumcise Titus. Was this because Titus had been baptized and thus circumcision was replaced? No, not at all. That was not Paul's explanation. If circumcision was replaced by baptism Paul should have explained that at this occasion. Also, if that was a true principle Paul would have been inconsistent to circumcise Timothy. He opposed Titus being circumcised so that "the truth of the gospel might continue with you" (Gal. 2:5). Those who tried to compel Titus to be circumcised were seeking to take away the liberty of believers "that they might bring us into bondage" (Gal. 2:4). Paul refused because of a gospel principle. Salvation was by grace alone. To insist on circumcision was to nullify grace and bring the bondage of the law. Circumcision is part of the Old Covenant of law. As Stott writes on this portion,

> "To introduce the works of the law and make our acceptance depend on our obedience to rules and regulations was to bring a man into bondage again."[*]

If the Gentile Christians had been compelled to be circumcised the gospel principle of freedom from bondage to law would have been surrendered. Although baptism is required of believers it is not bondage to law. Thus, circumcision and baptism cannot be equated nor are they parallel.

Paul did circumcise Timothy. Why? Timothy had a Jewish mother. To circumcise a Jew is far different than circumcising a Gentile. Timothy was circumcised as belonging to national Israel but baptized as belonging to spiritual Israel. Paul circumcised Timothy as a concession to the Jews and to keep from offending them unnecessarily and so to preserve unity. Yet if baptism took the place of circumcision Timothy should not have been circumcised after his baptism. This action of Paul's would have misled the whole church of God for all time and contradicted the truth, if it was so, that

---

[*] Stott, *The Message of Galatians*, 43.

baptism took the place of circumcision. These two actions of Paul prove conclusively that baptism did not take the place of circumcision.

What is the meaning of circumcision in regard to Abraham's seed? It was an external sign in the flesh that the one so circumcised was an Israelite after the flesh and it meant no more. It distinguished Israel from the other nations that were uncircumcised. Circumcision was a national sign and a legal ordinance.

David Kingdon objects to this by saying,

> "Circumcision, although it was taken up into the Mosaic Law and included within it, was initially bestowed not upon Moses but upon Abraham (see Gen. 17). Circumcision was enjoined on Abraham and his family before ever Israel became a nation. It was not a legal ordinance, but the sign in Abraham's flesh of God's gracious covenant with him and with his seed. Now if we accept this, as the evidence surely compels us to do, then we cannot interpret circumcision as a sign only of Israel's national separation to God. It was this of course, but its significance as a sign is not exhausted by describing it as a merely national sign. Whilst it was taken up into the Mosaic covenant it preceded it as the covenant sign by many generations, and thus it cannot be interpreted exclusively as a national sign."[*]

He reasons that because circumcision was to Abraham not Moses it was not "a sign only of Israel's national separation to God." Yet since it was to Abraham not to Moses it shows that it was a national sign. It was given when Israel as a nation began. Israel as a nation did not begin with Moses, it began with Abraham. Moses was not the father of the Jewish nation. The Jews rightly said, "Abraham is our father" (John 8:39). God's promise to Abram was, "My covenant is with you, and you shall be a father of many nations" (Gen. 17:4). One of these nations was Israel. If circumcision had been first given to Moses the argument would be as follows: Circumcision is not a national sign since the nation of Israel existed for over 400 years before

---

[*] Kingdon, 27-28.

circumcision was given. But since circumcision was given to the father of the nation for the whole nation it is a national sign.

Mr. Kingdon also states that circumcision, "was not a legal ordinance, but the sign in Abraham's flesh of God's gracious covenant with him and with his seed." It is true that all God's dealings with men are gracious in a certain sense but circumcision was a legal ordinance. As Paul in Galatians tells them, "I testify again to every man who becomes circumcised, that he is a debtor to keep the whole law" (Gal. 5:3). Circumcision is firmly joined to law by the apostle. It is a legal ordinance. Paul then enforces this in the very next verse, "You who attempt to be justified by law; you have fallen from grace" (Gal. 5:4). For the Galatians to be circumcised is to attempt to be justified by law.

Circumcision belongs to the covenant of works not the Covenant of Grace. The covenant of circumcision could be broken, "And the uncircumcised male child, who is not circumcised in the flesh of his foreskin, that person shall be cut off from his people; he has broken My covenant" (Gen. 17:14). But the Covenant of Grace is inviolable. The Covenant of Grace made with Abraham was "to you and your seed" that the apostle defines as singular seed not plural seeds. The singular seed is Christ (see Gal. 3:16). Thus God said the Covenant of Grace made with Abraham was made "to your seed," even Christ. This covenant is made through Christ with Abraham's spiritual seed but the covenant of circumcision was made with Abraham and all his physical seed. It was a legal covenant made with the nation of Israel. The two covenants that were made with Abraham are symbolized by his two sons Isaac and Ishmael.

> "For it is written that Abraham had two sons: the one by a bondwoman, the other by a freewoman. But he who was of the bondwoman was born according to the flesh, and he of the freewoman through promise, which things are symbolic. For these are the two covenants" (Gal. 4:22-24).

Ishmael was circumcised and so included in the covenant of circumcision. He was never in the Covenant of Grace although he was in the

Abrahamic covenant of circumcision. This covenant of circumcision was not made with Ishmael as an individual but God rather entered into the covenant of circumcision with Abraham. The covenant of circumcision is a covenant of works and it included all Abraham's physical seed. It was purely a legal covenant with conditions of obedience to the law and could be broken.

Isaac, however, as a "child of promise" was in the Covenant of Grace. The covenant (of Grace) was only with Isaac not Ishmael. "As for Ishmael, I have heard you . . . but my covenant I will establish with Isaac" (Gen. 17:20-21). Thus this Covenant of Grace was not made with all of Abraham's seed. It was made with his one seed or offspring, Christ, and through Him with all the children of promise. So Paul writing to the Galatian believers is able to say, "Now you, brothers, like Isaac, are children of promise" (Gal. 4:28), and so "the blessing of Abraham might come upon the Gentiles in Christ Jesus, that we might receive the promise of the Spirit through faith" (Gal. 3:14). "So then he is the father of all who believe but have not been circumcised" (Rom. 4:11).

Thus we see that there were two covenants made with Abraham represented by his two sons Ishmael and Isaac. All children enter the covenant of works by natural birth but all the "children of promise" who are born supernaturally, as Isaac, enter the Covenant of Grace by spiritual birth and through faith. "For you are all sons of God through faith in Christ Jesus" (Gal. 3:26). Even so the promise is sure to all Abraham's offspring,

> "Therefore it is of faith that it might be according to grace, so that the promise might be sure to all the seed, not only to those who are of the law, but also to those who are of the faith of Abraham, who is the father of us all" (Rom. 4:16).

Grace never comes through physical descent. It never comes by law. It never comes through a physical rite. The two covenants must never be confused nor reduced to just one. Grace and works are mutually exclusive. So the two covenants cannot be mixed. We are either in the one covenant or the other. Let us fear lest we come short of the promise found only in the Covenant of Grace.

22

Who Are Under the Covenant of Works?

The covenant of works was not only made with Adam but with all his seed. So when Adam fell his whole lineage fell with him and "so death came upon all men because all sinned" in Adam. Was the first covenant annulled by that fall? No, not at all. Every man is born in Adam and is obliged to keep the law. All men are born "under the law." Thus we read that Christ was, "born of a woman, born under the law, to redeem those who were under the law" (Gal. 4:4-5). Christ finds all he came to redeem under the law. And since redemption is only "in Christ" none are redeemed until by faith they are united with their Redeemer. Men are "justified freely by His grace through the redemption that is in Christ Jesus." There is no redemption outside of Christ. But to believers it is written, "But of Him you are in Christ Jesus, who became for us wisdom from God—and righteousness and sanctification and redemption" (1 Cor. 1:30). All this found in Him.

Another proof that all men are born in Adam and so under the law as a covenant of works is that sin rules over every natural man. Why is this? It is because men are under the law. Not until a man is set free from the law and put under grace can it be said that sin shall not have dominion over him (see Rom. 6:14).

All without exception are children of wrath. Even the elect of God such as the saints at Ephesus "were by nature children of wrath, just as others" (Eph. 2:3). Paul includes himself for he says, "We all . . . were by nature children of wrath." He had been circumcised and born into the commonwealth of Israel but he still was born under the old covenant "dead in trespasses and sins." Likewise, even those born to believers in the church are under the old covenant, the covenant of works and so subject to the curse of the law. No infant is born naturally into the Covenant of Grace. All are born under the law.

"Whatever the law says, it says to those who are under the law, that every mouth may be stopped and all the world may become guilty before God" (Rom. 3:19). The law speaks to those who are under it, that every mouth may be stopped and all the world may become guilty. Thus every person, yes, the whole world, is under the law until saved by grace.

"Who are now under the covenant of works? There is a vulgar prejudice abroad which supposeth that the first covenant was repealed and disannulled upon the fall, and that God now dealeth with us upon new terms; as if the Covenant of Grace did wholly extrude and shut out the former contract, wherein they think Adam only was concerned. But this is a gross mistake, because it was made not only with Adam, but with all his seed. And every natural man, whilst natural, whilst merely a son of Adam, is obliged to the tenor of it. The form of the law runneth universally, 'Cursed is every one that,' &c., Gal. 3:10; which rule brooketh no exception but that of free grace and interest in Christ. And therefore every child, even those born in the church, are obnoxious to the curse and penalty of it: 'Children of wrath, even as others,' Eph. 2:3; and therefore are natural men described by this term, 'Those that are under the law,' Gal. 4:5; that is, under the bond and curse of the law of works. If the law of works had been repealed and laid aside presently upon Adam's fall, Christ had not come under the bond and curse of it as our substitute and surety, for he was to take our debt upon him, to submit to the duty and penalty of our engagement; therefore it is said, in the place last quoted, he was 'made under the law, to redeem them that were under the law.' So also Gal. 3:13, 'He was made a curse for us;' that is, in our room and place. And, again, the law is not repealed, because it is an unchangeable rule, according to which God proceedeth, 'Not a pick of the law shall pass away,' Mat. 5:18, till all be fulfilled, either by the creature, or upon the creature, by us, or by our surety. It is the covenant of works that condemneth all the sons of Adam. The rigour of it brought Christ from heaven to fulfil it for believers. Either we must have Christ to fulfil it, or for the breach of it we must perish for ever. And therefore our apostle saith, that at the day of judgment God proceedeth with all men according to the two covenants; some are, 'judged by the law of liberty,' and some, 'have judgment without mercy.' The two covenants have two principal confederate parties that contracted for them and their heirs—Adam and Christ; therefore, as long as thou are Adam's heir, thou has Adam's engagement upon thee. The covenant of works was made with Adam and his seed, who were all natural men. The Covenant of Grace with Christ and his seed, who are believers, Isaiah 53:10. God will own no interest in them that claim by Adam. As Abraham was to reckon his seed by Isaac, not by Ishmael, 'In Isaac shall thy seed be called;' so God's children are reckoned by Christ. Others that have but a common interest, cherish a vain hope: 'God that made them will not save them.' Isaiah 27:11."[*]

Whether an infant is born of godly or heathen parents makes no difference as to their sinful and corrupt state. "There is no difference for all have sinned and fall short of the glory of God" (Rom. 3:22-23). *Sinned* is in the aorist tense representing a past action pointing to original sin. Meyer says, "The sinning of each man is presented as an historical fact of the past." However, the verb "come short" is in the present tense. The abiding consequence of original sin is a continual coming short of the glory of God. All without exception are included.

"For, 'as in water face answereth to face, so the heart of man to man' (Prov. 27:19). Adam's fall has framed all men's hearts alike in this matter. Hence the apostle (Rom. 3:10-18), proves the corruption of the nature, hearts, and lives of all men, from what the psalmist says of the wicked in his day (Psa. 5:9; 10:7; 14:1-3; 36:1; 140:3); and from what Jeremiah says of the wicked in his day (Jer. 9:3), and from what Isaiah says of those that lived in his time (Isa. 57:7-8), and concludes

---

[*] Manton, *Manton's Complete Works*, Volume 4, 288.

(vs. 19), 'Now we know that what things soever the law saith, it saith to them who are under the law; that every mouth may be stopped, and all the world may become guilty before God.'"*

Writing further on the sinfulness of man's natural state Boston continues,

"It appears from that text of Scripture (Job 14:4), 'Who can bring a clean thing out of an unclean? Not one.' Our first parents were unclean, how then can we be clean? How could our immediate parents be clean? How can our children be so? The uncleanness here referred to, is a sinful uncleanness; for it is such as makes man's days full of trouble; and it is natural, being derived from unclean parents; 'Man is born of a woman' (verse 1), 'And how can he be clean, that is born of a woman?' (Job 25:4). The omnipotent God, whose power is not here challenged, could bring a clean thing out of an unclean, and did so in the case of the man Christ: but no other can. Every person that is born according to the course of nature is born unclean. If the root be corrupt, so must the branches be. Neither is the matter mended, though the parents be sanctified ones; for they are but holy in part; and that by grace, not by nature, and they beget their children as men, not as holy men. Wherefore, as the circumcised parent begets an uncircumcised child, and after the purest grain is sown, we reap chaff with the corn; so the holiest parents beget unholy children, and cannot communicate their grace to them, as they do their nature; which many godly parents find true, in their sad experience. Consider the confession of the psalmist David (Psa. 51:5), 'Behold, I was shapen in iniquity, and in sin did my mother conceive me.' He ascends from his actual sin, to the fountain of it, namely, corrupt nature. He was a man according to God's own heart, but from the beginning it was not so with him. He was begotten in lawful marriage: but when the lump was shapen in the womb, it was a sinful lump. Hence the corruption of nature is called the 'old man' being as old as ourselves, older than grace, even in those that are sanctified from the womb.

---

* Boston, 62.

Hear our Lord's determination of the point (John 3:6). 'That which is born of the flesh is flesh.' Behold the universal corruption of mankind—all are flesh! Not that all are frail, though that is a sad truth too: yea, and our natural frailty is an evidence of our natural corruption, but that is not the sense of the text. The meaning of it is: all are corrupt and sinful, and that naturally. Hence our Lord argues that because they are flesh, therefore they must be born again, or else they cannot enter into the kingdom of God (verses 3-5). And as the corruption of our nature shows the absolute necessity of regeneration, so the absolute necessity of regeneration plainly proves the corruption of our nature; for why should a man need a second birth, if his nature were not quite marred in his first birth?"[*]

That all without exception are born in Adam with corrupt hearts and so under the law and its curse is seen by the inclination of all children to evil.

"Is not the way of evil the first way which the children of men go? Do not their inclinations plainly appear on the wrong side, while yet they have no cunning to hide them? In the first opening of our eyes in the world, we look a-squint, hell-ward, not heaven-ward. As soon as it appears that we are rational creatures, it appears that we are sinful creatures (Psa. 58:3). 'The wicked are estranged from the womb; they go astray as soon as they be born.' (Prov. 22:15). 'Foolishness is bound in the heart of a child: but the rod of correction shall drive it far from Him.' Folly is bound in the heart, it is woven into our very nature. The knot will not unloose; it must be broken asunder by strokes. Words will not do it, the rod must be taken to drive it away; and if it be not driven far away, the heart and it will meet and knit again. Not that the rod of itself will do this: the sad experience of many parents testifies the contrary; and Solomon himself tells you (Prov. 27:22), 'Though thou shouldest bray a fool in a mortar among wheat with a pestle, yet will not his foolishness depart from him;' it is so bound in his heart."[†]

[*] *Ibid.*, 65-66.
[†] *Ibid.*, 102-03.

Also, the natural religion of all men is a works religion thus showing that all are born in the covenant of works and not the Covenant of Grace.

> "None of Adam's children are naturally inclined to receive the blessing in borrowed robes; but would always, according to the spider's motto, 'owe all to themselves:' and so climb up to heaven on a thread spun themselves. For they 'desire to be under the law' (Gal. 4:21), and 'go about to establish their own righteousness' (Rom 10:3)."[*]

> "The law was Adam's covenant; and he knew no other, as he was the head and representative of all mankind, that were brought into it with him, and left under it by him, though without strength to perform the condition thereof. Hence, this covenant is interwoven with our nature; and though we have lost our father's strength, yet we still incline to the way he was set upon, as our head and representative in that covenant; that is, by doing, to live. This is our natural religion, and the principle which men naturally take for granted (Matt. 19:16), 'What good thing shall I do, that I may have eternal life?' "[†]

> "Such is the natural propensity of man's heart to the way of the law, in opposition to Christ, that, as the tainted vessel turns the taste of the purest liquor put into it, so the natural man turns the very gospel into law, and transforms the Covenant of Grace into a covenant of works . . . Great is the difficulty, in Adam's sons, of their parting with the law as a covenant of works. None part with it, in that respect, but those whom the power of the Spirit of grace separates from it."[‡]

The doctrine I have sought to prove and that I believe scripture and experience abundantly teaches is *all infants are born in the Covenant of Works.* They are all born in Adam. Only the regenerated are born in Christ but this is a spiritual not a natural birth. Further, only those in Christ by faith are in

---

[*] *Ibid.,* 113.
[†] *Ibid.,* 118-19.
[‡] *Ibid.,* 120-21.

the Covenant of Grace. Infant baptism is contrary to original sin and the corruption of nature through the fall and in practice denies these fundamental doctrines.

An objection that is made is that the Covenant of Works is no longer in force and as such does not now exist. Dr. J. O. Buswell Jr. states in a heading of his *Systematic Theology*, "The Covenant of Works No Longer Open."[*] He regards men as not being under the Covenant of Works and that it is not now in effect. Does he mean that there is therefore only one covenant now in operation? Are then all men under the Covenant of Grace? Or are unsaved men not under any covenant? If they are not under any covenant then are they not responsible to God their Creator to keep His laws? Are unsaved men "under the law"? Is the headship of Adam as their covenant head still valid? Can they be considered to be in the same covenant as Adam? Are they "in Adam"? I don't think Dr. Buswell has given due consideration to these questions nor to the consequences if the Covenant of Works has been abrogated in relation to the unsaved.

Dr. Buswell writes,

> "It is my contention that no scripture, even hypothetically, offers eternal life on the condition of obedience or meritorious works of any kind." The words, "This do and thou shalt live" (Luke 10:28) were spoken to the lawyer who had just enunciated the principle of love to God with all the heart, soul, strength, and mind together with appropriate love to the neighbour."[†]

Dr. Buswell is quite right to say that fallen man could not commend himself to God. However, this is not the same as denying that eternal life is promised on condition of obedience. No clearer verse could be given than Luke 10:28 to declare that eternal life is offered on the condition of obedience. Christ had asked the lawyer, "What is written in the law?" and when the lawyer quoted the summation of the law Christ answered, "Do this and you will live." Whether he was saved or unsaved does not effect the issue.

---

[*] Buswell, *Systematic Theology*, 312.
[†] *Ibid.*, 313.

Christ promised eternal life on the condition of obedience to the law.

Of course, the lawyer quoting the law is not the same as him keeping the law. Dr. Buswell is quite wrong to think the lawyer kept the law by loving the Lord with all his heart. The corrupt heart of the lawyer did not and indeed could not love God and his neighbor. Christ told the story of the Good Samaritan to reveal his sin of not loving his neighbor and so to produce a knowledge of his sin by the law (see Rom. 3:19-20). Why couldn't he commend himself to God? Because he had an inability to keep the law. Nevertheless the promise was "do this and you will live." Thus the law teaches that men are responsible to God. They must obey. Yet they cannot! They have an innate inability. Here are the two jaws of the vice to crush all men's hope in themselves.

Dr. Buswell objects to Romans 2:6 being used to teach that the Covenant of Works is still in effect by saying that the works in Romans 2:6 are an evidence of faith. The verses say, "Who will render to each one according to his deeds. Eternal life to those who by patient continuance in doing good seek for glory, honor, and immortality" (Rom. 2:6-7). He fails to understand the argument of Romans 1-3. All of Romans chapter two is about the judgment of God. It is written to bring the sinner to the place of Romans 3:19-20 where he, having a knowledge of his sin, sees himself guilty before God with nothing to say. Not until Romans 3:21 does Paul get into the gospel with the glorious words "but now." Romans 2:6 is not speaking of works as an evidence of faith. That is not the context. The context is the judgment of God to be given with justice. In fact, Romans does not deal with the evidences of faith as James and 1 John does. Romans 2:6-7 stands firm, "God will render to each one according to his deeds, eternal life to those doing good." The Covenant of Works is still in effect as all will surely find to be the case on the day of judgment.

Dr. Buswell's interpretation of Romans 10:5, "For Moses writes about the righteousness which is of the law, 'The man who does those things shall live by them'" is that it is not speaking about eternal life but "an outward sphere in which God's people may conduct their lives."[*] Paul in Romans

---

[*] *Ibid.*, 318.

10:5-13 is contrasting the two methods of obtaining righteousness; by works and by faith. His purpose is to show the former to be impossible while the other is reasonable and easy. Paul is not speaking only of life in this world but includes man's existence in the world to come. He means life in its fullest and most extensive meaning. Who can deny that "the Lord promises eternal life to those who would keep the law . . ." as Calvin writes on this verse in Romans?

The Covenant of Works that was made with Adam included the whole human race. The great promise was the promise of eternal life. The condition was complete and perfect obedience. The penalty that was threatened was death. Although Adam fell and the whole human race fell with Adam the Covenant of Works is still in force. All infants are born in Adam and born into the Covenant of Works. They are "under law." It is true that man lost all ability to good but he is still under law and obligated to keep the law. God's claim to obedience is not done away with. The wages of sin is still death and a perfect obedience is still required to merit eternal life. This promise as well as the threatening still holds. Man always owes God a perfect obedience. It is true that man after the fall cannot fulfill the condition but nevertheless the covenant stands. The proper answer to the question, "What good thing shall I do that I may have eternal life?" is still, as Christ said, "Keep the commandments." Christ's answer is the right answer to all those who are not convinced of their lost and hopeless condition. Those who hold to this are not "giving ground to modern dispensationalism" as Dr. Buswell accuses them. Rather it is those who would answer the rich young ruler differently who are erring in the direction of a false dispensationalism.

23

The Abrahamic Covenant

A COVENANT OF GRACE

T he covenant with Abraham is carefully explained by Paul in Galatians chapters 3 and 4 to the Galatians who "desired to be under law" (4:21). A key term that Paul used is "promise." I count the noun as being used 8 times in chapter 3 and twice in chapter 4. The verb is used once in chapter 3 or eleven times in all. The word *promise* is used 4 times in Romans 4 which is also about Abraham and justification. The promisor is God and so the promise or promises are sure. They cannot fail of their fulfillment. Promises are not like offers in that they are given to a specific people. They are not thrown out promiscuously but given to particular individuals who all receive them by faith. Paul joins another word with promise. This is the word believe or faith. In Romans 4 the word *grace* is also linked with promise and faith. These words speak to us of the Covenant of Grace.

The covenant was made with Abraham and his seed. Paul, speaking by the Holy Spirit, defines this seed as not Abraham's descendants but one particular descendant, Christ. "Now to Abraham and his Seed were the promises made. He does not say, 'And to seeds,' as of many, but as of one, 'And to your Seed', who is Christ" (Gal. 3:16). This further proves that it is the Covenant of Grace that was made with Abraham or as some call it the covenant of redemption being one and the same.

In both Galatians 3 and Romans 4 the promise and the principle it is based on is differentiated from the law and the principle the law is based on.

> "'These two things (as I do often repeat)', comments Luther, 'to wit, the law and the promise, must be diligently distinguished. For in time, in place, and in person, and generally in all other circumstances, they are separate as far asunder as heaven and earth ...' Again, 'unless the Gospel be plainly discerned from the law, the true Christian doctrine cannot be kept sound and uncorrupt.' What is the difference between them? In the promise to Abraham God said, 'I will... I will... I will...' But in the law of Moses God said, 'Thou shalt... thou shalt not...' The promise sets forth a religion of God—God's plan, God's grace, God's initiative. But the law sets forth a religion of man— man's duty, man's works, man's responsibility. The promise (standing for the grace of God) had only to be believed. But the law (standing for the works of men) had to be obeyed. God's dealings with Abraham were in the category of 'promise', 'grace' and 'faith'. But God's dealings with Moses were in the category of 'law', 'commandments' and 'works'."*

All the covenants may be summed up in two; the Covenant of Grace and the covenant of works. Thus, the covenant with Abraham was by promise, the Covenant of Grace.

THE COVENANTERS

In Genesis 17:7 God calls His covenant with Abraham an everlasting covenant. "And I will establish My covenant between Me and you and your seed after you in their generations, for an everlasting covenant, to be God to you and your seed after you." Spurgeon preaching on the blood of the everlasting covenant says,

> "As for the other side of the covenant this was the part of it, engaged and covenanted by Christ. He thus declared, and covenanted with his father: 'My Father, on my part I covenant that in the fullness of

---

* Stott, 86-87.

time I will become man, I will take upon myself the form and nature of the fallen race. I will live in their wretched world, and for my people will I keep the law perfectly. I will work out a spotless righteousness, which shall be acceptable to the demands of thy just and holy law. In due time I will bear the sins of all my people. Thou shalt exact their debts on me; the chastisement of their peace I will endure and by my stripes they shall be healed. My Father, I covenant and promise that I will be obedient unto death, even the death of the cross. I will magnify thy law, and make it honourable. I will suffer all they ought to have suffered. I will endure the curse of thy law, and all the vials of thy wrath shall be emptied and spent upon my head. I will then rise again; I will ascend into heaven; I will intercede for them at thy right hand; and I will make myself responsible for every one of them, that not one of those whom thou hast given me shall ever be lost, but I will bring all my sheep of whom by thy blood, thou hast constituted me the shepherd—I will bring everyone safe to thee at last'."*

God pictured the everlasting covenant, the Covenant of Grace to Abraham.

"Then He said to him, 'I am the Lord, who brought you out of Ur of the Chaldeans, to give you this land to inherit it.' And he said, 'Lord God, how shall I know that I will inherit it?' So He said to him, 'Bring Me a three-year-old heifer, a three-year-old female goat, a three-year-old ram, a turtledove, and a young pigeon.' Then he brought all these to Him and cut them in two, down the middle, and placed each piece opposite the other; but he did not cut the birds in two. And when the vultures came down on the carcasses, Abram drove them away. Now when the sun was going down, a deep sleep fell upon Abram; and behold, horror and great darkness fell upon him. Then He said to Abram: 'Know certainly that your descendants will be strangers in the land that is not theirs, and will serve them, and they will afflict them four hundred years. And also the nation whom they serve I will judge; afterward they shall come out with great possessions. Now as for you, you shall go to your fathers in peace; you shall be buried at a

---

* Spurgeon, *The New Park Street Pulpit*, No. 5, 419-20.

good old age. But in the fourth generation they shall return here, for the iniquity of the Amorites is not yet complete.' And it came to pass, when the sun went down and it was dark, that behold, there was a smoking oven and a burning torch that passed between those pieces. On the same day the Lord made a covenant with Abram" (Gen. 15:7-18).

The meaning of the dividing of the animals and birds into two piles is given in Jeremiah 34:18-19,

"And I will give the men who have transgressed My covenant, who have not performed the words of the covenant which they made before Me, when they cut the calf in two and passed between the parts of it—the princes of Judah, the princes of Jerusalem, the eunuchs, the priests, and all the people of the land who passed between the parts of the calf."

It was done when covenants were made. Those who covenanted passed together between the divided offering as a sign that they were covenanting and saying, "We will be in the same way cut in sunder, if we do not perform what we now promise." The passing of the "smoking oven and a burning torch" between the pieces symbolized the two who entered into the covenant. In every covenant there must be at least two parties since a covenant is defined as an agreement between two or more parties. The smoking oven symbolized the Father who is "a consuming fire." The wrath of God is depicted as a burning oven in Malachi 4:1. The same Hebrew word is used in Genesis 15:17. The burning torch symbolizes the second person in the covenant, the Son, who is "the light of the world."

Since it is an everlasting covenant it could only be entered into by the everlasting trinity. Thus Abraham could not be one who made the covenant and this is symbolized by Abraham being asleep when the covenant was made. Christ was his surety and made the covenant in his stead. In agreement with this Paul writes that the covenant was to the seed who would come "to whom the promise was made" (Gal. 3:19). The promise of eternal life was promised before time began. "In hope of eternal life which God, who cannot lie, promised before time began" (Titus 1:2). To whom was this promise that was made before the creation of man, made to? It was made to our precious Lord, "whose goings forth have been from of old, from everlasting" (Mic. 5:2).

ITS OBJECTS OR BENEFICIARIES

Most commentators agree that since it was made with Christ it included all His seed; that is His spiritual seed or those who are "sons of God through faith in Christ Jesus." Therefore, "the promise by faith in Jesus Christ might be given to those who believe" (Gal. 3:22). This makes it clear that the promise was not to Abraham's natural seed. The Covenant of Grace was made with Christ and to those in Him.

THE PROMISE

The promise in Genesis 17:7-8 was "to be God to you and your seed after you" and "I will be their God." This summed up all the spiritual blessings or promises found in the Covenant of Grace. Paul sums it up in Ephesians 1:3, "Blessed be the God and Father of our Lord Jesus Christ, who has blessed us with every spiritual blessing in the heavenly places in Christ." In Galatians 3 and Romans 4 it includes justification, the promise of the Spirit, the inheritance, adoption, and Christ himself (see Galatians 3:8, 14, 18, 26, 27, and 29). Of course, all these spiritual blessings are only to the true seed of Abraham not his natural seed. "And if you are Christ's, then you are Abraham's seed."

Thus, no Jewish infant that was circumcised was included in the Covenant of Grace made with Abraham for they were all by nature children of wrath, children of the flesh without life or faith at the time of circumcision. They were not in Christ but in Adam: not under grace but under law. Of course, some of these infants in their later years became God's spiritual people through the regeneration of the Spirit and then came into the Covenant of Grace through faith even as Abraham.

A COVENANT OF WORKS

The covenant with Abraham was a Covenant of Grace. It was also a covenant of works. That is two covenants were made with Abraham. This thought is not just mine. Dr. Hodge wrote,

> "It is to be remembered that there were two covenants made with Abraham. By the one his natural descendants through Isaac, were constituted a commonwealth—an external community; by the other his spiritual descendants were constituted into a church. The parties to the former covenant, were God, and the nation; to the other, God, and his true people. The promises of the national covenant, were national blessings; the promises of the spiritual covenant were spiritual blessings, as reconciliation, holiness, and eternal life. The conditions of the one covenant were circumcision, and obedience to the law; the conditions of the other were, and ever have been, faith in the Messiah, as 'the seed of the woman,' the Son of God, the Saviour of the world. There cannot be a greater mistake than to confound the national covenant with the Covenant of Grace, and the commonwealth founded on the one, with the church founded on the other. When Christ came, the commonwealth was abolished, and there was nothing put in its place. The church remained. There was no external covenant, nor promise of external blessings, on condition of external rites, and subjection. There was a spiritual society, with spiritual promises, on condition of faith in Christ."[*]

Please note important points in Hodge's statement. He says there is an important distinction between the national covenant and the Covenant of Grace and between the commonwealth and the Church. As he wrote, two covenants were made with Abraham. These two covenants are the covenant of circumcision and the Covenant of Grace. The covenant of circumcision was a legal covenant, a covenant of works. Its conditions "were circumcision and obedience to the law." Its promises were "external blessings, on condition of external rites and subjection." Thus the nation of Israel and its

---

[*] Hodge, *The Princeton Review*, October 1853, 684.

children were not in the Covenant of Grace but in the covenant of circumcision. None entered the Covenant of Grace except those who fulfilled its condition "faith in the Messiah, as the seed of the woman, the Son of God, the Saviour of the world."

The New International Version Study Bible lists two covenants with Abraham calling them the "Abrahamic 'A' covenant" and the "Abrahamic 'B' covenant." The former is described as "an unconditional promise," while the latter is said to be a "conditional divine pledge."

The covenant of circumcision was not the Covenant of Grace and to call it so is to confound and confuse things that are different. Circumcision is part of the law. The person circumcised was agreeing to keep the law. Paul wrote, "And I testify again to every man who becomes circumcised that he is a debtor to keep the whole law" (Gal. 5:3). J. A. Alexander in his commentary, *The Acts of the Apostles,* commenting on Acts 15:5 writes,

> "The last clause is explanatory of the one before it; to circumcise them was in fact to require them to observe the whole law, of which circumcision was the distinctive badge and sacramental seal."[*]

Note that he calls circumcision the distinctive badge and sacramental seal of the law *and not* of the Covenant of Grace.

THE COVENANTERS

The covenanters in this covenant of works was God and Abraham's descendants by birth or his natural seed. Or we could say as Hodge, "The parties to the former covenant (in which God constituted Abraham's descendants a commonwealth) were God and the nation."

THE PROMISES

I have said that this covenant of works made within the Abrahamic

---

[*] Alexander, *The Acts of the Apostles,* 75.

covenant was with Abraham's natural seed, his descendants by birth. The promises then were earthly promises or national blessings made to Abraham and all of Abraham's descendants. These blessings were the possession of the land of Canaan by all Abraham's seed, that this seed should be a countless multitude and that they would possess the gate of their enemies.

THE CONDITIONS

The conditions of this covenant of works were circumcision and obedience to the law. For this reason this covenant could be broken by the people or, we should rather say, it would be broken by the people. That it was broken by the people is again and again documented by Moses and the prophets. Time and again they were expelled from the land for disobedience. That God didn't completely destroy them was only due to God's mercy not to their faithfulness. Psalm 106 gives a summary of their sad history. Here is an excerpt,

> "Thus they were defiled by their own works, and played the harlot by their own deeds. Therefore the wrath of the Lord was kindled against His people, so that He abhorred His own inheritance. And He gave them into the hand of the Gentiles, and those who hated them ruled over them. Their enemies also oppressed them, and they were brought into subjection under their hand. Many times He delivered them; but they rebelled against Him by their counsel, and were brought low for their iniquity. Nevertheless He regarded their affliction, when He heard their cry; and for their sake He remembered His covenant, and relented according to the multitude of His mercies" (Psa. 106:39-45).

Also, no doubt the spiritual seed of Abraham that was mingled with the natural seed preserved the nation in the land of promise even for as long as they lived there.

Most Paedobaptists speak of the people of Israel being covenant breakers. In this they are quite right but they err greatly when they say they broke the Covenant of Grace. The Covenant of Grace is inviolable. It was the covenant of works that they broke again and again. For instance Louis Berkhof uses Isaiah 24:5 as an illustration of breaking the Covenant of Grace but that verse is speaking of those who "transgressed the laws and violated the statutes, broken the everlasting covenant. Therefore the curse has devoured the earth." It is speaking of the Covenant of Works. He also wrongly uses Esau, Korah, the making of the golden calf, the evil report of the spies and the sons of Eli as instances of breaking the Covenant of Grace.[*] Mr. Berkhof defines the Covenant of Grace as:

> "That gracious agreement between God and the elect sinner in Christ, in which God gives Himself with all the blessings of salvation to the elect sinner, and the latter embraces God and all His gracious gifts by faith."[†]

However, Esau, Korah, and the sons of Eli were neither elect sinners nor did they embrace God and all his gracious gifts by faith, so Mr. Berkhof contradicts his definition by using such examples.

---

[*] See Berkhof, *A Summary of Christian Doctrine*, 81-82.
[†] *Ibid.*, 76.

24

The Two Covenants Within the Abrahamic Covenant

God made two covenants with Abraham. As Stephen said, "He gave him the covenant of circumcision; and so Abraham begot Isaac and circumcised him on the eighth day." God also gave him the Covenant of Grace. Proofs of two covenants given to Abraham are:

(1.) *They were made at different times.* The Covenant of Grace was made with Abraham on his entrance into Canaan when God promised Abraham, "In you all the families of the earth shall be blessed" (Gen. 12:3). This was an unconditional promise. At that time, "Abram was seventy-five years old when he departed from Haran" (Gen. 12:4).

However, the covenant of circumcision was made twenty-four years later when Abraham was ninety nine years old. "This is My covenant which you shall keep, between Me and you and your descendants after you: Every male child among you shall be circumcised" (Gen. 17:10). "Abraham was ninety-nine years old when he was circumcised" (Gen. 17:24).

This is further verified by Moses and Paul. Moses wrote, "Now the sojourn of the children of Israel who lived in Egypt was four hundred and thirty years" (Exod. 12:40). Paul wrote that there was 430 years between the promise to Abraham and the giving of the law, ". . . the law, which was four hundred and thirty years later, cannot annul the covenant that was confirmed before by God in Christ" (Gal. 3:17). The promise was given to Abraham at the beginning of his sojourn in Canaan shortly after he left Haran while the law was given shortly after the Israelites went out from Egypt. Thus

226

the time of their sojourn was 430 years as was the time from the promise to Abraham until the law was given. The covenant of circumcision, however, was made with Abraham twenty-four years after the promise of the Covenant of Grace was given to him. Thus Paul in Galatians 3:17 is not referring to the covenant of circumcision made in Genesis 17 but to the Covenant of Grace made in Genesis 12. It is a different covenant.

(2.) *They are made with different people.* The Gentiles are not in the covenant of circumcision while they are in the Covenant of Grace. If the covenant of circumcision is the same as the Covenant of Grace made with Abraham how can the Gentiles be included? They cannot. The covenant of circumcision was to Abraham's natural seed. It only included Israelites. There was no provision for proselytes in the Abrahamic covenant. It was, "Every male child among you shall be circumcised" (Gen. 17:10). Thus, Ishmael was in the Abrahamic Covenant. Yet God had said his Covenant was with Isaac not Ishmael, "As for Ishmael, I have heard you. But my covenant I will establish with Isaac" (Gen. 17:20-21). But wasn't Ishmael in the Abrahamic covenant? Yes, but he was in the covenant of works not the Covenant of Grace.

However, the Covenant of Grace made with Abraham did include Gentiles. As Paul says, "Now to Abraham and his Seed were the promises made. He does not say, 'And to seeds' as of many, but as of one, 'And to your Seed,' who is Christ" (Gal. 3:16), and "And if you are Christ's, then you are Abraham's seed, and heirs according to the promise" (Gal. 3:29). The Covenant of Grace to Abraham was to his seed even Christ and thus with all those in Christ whether Jew or Gentile. Note Romans 4:11,

> "And he received the sign of circumcision, a seal of the righteousness of the faith which he had while still uncircumcised, that he might be the father of all those who believe, though they are uncircumcised, that righteousness might be imputed to them also."

Believers are connected with uncircumcised Abraham by faith. Jews are connected with circumcised Abraham by birth. The first is the Covenant of Grace. The second is the covenant of circumcision. Thus, Ishmael was in the

Abrahamic Covenant.

(3). *One covenant is conditional, one is unconditional.* The covenant of circumcision had conditions. It was a legal covenant. The circumcised person was under the law and was required to observe the whole law. As Paul wrote, "And I testify again to every man who becomes circumcised that he is debtor to keep the whole law" (Gal. 5:3). But the Covenant of Grace is without conditions. It is a covenant of promise founded on God's, "I will." All conditions are met by Christ and so the Spirit himself who is the sum of all good is poured out by Christ.

> "This Jesus has God raised up, of which we are all witnesses. Therefore being exalted to the right hand of God, and having received from the Father the promise of the Holy Spirit, He poured out this which you now see and hear" (Acts 3:32-33).

Thus repentance and faith, which some call conditions, are gifts of God through His Spirit (see Acts 11:18; Ephesians 2:8-9).

> "Many excellent divines, in consequence of the distinction which they made between the covenant of redemption and the Covenant of Grace, were led to speak of faith as the condition of the latter covenant. But the term, as used by them, signifies not a meritorious or procuring cause, but simply something which goes before, and without which the other cannot be obtained. They consider faith merely as a condition of order or connection, as it has been styled, and as an instrument or means of obtaining an interest in the salvation offered in the gospel. This is very different from the meaning attached to the term by Arminians and Neonomians, who represent faith as a condition on the fulfillment of which the promise is suspended. The Westminster Assembly elsewhere affirm, that God requires of sinners faith in Christ, 'as the condition to interest them in him.' But this is very different from affirming that faith is the condition of the Covenant of Grace. That faith is indispensably necessary as the instrument by which we are savingly interested in Christ, and personally instated in the covenant, is a most important truth, and this is all that is intended by the Westminster Divines.

They seem to have used the term condition as synonymous with instrument; for, while in one place they speak of faith as the condition to interest sinners in the Mediator, in other places they affirm, that 'faith is the alone instrument of justification,' and teach, that 'faith justifies a sinner in the sight of God, only as it is an instrument by which he receiveth and applieth Christ and his righteousness.' As the word condition is ambiguous, apt to be misunderstood, and is frequently employed in an unsound and dangerous sense, it is now disused by evangelical divines."[*]

(4.) *The one covenant is violable the other is inviolable.* The covenant of circumcision was a covenant that could be broken. God said of such covenant breakers, "He has broken my covenant" (Gen. 17:14), speaking of the covenant of circumcision. But the Covenant of Grace is inviolable. It cannot be broken. God will not break it and God will so work in his people that they will not break it. "And I will make an everlasting covenant with them, that I will not turn away from doing them good; but I will put my fear in their hearts so that they will not depart from Me" (Jer. 32:40).

(5.) *The one covenant includes the unregenerate, while the other includes only the regenerate.* The covenant of circumcision made with Abraham's natural seed includes many ungodly and unbelievers such as Ishmael, Esau, the wicked who fell in the wilderness, and all the faithless Jews down through history. But the Covenant of Grace made with Abraham's spiritual seed includes only the regenerate. It is only to the "children of promise."

(6.) *One covenant has curses; the other has only blessings.* The breakers of the covenant of circumcision were under a severe penalty. They were under the curse of the law. "And the uncircumcised male child, who is not circumcised in the flesh of his foreskin, that person shall be cut off from his people; he has broken My covenant" (Gen. 17:14). However, the Covenant of Grace has no curses. The curse of the law has been borne by the head of the covenant, even our beloved Savior. He has redeemed all those in the Covenant of Grace from the curse of the law.

The above six statements give proof that there were two covenants

---

[*] Shaw, *An Exposition of the Westminster Confession,* 396.

made with Abraham. Abraham's natural seed are in the covenant of circumcision. His spiritual seed are in the Covenant of Grace. Therefore the argument that all Abraham's natural seed were in the Covenant of Grace is false and falls to the ground. This argument is said to be,

> "the grand turning point on which the issue of the controversy very much depends; and that if Abraham's covenant which included his infant children, and gave them a right to circumcision, was not the Covenant of Grace, then it is confessed, that the main ground is taken away, on which the right of infants to baptism is asserted; and consequently the principal arguments in support of the doctrine are overturned.""

Just as Abraham's descendants were not born into the Covenant of Grace believers' children are not born into the Covenant of Grace. All infants, including the children of believers, are born in sin and are born in Adam not in Christ. They are all born under the law and can only be redeemed by the head of the new covenant to whom only believers are united. It is only "those who are of faith (that) are blessed with believing Abraham" (Gal. 3:9). "Therefore know that only those who are of faith are sons of Abraham" (Gal. 3:7). Entrance into the Covenant of Grace is not by natural birth. It is by spiritual birth alone and that is evidenced by faith.

Thus we see that infant baptism is founded on a false premise. Dr. Vos wrote, "The real proof of Infant Baptism depends on the truth that the children of believers are included in the Covenant of Grace" but the children of believers are not included in the Covenant of Grace unless they are believers. John Owen said,

> "This covenant was, that God would be 'a God unto Abraham and to his seed,' which God himself explains to be his infant seed—Gen. 17:12—that is , the infant seed of every one of his posterity who should lay hold on and avouch that covenant as Abraham did, and not else."

---

* Bostwick, *Fair and Rational Vindication of Infant Baptism*, 19.

But this is false since as Paul explains in Galatians 3:16 the promise was not to Abraham's infant seed but to Abraham's seed "who is Christ." Likewise the Heidelberg Catechism which says that infants should be baptized, "since they as well as adults are included in the covenant and the Church of God," is false. Infants are not included in the Covenant of Grace but are all born under the covenant of works. "That which is born of the flesh is flesh" even if born of believing parents. Grace does not come by birth. Rather spiritual birth comes by grace. A description of God's children is "as many as received Him . . . even those who believe in His name: who were born, not of blood, nor of the will of the flesh, nor of the will of man, but of God" (John 1:12-13).

Are there evidences of this new birth? Yes, the new birth always evidences itself. It never exists in isolation. Who is born of God? "Everyone who loves is born of God" (1 John 4:7). "Whoever is born of God does not sin" (1 John 5:18). "Whatever is born of God overcomes the world" (1 John 5:4). "Whoever believes that Jesus is the Christ is born of God" (1 John 5:1). Can a person be regenerate and it not be evidenced? Dr. John Murray rightly says he cannot.

> "When we put these texts together they expressly state that every regenerate person has been delivered from the power of sin, overcomes the world by the faith of Christ, and exercises that self-control by which he is no longer the slave of sin and of the evil one. That means, when reduced to its simplest terms, that the regenerate person is converted and exercises faith and repentance. We must not think of regeneration as something which can be abstracted from the saving exercises which are its effects . . . This simply means that all of the graces mentioned in these passages are the consequences of regeneration and not only consequences which sooner or later follow upon regeneration, but fruits which are inseparable from regeneration . . . He is immediately a member of the kingdom of God, he is spirit, and his action and behaviour must be consonant with that new citizenship . . . There are numerous other considerations derived from Scripture which confirm this great truth that regeneration is such a radical, pervasive, and efficacious transformation that it

immediately registers itself in the conscious activity of the person concerned in the exercises of faith and repentance and new obedience."[*]

Yet many believe that children of believers are regenerate although they show no evidence that they are. Some say it must be assumed that they are regenerate. Rather than assuming something that has no evidence it would be far safer to wait for the evidences of regeneration before assuming it exists for as J. C. Ryle wrote,

> "Many divines maintain that we may call people 'regenerate' in whom none of the marks just described are seen, or even were seen since they were born. They tell us, in short, that people may possess the gift of the Spirit, and the grace of Regeneration when neither the gift nor the grace can be seen. Such a doctrine appears to me dangerous in the highest degree."[†]

He is right! Such doctrine is dangerous in the highest degree. It brings the world into the church. The time to baptize a child is when he evidences regeneration, not before. Baptizing infants is sure to bring the unregenerate into the church with all its attendant evils and confusion tending to the serious weakening of the church and its testimony.

---

[*] Murray, *Redemption Accomplished and Applied*, 103-05.
[†] Ryle, *Knots Untied*, 132.

25

The New Covenant—The Covenant of Grace

In distinction to the Old Covenant that was fleshly and carnal "which stood only in meats and drinks and divers washings and carnal ordinances" (Heb. 9:10), the New Covenant is a spiritual covenant with spiritual not carnal qualifications. Thus eunuchs who were barred from the old covenant by physical disability are given in God's house under the New Covenant "a place and a name better than of sons and daughters" (Isa. 56:4). Indeed God says to these eunuchs who keep His Sabbaths and choose the things that please Him and take hold of His covenant, "I will give them an everlasting name that shall not be cut off " (Isa. 56:5). Were the Ammonites and Moabites barred from the congregation of the Lord under the old covenant because of physical birth?

Under the new there is now no distinction "but in every nation he that feareth Him and worketh righteousness is accepted with Him" (Acts 10:35). There are now no such cultural, racial or national distinctions but "all are one in Christ Jesus" for "there is neither Jew nor Greek, there is neither bond nor free, there is neither male nor female" (Gal. 3:28). The wall of partition is broken down. Praise Him! Now, "neither circumcision avails any thing nor uncircumcision" for all such outward distinctions are done away with in Christ. Only a new creature avails under the New Covenant (Gal. 6:15).

Only the Jewish nation and their proselytes were accepted into the old covenant. Not so now. Now all nations lay hold of the New Covenant by faith entering not by physical birth but by spiritual birth for it is "not of blood, nor of the will of the flesh, nor of the will of man but of God." Human descent is done away with.

Our Lord made this very clear to Nicodemus, a "covenant" child and a circumcised Israelite when he told him that he needed to be born again. Regardless of his ancestry, his sign of the covenant or natural birth he was outside the New Covenant and the kingdom of God. For "except a man be born again he cannot see the kingdom of God." What did his circumcision avail? Nothing. It was useless to bring either him or his children the spiritual blessings of the New Covenant. What does infant baptism avail? It is useless to bring the child the spiritual blessings of the New Covenant. Can a rite produce life? Can it unite to Christ? Does it signify anything if the reality it is supposed to signify is absent?

Why was the New Covenant made? It was made because the Old Covenant made with Israel was deficient. "The law made nothing perfect" (Heb. 7:19). It was annulled "because of its weakness and un-profitableness" (Heb. 7:18). "For if that first covenant had been faultless then no place would have been sought for a second" (Heb. 8:7). "He has made the first obsolete" (Heb. 8:13). Indeed the Old Covenant of law is called "the ministry of death written and engraven on stones" (2 Cor. 3:7), and the "ministry of condemnation" (2 Cor. 3:9), and so said to be "passing away" (2 Cor. 3:11). This leads Paul to exult in "God who also made us sufficient as ministers of the new covenant" (2 Cor. 3:6), and "the ministry of righteousness that exceeds much more in glory" (2 Cor. 3:9).

The Paedobaptist has to insist that there is only one covenant and must strongly oppose any teaching that says that the Old Covenant was annulled, has passed away and has been replaced by the New Covenant. For if there are two covenants and Israel was under the Old Covenant while the church is under the New Covenant their whole argument for infant baptism based on one covenant falls to the ground. But if Israel was under the Covenant of Grace how could they be cast off? Isn't the Covenant of Grace sure to all the seed? How then could Israel be cast off? Wasn't the New Covenant instituted because it is an inviolable covenant? Hasn't God sworn, "That I would not be angry with you nor rebuke you, For the mountains shall depart and the hills be removed, but My kindness shall not depart from you, nor shall My covenant of peace be removed, says the Lord, who has mercy on you" (Isa. 54:9-10)? This is the chapter quoted from by Paul in Galatians 4:27 referring to the two covenants. If the church is under the same covenant as Israel isn't the church able to be cast off? Why won't God cast off the church? What guarantee do we have that we will not finally be lost? No, Israel was not under the Covenant of Grace. Israel was under the Old Covenant which was conditional. It was a legal covenant. Israel failed to keep the conditions of the covenant so she was cast off. God, speaking of the Old Covenant made with Israel when he brought them out of Egypt says, "My covenant which they broke" (Jer. 31:32). However, the church is under the New Covenant which was instituted and established by the blood of our Savior. It "was established upon better promises" (Heb. 8:6). It is a better covenant. His promise is,

> "My mercy I will keep for him forever and my covenant shall stand firm with him. His seed also I will make to endure forever . . . if his sons forsake my law and do not walk in my statutes . . . I will visit their transgression with the rod . . . Nevertheless my lovingkindness I will not utterly take from him nor allow my faithfulness to fail. My covenant I will not break nor alter the word that has gone out of my lips" (Psa. 89:28-30, 32-34).

Aren't these better promises? Praise the Lord for the New Covenant of Grace. The conditions of the covenant are secured for us by our Surety such that the New Covenant is inviolable. This is abounding grace, marvelous grace, triumphant grace!

> "Now may the God of peace who brought up our Lord Jesus from the dead, that great Shepherd of the sheep, through the blood of the everlasting covenant, make you complete in every good work to do His will, working in you what is well pleasing in His sight, through Jesus Christ, to whom be glory forever and ever. Amen" (Heb. 13:20-21).

26

Who Are Members In the Covenant of Grace?

The writer of Hebrews calls those who inherit the promises "heirs of the promise" and describes them as those who have "fled for refuge to lay hold of the hope set before us" (Heb. 6:17). Those who have not fled to this refuge are thus outside the Covenant of Grace.

Another term used for those who are in the Covenant of Grace and so obtain its blessings is "children of promise" (Rom. 9:7-8; Gal. 4:28). Hodge defines this term as follows,

> "It may mean, according to a common force of the genitive, children in virtue of a promise. This suits the context exactly. It assigns to the genitive "promise" in this clause the same force that flesh has in the preceding. Isaac was not born after the ordinary course of nature, but in virtue of a divine promise. See Gal. 4:23, where the expressions born after the flesh, and born by promise, are opposed to each other. It is, of course, implied in the phrase children in virtue of a promise, that it is by a special interposition that they become children, and this is the sense in which Paul applies the expression to believers generally. In. Gal. 4:28, he says, 'We, as Isaac was, are the children of promise.' Believers, therefore, are children of the promise in the same sense as Isaac. The birth of Isaac was *kata pneuma*, supernatural; believers also are the children of God in virtue of a spiritual or supernatural birth. This is the main idea, although not the full meaning. The children of promise are those to whom the promise belongs. This is what the apostle has specially in view in the passage in Galatians. He there desires to show that believers are the true

children of Abraham, and heirs of the promise made to the father of the faithful. This idea, therefore, is not to be excluded even here. Isaac was not only born in virtue of a promise, but was, on that account, heir of the promised blessing. The former, however, as just stated, is the prominent idea."[*]

Thus, since "children of promise" means those born supernaturally by the Spirit, the Covenant of Grace includes only the regenerate. Professor Berkhof therefore is wrong to say "unregenerate persons may temporarily be in the covenant as a purely legal relationship." I cannot agree with his statement when he speaks of being in the covenant "temporarily" and as "a purely legal relationship." No unregenerate are ever in the Covenant of Grace and anyone who is in the Covenant of Grace is not in the covenant temporarily or legally. Mr. Berkhof changes grace into law and would take away all our hope by making the covenant that is "sure to all the seed" but a temporary provision. He makes these statements to include infants in the Covenant of Grace but by so doing he gives up the grace and certainty of the covenant. He must give up infants being in the covenant or the grace and certainty of the covenant. He cannot hold both. Wouldn't it have been better for him to have given up infants being in the covenant?

Let us be persuaded that all those in the Covenant of Grace will partake of all the blessings of it, not temporarily but for evermore. "At thy right hand there are pleasures for evermore" (Psa. 16:11). "For the mountains shall depart and the hills be removed, 'But My kindness shall not depart from you, nor shall My covenant of peace be removed,' says the Lord, who has mercy on you" (Isa. 54:10).

Mr. Berkhof has to admit, "children of believers, however, enter the covenant as a legal arrangement by birth, but this does not necessarily mean that they also at once enter it as a communion of life, nor even that they will ever enter it in that sense." All is uncertain in the Covenant of Grace according to that statement.

Let us turn to the infallible Word that assures all who are in the

---

[*] Hodge, 307.

covenant that they will receive the promise of it and that promise is nothing short of "the eternal inheritance."

> "And for this reason He is the Mediator of the new covenant, by means of death, for the redemption of the transgressions under the first covenant, that those who are called may receive the promise of the eternal inheritance" (Heb. 9:15).

God's purpose is that they may receive the promise of eternal inheritance. His purpose cannot fail of fulfillment. This verse further describes the ones for whom Christ is mediator of the new covenant as "those who are called." He is speaking of those who are "called by the gospel" none of whom will come short of "the obtaining of the glory of our Lord Jesus Christ" (2 Thess. 2:14). This definition necessarily excludes all infants from being in the Covenant of Grace. Infants have not been called by the gospel.

ITS REQUIREMENTS

All the requirements of the Covenant of Grace are fulfilled for those in the covenant by their "surety of a better covenant," the Lord Jesus Christ (Heb. 7:22).

> " 'The Greek work for *surety* properly means a bondsman: one who pledges his name, property or influence, that a certain thing shall be done. When a contract is made, a debt contracted, or a note given, a friend often becomes the surety in the case, and is himself responsible if the terms of the contract are not complied with' (A. Barnes). A *surety* is one who agrees to undertake for another who is lacking in ability to discharge his own obligations. Whatever undertaking the surety makes, whether in words of promise, or in the depositing of real security in the hands of the arbitrator, or by any other personal engagement of life or body, it implies the defect of the person for whom any one becomes surety. The surety is sponsor for another, standing in the room of and acting for one who is incompetent to act for himself: he represents that other person, and pledges to make

good his engagements. Thus, Christ was not a Surety for God, for He needed none; but for His own poor, failing and deficient people, who were unable to meet their obligations, incapable of discharging their liabilities. In view of this, Christ agreed to undertake for them fully pay all their debts, and completely satisfied every demand which God had against them.'"*

As Dr. Berkhof writes, "God gives man all that He requires of him."[†] Thus the covenant is as Dr. Berkhof continues, "an eternal and inviolable covenant." However, he contradicts himself in the same sentence by saying, "though men may break it." The covenant is not inviolable if men may break it. Inviolable means "secure from violation" according to Webster's Collegiate Dictionary. The reason he wants to make the Covenant of Grace subject to violation is so that he could fit infants, who grow up to be clearly ungodly, into the covenant as covenant breakers. However, if some are "covenant breakers" he cannot say, "God gives man all He requires of him." The covenant breakers must have been deficient in something to be called covenant breakers.

It is true that Christ fulfills all conditions for his covenant people but this does not mean they enter the covenant unconsciously or in ignorance, with their eyes closed. All enter being conscious of their guilt and lost condition. All enter by repentance and faith in the Lord Jesus Christ. Need we say that this faith is an intelligent act? It is also required that such believers make a profession of their faith. This is called in the Old Testament covenanting with God.

> "Gather My saints together to Me, those who have made a covenant with Me by sacrifice. But to the wicked God says: 'What right have you to declare my statutes or to take My covenant in your mouth seeing you hate instruction and cast My words behind you.'" (Ps. 50:5, 16-17).

---

* Pink, *Hebrews*, 407.
† Berkhof, 77.

These words imply that God's people made or literally "cut" a covenant with God by sacrifice and by professing the covenant; that is taking it into their mouths.

Jonathan Edwards, writing on who should be admitted to the church of Christ writes,

> "There is no one thing that the Covenant of Grace is so often compared to in scripture, as the marriage covenant; and the visible transaction, or mutual profession, there is between Christ and the visible church, is abundantly compared to the mutual profession there is in marriage. In marriage the bride professes to yield to the bridegroom's suit and to take him for her husband, renouncing all others, and to give up herself to him to be entirely and forever possessed by him as his wife. But he that professes this towards Christ, professes saving faith. They that openly covenanted with God according to the tenor of the institution, Deut. 10:20, visibly united themselves to God in the union of that covenant. They professed on their parts the union of the covenant of God which was the Covenant of Grace. It is said in the institution, 'thou shalt cleave to the Lord, and swear by His name;' or as the words more literally are, 'thou shalt unite unto the Lord, and swear into His name.' So in Isaiah 56 it is called a 'joining themselves to the Lord.' But the union, cleaving, or joining of that covenant, is saving faith, the grand condition of the covenant of Christ, by which we are in Christ. This is what on our part brings us into the Lord. For a person explicitly or professedly to enter into the union or relation of the Covenant of Grace with Christ, is the same as professedly to do that which on our part is the uniting act, and that is the act of faith. To profess the Covenant of Grace is to profess it, not as a spectator, but as one immediately concerned in the affair, as a party in the covenant professed; and this is to profess that in the covenant which belongs to us as a party, or to profess our part in the covenant; and that is the soul's believing acceptance of the Saviour. Christ's part is salvation, our part is a saving faith in Him; not a feigned but an unfeigned faith; not a common, but special and saving faith; no other faith is the condition of the Covenant of

Grace."*

This same profession or confession is found in the New Testament and is called "confession unto salvation." (Greek, *eis*—"into" or "unto").

> "That if you confess with your mouth the Lord Jesus and believe in your heart that God has raised Him from the dead, you will be saved. For with the heart one believes to righteousness, and with the mouth confession is made to salvation" (Rom. 10:9-10).

"Professing faith in Christ was visibly owning the Covenant of Grace, because faith in Christ was the grand condition of the covenant."†

In this sense all believers "make" or "cut" a covenant with God. They enter into covenant by faith and by the profession of this faith. All (including infants) who do not make such a covenant are not in it, for the conditions, in the sense of what I have written, must be fulfilled. The covenant must be owned.

---

* Edwards, *Works*, Volume 1, 443.
† *Ibid.*, 444.

27

Dr. Murray's Questions

D r. John Murray asked a series of questions under the heading, "The Continuance of this Privilege." He wrote,

"The gospel dispensation is the unfolding of the covenant made with Abraham, the extension and enlargement of the blessing conveyed by this covenant to the people of the Old Testament period. Abraham is the father of all the faithful. They who are of faith are blessed with faithful Abraham. We come now to the question which cannot be suppressed or evaded and which cannot be pressed with too much emphasis. If children born of the faithful were given the sign and seal of the covenant and therefore of the richest blessing which the covenant disclosed, if the New Testament economy is the elaboration and extension of this covenant of which circumcision was the sign, are we to believe that infants in this age are excluded from that which was provided by the Abrahamic covenant? In other words, are we to believe that infants now may not properly be given the sign of that blessing which is enshrined in the new covenant? Is the new covenant in this respect less generous than was the Abrahamic? Is there less efficacy, as far as infants are concerned, in the new covenant than there was in the old? Are infants in the new dispensation more inhabile to the grace of God? These are questions that cannot be lightly dismissed.

If infants are excluded now, it cannot be too strongly emphasised that this change implies a complete reversal of the earlier divinely instituted practice. So we must ask: do we find any hint or intimation of such reversal in either the Old or the New Testament? More pointedly, does the New Testament revoke or does it provide any intimation of revoking so expressly authorised a principle as that of the inclusion of infants in the covenant and their participation in the covenant and seal? This practice had been followed, by divine authority, in the administration of the Covenant of Grace for some two thousand years. Has it been discontinued?"[*]

He had confidence that these questions were unanswerable except to support infant baptism. Dr. Murray assumes that children born of the faithful are in the Covenant of Grace so that the promises belong to them. He then makes a number of logical inferences from this assumption. However, his assumption is false. Children born to believers are born under the law just as all children are. Only believing or faithful seed are in the Covenant of Grace and the spiritual promises only pertain to them. As Owen says, when commenting on the Abrahamic covenant,

> "This is that which God engageth himself unto in this Covenant of Grace, that he will for everlasting be a God to him and his faithful seed. Though the external administration of the covenant was given to Abraham and his carnal seed, yet the effectual dispensation of the grace of the covenant is peculiar to them only who are the children of the promise."[+]

Dr. Murray's assumption being false causes all his arguments to fall to the ground even though his inferences may be as the Westminster Confession says, "good, and necessary consequences." Yet basic presuppositions must come from scripture. I would like to try to answer his questions one by one. He wrote that his question "cannot be suppressed or evaded and which cannot be pressed with too much emphasis." I would like to break up his questions into small units to make them easier to answer.

(1.) "If children born of the faithful were given the sign and seal of the

---

[*] Murray, 51-52.
[+] Owen, Volume 11, 205-06.

covenant . . ."

The sign of the covenant was not given to the children of the faithful but to all the natural seed or offspring of Abraham. Every Israelite child was circumcised whether his parents were faithful or unfaithful, whether they were godly or ungodly. God's command was "Every man child among you shall be circumcised" (Gen. 17:10). There were no exceptions.

(2.) "(They) were given the sign and seal of the covenant . . ."

All the Israelite male children were circumcised. Circumcision was the sign of the covenant of circumcision. Circumcision was not part of the Covenant of Grace but part of the Covenant of Works. The matter that the apostles and elders came together to consider was whether "it was needful to circumcise them (the Gentiles) and to command them to keep the law of Moses" (Acts 15:5). In verse one it was called "circumcised after the manner of Moses." Circumcision is part of the Law of Moses, part of the covenant of law. Circumcision and the law are joined firmly together, "For I testify again to every man that is circumcised, that he is debtor to do the whole law" (Gal. 5:3). For a Galatian to be circumcised was to be "justified by the law" and "fallen from grace" (verse 4). All children are born in the Covenant of Works. To enter the Covenant of Grace a person needs to be born again. Nicodemus had been circumcised and was a child of that covenant but he was not in the Covenant of Grace. Infants are in Adam, not in Christ. Only faith unites to Christ the Covenant head and so introduces into the Covenant of Grace. Only the spiritual children of Abraham are in Christ, not his natural children. "Know ye therefore that they which are of faith, the same are the children of Abraham" (Gal. 3:7).

It is true that God said his Covenant of Grace was, "to you and your seed," but who is this seed? Paul identifies this seed to be one descendant only, even Christ. "Now to Abraham and his seed were the promises made. He saith not, And to seeds as of many (descendants); but as of one (descendant), And to thy seed (singular), which is Christ" (Gal. 3:16). "And to thy seed" is a quotation from Genesis 17:7-8. The Covenant of Grace is with Christ and those in Him by faith not with Abraham's physical seed. This is a major error of Dr. Murray.

Although every male child was circumcised, obviously the whole nation was not in the Covenant of Grace. Anyone who enters the Covenant of Grace has entered a sure covenant with sure promises. But the promise of the covenant is only "given to those who believe." They are the "heirs of promise" and it is to them that God confirms the promise even by an oath. They all receive eternal life and none can be lost. "This hope we have as an anchor of the soul, both sure and steadfast, and which enters the Presence behind the veil" (Heb. 6:19). This is not true for all the circumcised Israelites. They did not attain to the law of righteousness and so were lost. Why? "Because they did not seek it by faith, but as it were, by the works of the law" (Rom. 9:31-32).

(3.) "(They) were given the richest blessing which the covenant disclosed."

Since the circumcised Israelite infants were not in the Covenant of Grace they did not receive its richest blessing. The richest blessing was to have God as a God to them which includes all the spiritual blessing of Ephesians 1:3, "every spiritual blessing in the heavenlies in Christ." Did every circumcised infant receive those blessings? The overwhelming majority were "a disobedient and contrary people" (Rom. 10:21) and died in their sins. As Dr. Murray wrote in this section, "They who are of faith are blessed with faithful Abraham." Infants are not of faith so they are not blessed with faithful Abraham.

(4.) "If the New Testament economy is the elaboration and extension of this covenant..."

The New Testament economy is not the elaboration and extension of the old covenant which the Israelites and their children were under. The New Testament is an elaboration and extension of the Covenant of Grace. The Covenant of Grace that included Abraham was made with Christ, the seed of Abraham. This "New" covenant is not an extension of the old covenant of works that the natural seed of Abraham were under. Rather the new covenant is with Abraham's spiritual seed.

(5.) "... are we to believe that infants in this age are excluded from that which was provided by the Abrahamic Covenant?"

What was provided to infants by the Abrahamic covenant? Infants being born Israelites, received the national blessings. As I have written under the heading "The Abrahamic Covenant" the Abrahamic covenant was divided into two covenants. The one was made with Abraham's natural seed, the nation of Israel, and the other with Abraham's spiritual seed. The former is the covenant of circumcision or the covenant of law. The latter is the Covenant of Grace. Israelite infants, born under law, received circumcision, the sign of that covenant, and received the blessings of the nation while they were obedient. This included the land of Canaan. When they were disobedient they lost the land and the blessings. They then came under the curse. Gentile infants are of-course excluded from that covenant. The elect in this age are "a chosen generation, a royal priesthood, a holy nation, His own special people." They are the "living stones being built up a spiritual house." and as such receive the promises of the Abrahamic Covenant of Grace upon faith in the seed, Jesus Christ.

(6.) "In other words, are we to believe that infants now may not properly be given the sign of that blessing which is enshrined in the new covenant?"

Since all infants are born in Adam and under the law, none are given the blessing of the new covenant in infancy. This is as true of infants born now as it was true of infants born before Christ. The Covenant of Grace is only entered through the new birth not through physical birth. Union with its head is only by faith. These are basic gospel truths that are being denied.

(7.) "Is the new covenant in this respect less generous than was the Abrahamic?"

The covenant of circumcision, which is part of the Abrahamic, still continues today to the Jews with the same national promises as before. The new Covenant of Grace and the Abrahamic Covenant of Grace are the same covenant with the same eternal blessings. However, no unbelievers are in the Covenant of Grace. They never were. Dr. Murray improperly assumes all the Israelites were born into the Covenant of Grace. This is not so. They were all born under law.

(8.) "If infants are excluded now, it cannot be too strongly emphasized that this change implies a complete reversal of the earlier divinely instituted practice."

Yes, infants are excluded now from the Covenant of Grace but this is not a complete reversal from before since infants being born in sin have always been excluded from the Covenant of Grace until they are regenerated, repent and believe.

Part 5

THE CHURCH

28

Definition and Membership

DEFINITION OF A CHURCH

I think it is necessary at the outset to define the church lest there be confusion. If we can agree on the definition of the church we will have gone a long way to resolving our differences in regard to who belongs to the church, what are the qualifications to be a member of the church and other allied issues. The definition should be simple and basic; not including unnecessary additions or even desirable features that are not required to define a primitive church.

The Greek word *ekklesia* that we translate as "church" is, of course, a New Testament word. It is generally agreed that *ekklesia* is broadly defined as an assembly. The kind of assembly is not defined by the term alone. The scriptural context defines the kind of assembly. In Acts 19 the word *ekklesia* is used three times and translated assembly. That was an assembly of the Ephesian town people.

Ekklesia is also used in Acts 7:38 which is speaking of the congregation (NKJV or NASV) or assembly (NIV) of the Israelites in the wilderness. It should not be translated "church" as the KJV does. Church is a New Testament word defining a New Testament concept. The Church is His new creation as the well-known hymn says. The Church is "this one new man" created in Himself through the cross, "so as to create in Himself one new man from the two thus making peace . . . through the cross" (Eph. 2:15-16). Before the cross there was no church since the church is "built on the foundation of the apostles and (New Testament) prophets, Jesus Christ Himself being the chief cornerstone" (Eph. 2:20). Isaiah wrote, "Behold, I lay in Zion a stone for a foundation" (Isa. 28:16). When was this foundation laid? After the builders rejected Jesus by their crucifixion of him, God raised him up to be the chief cornerstone. "The stone which the builders rejected has become the chief cornerstone" (Matt. 21:42, see Acts 4:10-11). Once the foundation was laid the church could be "built together for a habitation of God in the Spirit." It could be built on the foundation of the redemption of Christ accomplished on the cross.

For this reason it is confusing if the term Jewish church is used for the Jewish nation in Old Testament times. There was no instituted church then. The foundation was yet to be laid. The two terms Jewish and church are also contradictory since the Jewish nation was characteristically "stiff-necked and uncircumcised in heart" (Acts 7:51). The church, however, are circumcised in heart. As Paul tells the Philippian church, "We are the circumcision" (Phil. 3:3). Thus Jewish and Church signify two distinct peoples with two opposite traits or characteristics. Thus the phrase Jewish church is unscriptural, contradictory and confusing.

MEMBERSHIP

Also, the term Jewish speaks of a provincial and national body but the church is a universal body. It transcends nationalities and all peoples. There are no national churches in scripture. There should be no such thing as a Jewish church or Russian church or Indian church or whatever. The church is

> "the new man who is renewed in knowledge according to the image of Him who created him; where there is neither Greek nor Jew, circumcised nor uncircumcised, barbarian, Scythian, slave nor free, but Christ is all and in all" (Col. 3:10-11).

The church is the saints who have been called out of the world and out of all their nationalistic distinctions and gather or rather "are gathered together" in Christ's name. The second reference to the church in the New Testament is found in Matthew 18:17. (The first reference to church is Matt. 16:18). In that context it is stated, "For where two or three are gathered together in my name, I am there in the midst of them" (Matt. 18:20). The gathering of a church, is "in His name" that is, it is a gathering in Christ's power and authority. A church is a gathering for the ends and purposes that Christ has appointed. Previously, Christ gave the instruction, "tell it to the church," in verse 17, so there is the implication that the church has power and authority. The power and authority has been given by Christ the anointed one.

They have power to bind and loose on earth such that it is bound or loosed in heaven (Matt. 18:18), or as the authority is called in Matthew 16:19, "The keys of the kingdom of heaven," that were representatively given to Peter. Thus we read that the Corinthian church gathered "in the name of our Lord Jesus Christ and with the power of our Lord Jesus Christ" (1 Cor. 5:4). Because of this the verb "gathered together" in Matthew 18:20 and 1 Corinthians 5:4 is in the passive voice. They do not gather themselves but He gathers them together by His Spirit. They don't gather but are gathered together by Him and unto Him, having been called out of the world. They are "the called," by the gospel.

Who are these that are the church who are gathered together? They are the saints. Those who gather are brothers in the Lord. See verse 15 in this context where a member of the church is called "brother." In the context of Matthew 16 they are those who confess faith in Christ even as Peter who said, "You are the Christ, the son of the living God" (Matt. 16:16). Later Peter called those who had come to Christ the living stone, as like unto Him and so "living stones . . . Built up a spiritual house" (1 Pet. 2:5).

His name, *Petros*, Peter, which Christ here anew gives him, with the reason of it, namely, "upon the rock," in an allusion to *Petra*, signifying one built on the rock, and so of the same nature with the rock.*

Nothing but living stones belong to the church, living stones that confess their faith in Christ. They meet, "In my name" says Christ, that is, those who profess His name and obey His commands.

---

* Goodwin, *Works*, Volume 11, 57.

Further, the believers gathered as a local church are a stated company or a body. Although they are called out of the world and gathered by Christ they also form themselves into a body for prayer, fellowship, worship, teaching and discipline. For this reason there is membership which can be numbered and specific members who make up the local body.

Quoting Goodwin again,

> "And that the churches then in the primitive times of Christianity were such bodies is evident, for, 1 Cor 14, the apostle calls not only a particular church an whole church, but further, he speaks of that church as importing a stated union in relation to meeting actually: If the whole church, says he, verse 23, come together.
>
> They were therefore a church in order to meeting, even when they met not, and are at home, in respect that the union and bond to the same laws and ordinances still remained. They were not a church simply because they met or when they met, but they, the same persons, were to meet because they were a church in a stated and constant relation."*

A local church is of the same nature as the one universal church. The church of God and the churches of God do not differ in essence. The nature of all local churches should be the same everywhere. Thus the seven golden lampstands that signify the seven churches in Revelation were separate and distinct but made out of the same lump and so of the same nature. The local church is the manifestation of the universal church in this world. Is the universal church made up of only the elect? Then ideally local churches are to be made up of only the elect who are all to "proclaim the praises of Him who called them out of darkness into His marvelous light" (1 Pet. 2:9). Christ, as the head of the churches, walks among the golden lampstands that are holding forth the Word of life. When a church walks in the fear of the Lord and the comfort of the Holy Spirit they are a glorious church indeed.

It is true that the unsaved are sometimes found in local churches due to the fact that admittance to a local congregation is determined by men who

_____

* *Ibid.*, 62.

are fallible.

> "So as though before God, and as to his knowledge, others than saints may be in a church, yet none but such as are to us and in our judgments saints and holy, and of whom (as the apostle says, Philip. i. 6, 7) it is meet for us to think they have a work wrought, knowing their election, 1 Thess. i. 5, are to be admitted by us into church fellowship. By us there are none to be admitted, but such as to us are saints. So then to us a church instituted is all holy, and justified, and elected, and sanctified."*

From the above I think it should be clear that only believers belong to the church, not believers and their children, at least not until the children are believers themselves. Infants neither qualify as believers nor are they able to function in the church in any way. They are not living members by which every part does its share causing growth of the body for the edifying of itself in love (Eph. 4:16). The church is to glorify God with one mouth and one mind (Rom.15:6), and so in the context of the institution of the church we read of their oneness, their agreement, "If two shall agree . . ." (Matt. 18:19). Only those of like precious faith can have this relation and unity.

To sum up, I quote Thomas Goodwin:

> "As the church mystical is a company of saints, so is the church instituted also to be. So was the church of Corinth: 1 Cor. 1:2, To the church at Corinth, called to be saints. And it is a company of such as are elect: so 1 Peter. 5:13. The church which was at Babylon, is said to be elect together with them; that particular church was such.
>
> For to all callings there is to be a qualification. Because these are to make up a body to Christ, as well as the mystical, therefore they must be answerable to their head. It would be very unsuitable, to join monstrous members to such a glorious head.
>
> These are called to fellowship with Christ and his saints. And as moral virtues fit persons to have communion with men, so grace only qualifies men to have communion with Christ and saints. Their

---

* *Ibid.*, 294.

fellowship, and meetings, and transactions, are to be with one accord, Acts 4:32, and with one heart. Now faith will give them that. The believers met with one mind, Acts 4:32; and they only can and will do so. There is to be an agreement, an harmony, in a church and one false string makes a discord. There must be agreeing in principles to fit men for church fellowship.

The ends of church fellowship are the form of it. Now, therefore, such matter is only to be taken in, as may comply and be serviceable to those ends. Christ, when he makes any institution to an end, makes it such as may attain that end, or else it is in vain, and so not an ordinance. Therefore, those who have not the Spirit of Christ, and have no spiritual gifts and graces, have but the spirit of this world, and are unfit, and will be so far from edifying the church, that (as Solomon says, Eccles. 9:18) "One sinner will destroy much good." And are such persons also fit to reprove, to judge, and thereby to preserve the church pure? Since they are such whom Christ calls swine, they are so unfit to reprove, as they are not fit to be reproved, Matt. 7:6. And it is of such the apostle speaks, 1 Cor. 2:14, that they cannot receive things spiritual, but they are foolishness unto them, and therefore they are unfit to judge those within, for the spiritual man only judgeth all things, and is judged of none, 1 Cor. 2:14."*

Calvin's marks of a true church are:

"Wherever we see the Word of God purely preached and heard, and the sacraments administered according to Christ's institution, there it is not to be doubted, a church of God exists."†

This is quite insufficient as marks of a true church since he defined a church apart from its membership. His marks only apply to the pastor or leadership of the church. Too, his marks are outward things that can exist apart from true life. The unregenerate can preach and even say, Have we not prophesied in your name? (See Matt. 7:22). Many apostate churches

---

* *Ibid.*, 293-94.
† Calvin, *Institutes*, Book 4:1:9, 1023.

administer the sacraments. Calvin's definition leaves out the mutual responsibility of believers and the corporate priesthood of all believers. A better definition is when he defines the true church membership saying,

> "Sometimes by the term 'church' it means that which is actually in God's presence, into which no persons are received but those who are children of God by grace of adoption and true members of Christ by sanctification of the Holy Spirit."[*]

PAEDOBAPTISTS DEFINITION OF THE CHURCH

Having sought to establish a definition of church we come to a major argument that our Paedobaptist brethren use.

> "The Bible teaches that the people of God in the Old Testament and the people of God in the New Testament are one and the same people. Both Old and New Testament believers are saved by grace through faith in the Saviour . . . God's people (*i.e.*, the church) have always been spiritual in nature."[†]

Since he is saying that believers are the people of God we agree since believers do belong to the church as we defined it. However, on this same page Mr. Booth says, "In the Old Testament he included believers and the children of believers in the membership of his church."

In this statement he has ignored his statement that the people of God are believers and then redefined the church by including unbelievers and calling the whole nation of Israel the church even though there was only a remnant that were believers. Here is a major error and it fails to listen to Paul's argument "that they are not all Israel who are of Israel" (Rom. 9:6). In other words the nation of Israel was in reality two people. Paul defines them "as children of the flesh" and "children of the promise." The children of the promise are the true Israel. The children of the flesh are not the true Israel. Thus there are two peoples who are called the people of God. Yes, God has

---

[*] *Ibid.*, 1021.
[†] R. Booth, 73.

only one true church throughout the ages as Mr. Booth rightly says, on the same page,

> "God has always made the same spiritual demands on his people—justification by faith alone, wholehearted devotion to him and true spiritual worship. Nothing less has ever been acceptable."[*]

But Mr. Booth fails to see that he is describing the remnant of Israel and not the nation of Israel. The nation of Israel was not God's spiritual people since they were not justified by faith but rather sought righteousness "by the works of the law for they stumbled at that stumbling stone" (Rom. 9:32). Not being believers they were not the church as Paul wrote in Romans 9:27, "Though the number the children of Israel be as the sand of the sea the remnant will be saved." Most of the Jews were cut off as Paul continues, "He will finish the work and cut it short in righteousness." The word rendered "He will finish" means bring to an end. Apart from the seed or the remnant (the word is "remnant" in the Hebrew; see Isaiah 1:9) the nation would have been as Sodom and Gomorrah. And as Isaiah said before: "Unless the Lord of Sabaoth had left us a seed, we would have become like Sodom, and we would have been made like Gomorrah" (Rom. 9:29). Evidently the nation was not God's true people nor did they belong to those believers who were justified by faith and part of God's church. It was only the seed or remnant that was such. "The rest were hardened" (Rom.11:7). The nation was God's people in name only.

---

[*] *Ibid.*

29

The Commonwealth of Israel and the Church

T he argument that infants should be baptized is based on the Paedobaptist belief that the Church and the Commonwealth of Israel are one and the same. Their argument is that God included believers and their children in the Old Testament Church so believers and their children are also included in the New Testament Church since the Old Testament and New Testament Church are one and the same. Charles Hodge wrote, "The Commonwealth of Israel was the Church."[*]

The Jews believed that since the promises were to them all their physical seed were included and being God's children they would obtain all God's blessings. The Jews believed that the blessings arising from the coming of the Messiah would be given to all Israelites. How different were the results from their anticipations. Today some Christians also believe that all their physical seed are in the Covenant of Grace and so to them belong the promises. They are as equally wrong as were the Jews.

In Romans 9 to 11 Paul fully vindicated God from injustice. God's blessings are only given to those who believe. They are not given to any infants through physical birth. They are only to the elect, such as Isaac and Jacob. But even the elect do not obtain the blessings until they come to believe. Even the elect have no hope and are without God in the world until by the new birth they enter the Covenant of Grace.

That Israel had great privileges cannot be denied but privilege is not grace. It should be noted that the privileges of the Jews that are given in

---

[*] Hodge, *Systematic Theology*, 3:548-49.

Romans 9:3-4 describe Israel "according to the flesh," not as regenerate. Although to Israel "according to the flesh . . . belongs the adoption as sons and the glory and the covenants and the giving of the Law and the temple service and the promises" they as a body were doomed to destruction. Their adoption separated them from the idolatrous nations to the privileges of the Jewish commonwealth but did not give them an inalienable interest in the Divine favor. That is only the possession of the individual believer, not of any nation, whether in the old economy or today. They were "children of the kingdom" only in an outward sense and so being a rebellious and obstinate people they were to be "cast out into outer darkness" (Matt. 8:11-12). So far were their privileges from bringing blessing to the unbelieving Jews that they were the occasion of their delusion and punishment.

> "And David says: 'Let their table become a snare and a trap, a stumbling block and a recompense to them; Let their eyes be darkened, that they may not see, and bow down their back always'" (Rom. 11:9-10).

Haldane paraphrases this verse,

> "Let them experience misery and disappointment in their daily occupations and concerns, and let them find those things, of whatever description—whether sacred or common—which were calculated to be for their welfare and advantage, a snare, and a trap, and a stumbling-block, and a punishment to them."[*]

Privilege disregarded is lost. Their privileges were lost and given to the Gentiles "through their fall salvation is come unto the Gentiles" (Rom. 11:11).

---

[*] Haldane, *Romans*, 529.

30

The Characteristics of the Nation of Israel

Throughout the Old Testament Israel is portrayed as a wicked and rebellious nation. This description of the nation was applicable not only to a specific time of their history but described them throughout their history. God himself said,

> "They have rejected me, that I should not reign over them. According to all the works which they have done since the day that I brought them up out of Egypt, even to this day" (1 Sam. 8:7-8).

He said of them in Jeremiah's time, "This is a nation that does not obey the voice of the Lord their God nor receive correction" (Jer. 7:28).

References could be multiplied but I will only use Stephen's testimony that such was the nation from the beginning even until the times of the apostles. "You stiff-necked and uncircumcised in heart and ears! You always resist the Holy Spirit, as your fathers did, so do you" (Acts 7:51). Paul adds his voice to this,

> "... the Jews who killed both the Lord Jesus and their own prophets, and have persecuted us: and they do not please God and are contrary to all men, forbidding us to speak to the Gentiles that they may be saved, so as always to fill up the measure of their sins, but wrath has come upon them to the uttermost" (1 Thess. 2:15-16).

Indeed, the Jews who were outwardly God's people, are described as worse than the heathen. God speaking of Jerusalem says, "She has rebelled against my judgments by doing wickedness more than the nations, and against my statutes more than the countries that are all around her" (Ezek. 5:6). Christ likewise represented the guilt of the Jews as greater than Tyre and Sidon or even Sodom and Gomorrah (see Matt. 11:20-24; 10:15; Mark 6:11). What is the conclusion of this? It is as Moses said, "They have corrupted themselves, they are not his children, because of their blemish: a crooked and perverse generation" (Deut. 32:5).

An objection to this is that Israel is called God's people, his elect, his covenant people. How then can they be rejected of God and designated a rebellious nation and "not his children"? Jonathan Edwards is helpful here.

> "And with regard to the people of Israel, it is very manifest, that something diverse is oftentimes intended by that nation being God's people, from their being visible saints, visibly holy, or having those qualifications which are requisite in order to a due admission to the ecclesiastical privileges of such."[*]

Edwards is here saying that Israel being God's people was different to their being saints with the blessings and privileges that the true people of God have. He continues,

> "That nation, that family of Israel according to the flesh, and with regard to that external and carnal qualification, were in some sense adopted by God to be his peculiar people, and his covenant people. This is not only evident by what has been already observed, but also indisputably manifest from Rom. 9:3-5. "I have great heaviness and continual sorrow of heart; for I could wish that myself were accursed from Christ for my brethren, my kinsmen, ACCORDING TO THE FLESH, who are Israelites, to whom pertaineth the ADOPTION, and the glory, and the COVENANTS, and the giving of the law, and the service of God, and the PROMISES; whose are the fathers; and of whom, as concerning the flesh, Christ came." It is to be noted, that

---

[*] Edwards, 1:462.

the privileges here mentioned are spoken of as belonging to the Jews, not now as visible saints, not as professors of true religion, not as members of the visible church of Christ; but only as people of such a nation, such a blood, such an external and carnal relation to the patriarchs their ancestors, Israelites ACCORDING TO THE FLESH. For the apostle is speaking here of the unbelieving Jews, professed unbelievers, that were out of the Christian church, and open visible enemies to it, and such as had no right to the external privileges of Christ's people. So, in Rom. 11:28, 29 this apostle speaks of the same unbelieving Jews, as in some respect an elect people, and interested in the calling, promises, and covenants God formerly gave to their forefathers and as still beloved for their sakes. "As concerning the gospel, they are enemies for your sake; but as touching the election, they are beloved for the fathers' sakes: for the gifts and calling of God are without repentance." These things are not privileges belonging to the Jews now as a people of the right religion, or in the true church of visible worshippers of God; but as a people of such a pedigree or blood; and that even after the ceasing of the Mosaic administration.

On the whole, it is evident that the very nation of Israel, not as visible saints, but as the progeny of Jacob according to the flesh, were in some respect a chosen people, a people of God, a covenant people, an holy nation; even as Jerusalem was a chosen city, the city of God, a holy city, and a city that God had engaged by covenant to dwell in."[*]

Note how Edwards wrote that the people of Israel, although unbelievers, were in some respect an elect people, a covenant people, having part in the calling, promises, and covenants of God. It was in respect of them being born Jews. It had to do with them as a type of the true people of God. Although the same words are used to describe the New Testament church their meaning is quite different when applied to the unsaved Israelites than when applied to God's true people born of his Spirit and justified by Christ's blood through faith.

"Just as we must not equate the physical nation of Israel with the

---

[*] Edwards, 1:462 (capitalization retained from Edwards).

'Body of Christ,' so we must never give New Testament spiritual meaning to the physical blessings (which were only a type of the spiritual) that were experienced by every person born into the nation of Israel. This is true even when the same words are used in both cases. The nation of Israel, as a nation, was loved, chosen, redeemed, called, adopted, etc. by God, and every Israelite, without exception, experienced each one of these blessings in a physical sense regardless of their personal spiritual relationship to God. However, none of those blessings mean the same thing when the NT Scriptures apply them to individual believers or to the Church as the Body of Christ. The redemption from Egypt does not equal justification by faith, and national 'adoption' does not equal 'sons of God;' and election as a nation among nations is not equal to 'chosen in Christ before the foundation of the world' unto salvation, etc."*

Israel as a nation was not the true people of God but only in type. Therefore, the new covenant people of God are represented in the Old Testament as a people of greater purity and spirituality. The New Testament church are a different people from the nation of Israel.

Another reason that we should not use the condition of Israel under the old covenant as a guide to what are the qualifications for membership in the church is because the prophecies concerning gospel times speak of a great change. What made men acceptable for membership in Israel would no longer make men acceptable under the new dispensation that required spiritual worship, heart circumcision and inner holiness. As Isaiah 52:1 says, "For the uncircumcised (spiritually or in heart) and the unclean shall no longer come to you." They shall no longer be accepted as God's people and enter God's sanctuary, the church. Zechariah likewise speaks of the great alteration that was to be made *in that day.* "In that day there shall no longer be a Canaanite in the house of the Lord of hosts" (Zech 14:21).

The last 9 chapters of Ezekiel are a prophecy of the church in the days of the gospel. Ezekiel's temple that he prophesied of is the same temple that the Messiah was foretold to build, "The man whose name is the branch—he

---

* Reisinger, *Abraham's Four Seeds*, 43.

shall build the temple of the Lord" (Zech. 6:12). Ezekiel writing of this temple in the latter chapters of his prophecy wrote, "Thus says the Lord God; No foreigner, uncircumcised in heart or uncircumcised in flesh shall enter My sanctuary, including any foreigner who is among the children of Israel" (Ezek. 44:9). The context tells us that God told Ezekiel, "Mark well who may enter the house" (verse 5) and blamed Israel for bringing in foreigners, uncircumcised in heart and flesh. Thus it is speaking of admission into the visible church not the invisible church. By this circumcision of heart is meant regeneration.

> "The apostle tells us what was signified both by circumcision and baptism, Col. 2:11, 12. 'In whom also ye are circumcised with the circumcision made without hands, in putting off the sins of the flesh by the circumcision of Christ, buried with him in baptism; wherein you are also risen with him, through the faith of the operation of God.' Where I would observe by the way, he speaks of all the members of the church of Colosse as visibly circumcised with this circumcision; agreeable to Ezekiel's prophecy, that the members of the Christian church shall visibly have this circumcision. The apostle speaks, in like manner, of the members of the church of Philippi as spiritually circumcised, (*i.e.*, in profession and visibility,) and tells wherein this circumcision appeared. Philip. iii. 3. 'For we are the circumcision, which worship God in the spirit, and rejoice in Christ Jesus, and have no confidence in the flesh.' And in Rom. ii. 28, 29 the apostle speaks of this Christian and Jewish circumcision together, calling the former the circumcision of the heart. 'But he is not a Jew which is one outwardly, neither is that circumcision which is outward in the FLESH; but he is a Jew, which is one inwardly, and circumcision is that of THE HEART, in the spirit, not in the letter; whose praise is not of men, but of God.' And whereas in this prophecy of Ezekiel it is foretold, that none should enter into the Christian sanctuary or church, but such as are circumcised in heart and circumcised in flesh; thereby I suppose is intended, that none should be admitted but such as were visibly regenerated, as well as baptized with outward

baptism."[*]

That believers in the Old Testament belong to the Church (although they were not built on the foundation until the cross and resurrection) we readily grant. That all believers of all ages are saved the same way by the same Savior is a fundamental truth we must never give up. However I deny that the Commonwealth of Israel was the Church. I am going to use four arguments to prove that Israel, the Commonwealth, was not the Church.

---

[*] Edwards, 1:441.

31

The Commonwealth of Israel Not the Church

(1.) The character of the Church and Israel is different, composed of different people.

(2.) The Church and the Commonwealth of Israel were founded on different covenants.

(3.) The Church was not brought into visible existence until the New Testament age.

(4.) The Jewish commonwealth or Israel was the enemy of the Church.

T he character of the Church and Israel are different, composed of different people. Charles Hodge differs with the above statement. He wrote,

> "This is really the turning point in the controversy concerning infant church membership. If the Church is one under both dispensations; if infants were members of the Church under the theocracy, then they are members of the Church now, unless the contrary can be proved."*

I would like to use Dr. Hodge to answer his own argument,

> "The fallacy of this whole argument lies in the false assumption, that the external Israel was the true Church. It was not the body of Christ; it was not pervaded by the Spirit. Membership in it did not constitute

---

* Hodge, *Systematic Theology*, 3:555.

membership in the body of Christ. The rejection or destruction of the external Israel was not the destruction of the Church. The apostacy of the former was not the apostacy of the latter. The attributes, promises, and prerogatives of the one, were not those of the other. In short, they were not the same, and therefore, that the visibility of the one was that of the external organization, is no proof that the visibility of the Church is that of an external society. All this is included, not only in the express declaration of the Apostle, that the external Israel was not the true Israel, but is involved in his whole argument. It was, indeed, the main point of discussion between himself and the Jews. The great question was, is a man made a member of the true Israel, and a partaker of the promise, by circumcision and subjection, or by faith in Christ? If the former, then the Jews were right, and Paul was wrong as to the whole issue . . . Besides, if we admit that the external Israel was the true Church, then we must admit that the true Church apostatized: for it is undeniable that the whole external Israel, as an organized body, did repeatedly, and for long periods, lapse into idolatry. Nay more, we must admit that the true Church rejected and crucified Christ; for he was rejected by the external Israel, by the Sanhedrim, by the priesthood, by the elders, and by the people. All this is in direct opposition to the Scriptures, and would involve a breach of promise on the part of God. Paul avoids this fatal conclusion by denying that the external Church is, as such, the true Church, or that the promises made to the latter were made to the former.""

Thus when he says in his *Systematic Theology*, "if infants were members of the church under the theocracy, then they are members of the church now" he answers himself in the *Princeton Review*, "this whole argument lies in the false assumption that the external Israel was the true church." Infants were not members of the church under the theocracy. They were members of the external Israel but not the true church. As he wrote, "Membership in it (the external Israel) did not constitute membership in the body of Christ."

The nation of Israel was redeemed in type which was not the "eternal

---

* Hodge, *Princeton Review*, 683-84.

redemption" of believers so that a person could belong to Israel but be eternally lost. But a person cannot be a member of the church which is the body of Christ and be lost. When speaking of the nation Paul wrote, "They are not all Israel who are of Israel" but it could never be written, "They are not all the church who are of the church," if we use the scriptural definition of church; that is, "the church which is His body" (Eph. 1:22-23). Unbelievers are excluded.

John Murray wrote that Israel in the Old Testament was the church. He bases his statement on the translation of *ekklesia* in Acts 7:38 in the King James Bible as church. He wrote, "The organization of the people of God in the Old Testament is expressly called the church, Acts 7:38."*

The Greek word *ekklesia* which is used in Acts 7:38 is translated church in some translations. The word *ekklesia* is defined in Greek concordances as assembly. The character of the assembly is not defined by the Greek word. Thus, the word *ekklesia*, assembly, is also used to denote the assembly of the Ephesian people in the theater concerning the goddess Diana in Acts 19. Obviously, that was not the church and was translated assembly. In Acts 7:38 *ekklesia* stands for the assembly of the Jews, "He was in the *ekklesia*, or assembly, in the wilderness." Because the same word is used does not mean it is necessarily speaking of the same thing for words have many meanings as anyone notices when they use a dictionary. Just because the same Greek word is used does not mean its meaning is identical in both contexts. This is a fallacious argument. The character of the assembly is defined by the Biblical context.

Hodge's argument is based on the assumption that the Commonwealth and the Church are the same. If his argument is valid then it follows that all people who were in the "Church" as it existed before Christ came are members now. Those who were in the Commonwealth of Israel, which Hodge denominates the church, were the whole of Israel. Many of them were, "obstinate idolaters and impious wretches" (I use Jonathan Edwards' description of them).

Indeed, the majority had revolted against the Lord and lived scandalous

---

* Murray, 46.

lives. In the times of Christ it was the Jewish church that was the inveterate enemy of Christ and finally had him put to death. Yet they were all "covenant children" and members of the Commonwealth of Israel. In Christ's day the members of the Jewish church were the Sadducees, who denied a future state and the resurrection; the Pharisees, who believed in justification by the law; the Herodians, who conformed to the world; and multitudes who were ignorant and ungodly. By Hodge's argument such people are all members of the Church because such people were members of the Commonwealth. Obviously, his reasoning is false. The following paragraphs seek to show where his reasoning is false.

The Church is a company of believers requiring new spiritual life to enter into it. The commonwealth was a society into which its members were born by natural birth. The commonwealth was the shadow of which the church is the reality. The Jewish church or Israel had priests that "offered gifts according to the law, who serve unto the example and shadow of heavenly things..." (Heb. 8:4-5). The priest of the church is none other than the Lord of glory who ministers in the true tabernacle not made with hands having offered himself "an offering and a sacrifice to God." It is needless for me to write of the different law of the church, the different promises, another altar, another rest, another mountain, another covenant, another kingdom, another city, and so on, for it is all written in Hebrews. In short the one was earthly, the other heavenly, the one natural, the other spiritual, the one the shadow, the other the substance.

Dr. Hodge in the *Princeton Review*, October 1853, which I previously quoted, wrote very clearly of these distinctions,

> "It is to be remembered that there were two covenants made with Abraham. By the one his natural descendants through Isaac, were constituted a commonwealth—an external community; by the other his spiritual descendants were constituted in a church, (invisible of course, since, at that time, the only formal organization was that of the law.) The parties to the former covenant, were God, and the nation; to the other, God, and his true people. The promises of the national covenant, were national blessings; the promises of the

spiritual covenant (*i.e.*, the Covenant of Grace) were spiritual blessings, as reconciliation, holiness, and eternal life. The conditions of the one covenant (the old) were circumcision, and obedience to the law; the conditions of the other were, and ever have been, faith in the Messiah, as 'the seed of the woman,' the Son of God, the Saviour of the world. There cannot be a greater mistake than to confound the national covenant with the Covenant of Grace, (that is, the old covenant with the new) and the commonwealth founded on the one, with the church founded on the other. When Christ came, the commonwealth was abolished, and there was nothing put in its place. The church (now made visible) remained. There was no external covenant, nor promise of external blessings, on condition of external rites, and subjection. There was a spiritual society, with spiritual promises, on condition of faith in Christ. The church is, therefore, in its essential nature, a company of believers, and not an external society, requiring merely external profession as the condition of membership."*

The members of the Commonwealth of Israel entered it at the time of birth. They entered it as unregenerate and unsaved; as Abraham's natural seed. Entrance into the church was of the regenerate who had been saved. "And the Lord added to the church daily those who were being saved" (Acts 2:47). The visible entrance into the church was at baptism of those who received the word in faith. "Then those who gladly received his word were baptized, and that day about three thousand souls were added to them" (Acts 2:41).

Probably most if not all of those who were joined to the church on the day of Pentecost and soon after were in the Commonwealth previous to their entrance into the church. This shows that the Commonwealth and the church were separate and different entities. Membership in the Commonwealth of Israel was not the same as membership in the Church as shown by the above verses.

What was the condition of membership in the Commonwealth? The

---

* Hodge, *Princeton Review,* 684.

qualification was birth as an Israelite and circumcision. What is the condition of membership in the Church? Dr. Hodge, in the article quoted above rightly said,

> "In no part of the New Testament is any condition of membership prescribed other than that contained in the answer of Philip to the Eunuch who desired baptism, 'If thou believest with all thy heart thou mayest.' "[*]

Membership in the Commonwealth did not qualify a person to be a member of the Church nor did its lack disqualify a person from being a member of the Church. The conditions were different for membership because the Commonwealth and the Church were different. None are part of the church except those who have life, having been made alive by the Spirit and united to Christ.

> "For if Christ be the rock whereon the church is built, whereas he is a living stone, those that are laid and built on him must be lively (living) stones also, as this apostle assures us, 1 Peter 2:4, 5, they must be like unto Christ himself, partaking of his nature, quickened by his Spirit, so as it were, to be bone of his bones, and flesh of his flesh: Eph. 5:30. Nor can any be built on him but by a living faith, effectual in universal obedience."[†]

It is only by using a definition of church arrived at by reason rather than revelation that the Paedobaptist is able to justify the baptism of infants. Dr. Hodge sees the difficulty of defining the church as the scriptures do, as a company of believers. In his section on infant baptism he makes an amazing statement for a Paedobaptist.

> "Infant Baptism. The difficulty on this subject is that baptism from its very nature involves a profession of faith. It is the way in which by

---

[*] *Ibid.*, 685.
[†] Owen, 31.

the ordinance of Christ, He is to be confessed before men; but infants are incapable of making such a confession; therefore they are not the proper subjects of baptism. Or, to state the matter in another form: the sacraments belong to the members of the Church; but the Church is the company of believers; infants cannot exercise faith, therefore they are not to be baptized. In order to justify the baptism of infants, we must attain and authenticate such an idea of the church as that it shall include the children of believing parents . . ."[*]

Hodge then lists five definitions of church. His first is "the whole body of the elect," but this is not helpful to his purpose. He then gives a definition of *church* that he wants to use in his discussion of infant baptism: "In the present discussion, by the Church is meant what is called the visible Church; that is the whole body of those who profess the true religion."[†]

However, infants do not and cannot "profess the true religion" therefore infants are even excluded from the Church by that definition. Since that definition is not suitable Hodge turns to the Old Testament. He wrote, "The Commonwealth of Israel was the Church." Since Church is a New Testament word and concept why use the Old Testament for its definition? Hodge himself sees that it is a false position since he on page 543 says that the Roman Catholic theory of the Church is "derived from the ancient theocracy and from the analogy between the Church and a civil Commonwealth." From such an analogy Rome arrives at a false understanding of the Church but Hodge uses the same analogy. The error is that an analogy is only an analogy. It is not an equivalent. Dr. Murray writes perceptively of this,

> "Similitude here again does not mean identity . . . one of the simplest principles which must always guide our thinking namely, that analogy does not mean identity. When we make a comparison we do not make an equation."[‡]

---

[*] Hodge, *Systematic Theology*, Volume 3, 546.
[†] *Ibid.*, 547.
[‡] Murray, *Redemption Accomplished*, 168.

To use the Old Testament in such a way is rejected by Jonathan Edwards. He was writing on the qualifications for communion but it is also appropriate for our discussion in regard to infant baptism.

> "Whatever was the case with respect to the qualifications for the sacraments of the Old Testament dispensation, I humbly conceive it is nothing to the purpose in the present argument, nor needful to determine us with respect to the qualifications for the sacraments of the Christian dispensation, which is a matter of such plain fact in the New Testament. Far am I from thinking the Old Testament to be like an old almanack out of use; . . . But yet all allow that the Old Testament dispensation is out of date, with its ordinances; and I think, in a matter pertaining to the constitution and order of the New Testament church—a matter of fact, wherein the New Testament itself is express, full and abundant—to have recourse to the Mosaic dispensation for rules or precedents to determine our judgment, is quite needless, and out of reason.
>
> Since God uses great plainness of speech in the New Testament, which is as it were the charter and municipal law of the Christian church, what need we run back to the ceremonial and typical institutions of an antiquated dispensation, wherein God's declared design was, to deliver divine things in comparative obscurity, hid under a veil, and involved in clouds?
>
> We have no more occasion for going to search among the types, dark revelations, and carnal ordinances of the Old Testament, to find out whether this matter of fact concerning the constitution and order of the New Testament church be true, than we have occasion for going there to find out whether any other matter of fact, of which we have an account in the New Testament, be true."[*]

Bannerman writes,

> "The Scripture conception of the Church involves that of 'calling,' 'calling out,' or 'choosing,' and implies that the call has been, so far,

---

[*] Edwards, 465.

an effectual one, that it has been, to a certain extent at least obeyed. Further, there is general agreement that one great bond of union in this society or fellowship is a common faith or belief of some kind, with respect to God, that the Church is a fellowship of believers, 'a congregation of faithful men,'—of whatever sort the belief may be which binds them together, and to whatever relations to God and to each other it may give rise. Hence a favourite starting-point with the old divines of the Reformed Church in their treatises De Ecclesia was the fourteenth verse of the seventeenth chapter of Revelation. They held that the words which the angel spoke to the apostle in his vision set before us briefly and clearly what the Church of God is and has been in all ages. It means 'those that are with the Lamb, who is Lord of lords and King of kings, and they that are with Him are called, and chosen, and faithful.' "*

Thus infants are ruled out because they have not been called nor can they be termed faithful until they believe. Such a simple gathering as, "Two or three gathered together in my name" (Matt. 18:20), is a church but even that definition of the Church excludes infants. Usually the place of gathering is specified so we have the church at Jerusalem, the church at Antioch, and so on. The term in the singular denoted the separate local assemblies in those cities.

The members of these assemblies are called, "The elect of God" (Col. 3:12), "children of God by faith" (Gal. 3:26), "Sanctified in Christ Jesus, called to be saints" (1 Cor. 1:2), "Saints in Christ Jesus" (Phil. 1:1), "Followers of the Lord" (1 Thess. 1:6), "Beloved of God called to be saints" (Rom. 1:7).

> "No doubt can exist that these churches were, in the view of the inspired writers who addressed them, composed of persons truly converted to God. What has been said must not be understood to imply that none but true believers ever entered the primitive churches. We know from the Acts of the apostles, that Ananias, Sapphira, and Simon the Sorcerer, had a place for a time among the

---

* Bannerman, *The Scripture Doctrine of the Church*, 1.

true disciples of Jesus; and we know from the apostolic epistles, that false brethren were brought in unawares into the churches. But we are clearly taught that they were considered intruders, occupying a place that did not properly belong to them, and were ejected when their true character became apparent. Although, even in apostolic times, such men obtained admittance into the churches, they crept in unawares, and therefore, if we would tread in the footsteps of the apostles, we cannot plead their authority for admitting into the churches any who are not true disciples of Christ.

In our definition of a church, we have called it an assembly of believers in Christ. This definition tells what a church is according to the revealed will of God, and not what it becomes by the criminal negligence of its ministers and members, or the wicked craft of hypocritical men who gain admittance into it. When we study the word of God to ascertain what a church is, we must receive the perfect pattern as presented in the uncorrupted precepts of the word, and not as marred by human error and crime."[*]

Thus we see that the Commonwealth was composed of the nation of Israel, who were mostly unbelievers, and that it included all Jewish children but the Church is composed of believers and only includes believing children.

"A man could be admitted to the outward Israel without being received into the number of God's true people, and he could be excluded from the former without being cut off from the latter. The true Israel was not the commonwealth, as such, and the outward organization, with its laws and officers, though intimately related with the spiritual body as the true Church, did not constitute it."[†]

---

[*] Dagg, *Church Order*, 79-80.
[†] Hodge, *Princeton Review*, 681.

THE CHURCH AND THE COMMONWEALTH WERE FOUNDED ON DIFFERENT COVENANTS

The Covenant of Grace was entered into by the Trinity before the foundation of the world and so it is also denominated the everlasting covenant. It is therefore older than all the other covenants. However, it is also called the New Covenant. That is because it followed the Old Covenant, not in respect to its origin but in regard to its visible administration. The New Covenant in that regard began after the Old Covenant. Christ established the New Covenant after the Old had served its purposes, after He had fulfilled it, and after it had passed away.

The Commonwealth or the Jewish church was founded on the law, that is on the Old Covenant. The Jewish Church was typical and its sacrifices and priesthood which were according to the law were symbolic. It was external and earthly. Natural descent and physical circumcision gave a full right to all its privileges. Its visible existence began when it was organized by the law given from Mount Sinai. The covenant of the law was the charter of the Jewish church. The tabernacle of the Jewish church, its services and all its ritual pointed to the one who would come. Its priests and prophets typified the apostle and high priest of our confession. When He came the ceremonial law came to an end. It had accomplished its purpose. The charter expired and the Jewish church was discontinued.

Then the New Covenant came into visible administration when the Savior came making "the first (covenant) obsolete" (Heb. 9:13). The shadows ceased. The substance, the body, had come. Thus, the new covenant was dedicated by the death of the testator. As Christ said, "This cup is the new covenant in My blood, which is shed for you" (Luke 22:20). On this very covenant, "the New Covenant in His blood" is founded the church, the church of the firstborn; called by Christ "my Church." Believers don't come to the "mount that might be touched" where the law was given that founded the visible commonwealth.

(We) "have come to Mount Zion and to the city of the living God, the heavenly Jerusalem, to an innumerable company of angels, to the

277

general assembly and church of the firstborn who are registered in heaven, to God the Judge of all, to the spirits of just men made perfect, to Jesus the Mediator of the new covenant, and to the blood of sprinkling that speaks better things than that of Abel" (Heb. 12:22-24).

THE CHURCH WAS NOT BROUGHT INTO VISIBLE EXISTENCE UNTIL THE NEW TESTAMENT AGE

The word "church" only occurs three times in the gospels and these are all in Matthew. But it occurs a staggering 111 times in Acts to the Revelation. This is significant as to when the church began. The first time church is mentioned Christ speaks of it in the future tense. "Upon this rock I will build my church" (Matt. 16:18). Paul, writing of the church's foundation writes, "Having been built on the foundation of the apostles and prophets, Jesus Christ Himself being the chief cornerstone" (Eph. 2:20). Since prophets follows apostles in the word order Paul is probably writing of New Testament prophets. Another possible interpretation, which I believe is correct, is that apostles and prophets are not two separate groups but designations of the same men; that is, apostles who are prophets. It doesn't say "the foundation of the apostles and the prophets." There is a like construction in the same letter, "and some pastors and teachers" 4:11; that is, men who are pastors and teachers. I believe Ephesians 2:20 is speaking of the apostles being the foundation of the Church by their writing the Holy Scriptures. In writing the scriptures under the inspiration of the Holy Spirit they were prophets; analogous to the Old Testament prophets. Thus, Matthew 16:18 and Ephesians 2:20 point to the church beginning in the New Testament.

The church came into existence after Christ

"abolished in His flesh the enmity, that is, the law of commandments contained in ordinances, so as to create in Himself one new man from the two, thus making peace, and that He might reconcile them both to God in one body through the cross, thereby putting to death the enmity" (Eph. 2:15-16).

278

The old was abolished and completely done away with. It was replaced by the one new man. This new man is the Church consisting of Jew and Gentile. It is not the old modified or improved. It is a new man, a new humanity. It never existed before. It is absolutely new. The word translated "create" is *ktizo*. It is used of the creation of man (1 Cor. 11:9), the whole creation (Col. 1:16; Rev. 4:11) and the new creation (Eph. 2:10; 4:24). In every case it is used for a completely new entity that never existed before.

> "That is the truth: the Church is something absolutely new that has been brought into being, something that was not there before. It is comparable to what happened in the very beginning when God created the heavens and the earth. There was nothing there before God created. Creation means bringing into being something that was previously not there, non-existent; it is making something out of nothing."[*]

To fix the time of the Church coming into existence it is said that it was "through the cross." Christ reconciled "them both in one body through the cross." The one body is the Church. As the hymn says, "She is His new creation by water and the Word." What an astounding thing has been done! The Church has been created! It is one body! "Elect from every nation, yet one o'er all the earth." All are one in Christ Jesus. What is this glorious creation? It is "the Church which is His body, the fulness of Him Who fills all in all" (Eph. 1:22-23). It is nothing less than "a holy temple . . . a habitation of God in the Spirit" (Eph. 2:21-22).

The church is the body of Christ. It is called "the church, which is His body" (Eph. 1:22-23). It is the Holy Spirit that forms the spiritual body of Christ, "For by one Spirit we were all baptized into one body—whether Jews or Greeks, whether slaves or free—and have all been made to drink into one Spirit" (1 Cor. 12:13). This, likewise, puts the church in the new dispensation, the dispensation of the Spirit. We can say that the birth of the church was at Pentecost when the Spirit was poured out on the assembled

---

[*] Lloyd-Jones, *God's Way of Reconciliation*, 214.

believers, later called the Jerusalem church.

If a person wanted to argue that the church also began at the cross when Christ cried, "It is finished," we would not argue for at that moment the "veil of the temple was torn in two," and the whole sacrificial system of the temple came to an end. The Commonwealth was finished and Judaism was no more. The shadow disappeared to make way for the substance to shine in the light of day. The temple and all it stood for had fulfilled its day to be replaced by the spiritual temple; the church of the living God. The removal of the Jewish commonwealth was necessary for the introduction of the Christian church. Thus, the assumption that the Paedobaptist makes, "The Jewish society before Christ, and the Christian society after Christ are one and the same church, under different dispensations" is manifestly false. As R. B. C. Howell wrote,

> "Can that which is removed, and that which is placed in its stead, be after all substantially the same thing? Can the law be changed and still continue to be the same law?"[*]

Does this mean then that all the Old Testament saints are not in the church? Don't they belong to the body of Christ? Aren't they too, the bride of Christ? Yes, surely all the saints are one body. All belong to the one body, even the bride of Christ. Dagg writes beautifully of the place of the Old Testament saints.

> "The Scriptures represent a gathering of all things under Christ, both in heaven and on earth, at the time of his exaltation in human nature to supreme dominion. The Old Testament saints who had been saved by the efficacy of his blood before it was shed, and who had desired to understand what the Holy Ghost signified when it testified to their prophets concerning the sufferings of Christ, and the glory which should follow, were waiting in heaven for the unfolding of this mystery. Moses and Elias evinced their interest in this theme, when, during their brief interview with the Saviour on the mount of

---

[*] Howell, *The Covenants*, 116.

transfiguration, they discoursed of the decease which he was to accomplish at Jerusalem. The angels had desired to look into this mystery, but the fulness of time for its disclosure did not arrive until the man Christ Jesus entered the heavenly court, and was crowned with glory and honor. Then the angels gathered around and worshipped the Son. Then the saints drew near, and adored him as their Lord and Saviour. The proclamation was made throughout the courts of glory, and every inhabitant of heaven rendered willing homage to the Mediator. The Holy Spirit brought the proclamation down to Jerusalem on the day of Pentecost, that it might go thence through all the earth. They who gladly received it, were received into his royal favor, made citizens of the heavenly Jerusalem, and members of the great *ecclesia*.

In the words of Christ before cited, the church is represented as a building. The beginning of an edifice may be dated back to the first movement in preparing the materials. In this view the church was begun, when Abel, Enoch, Noah, and Abraham first exercised faith. But in another view, the building was commenced when the materials were brought together in their proper relation to Jesus Christ. To the Old Testament saints, until gathered under Christ with the saints of the present dispensation, Paul attributes a sort of incompleteness, which may be not unaptly compared to the condition of building materials not yet put together: 'These all, having obtained a good report through faith, received not the promise: God having provided some better thing for us, that they without us should not be made perfect.' "*

Following Dagg's teaching we can say that Christ's work of building His Church consists in two distinct operations. The one being the preparation of the materials and the other the building being erected on the foundation. The preparation of the materials is the making ready of the individual stones for the church which is likened to a majestic temple constructed of stones. However, these stones are "living stones," that is those, "begotten again unto a living hope by the resurrection of Jesus Christ from the dead" (2 Pet. 1:3).

---

* Dagg, *Church Order*, 138-39.

This is typified in the Old Testament by Solomon's temple. It was a magnificent edifice built of precious stones; quarried and perfectly shaped and fitted before they were brought to the temple site. "The temple, when it was being built, was built of stone made ready before it was brought thither, so that no hammer or chisel or any iron tool was heard in the temple while it was being built" (1 Kgs. 6:7). This work of making ready or finishing the stones at the quarry was begun with the Old Testament saints.

However, until the foundation was laid the temple could not be reared. God speaks of this foundation through His prophet Isaiah, "Behold, I lay in Zion for a foundation, a stone, a tried stone, a precious cornerstone, a sure foundation" (Isa. 28:16). Peter quotes this verse in 1 Peter 2:6 and ties it in with Psalm 118:22 which he quotes in verse seven, "The stone which the builders rejected (by crucifying Him), has become the chief cornerstone" (when God raised Him from the dead). Thus, Peter applies these Old Testament prophecies to the risen Christ, who was "disallowed indeed of men, but chosen of God and precious" (1 Pet. 2:4). Thus the actual building of the Church could not begin in Old Testament times because it was to be built upon Jesus Christ crucified and raised from the dead, as the sure foundation and the chief cornerstone.

Paul, in Ephesians chapter two, speaking about this same temple, the house of God, writes of God making Jew and Gentile "one new man." And so Old Testament saints and New Testament saints are reconciled "both to God in one body through the cross," such that all are, "members of the household of God, having been built on the foundation of the apostles and prophets, Jesus Christ Himself being the chief cornerstone, in whom the whole building, being joined together, grows into a holy temple in the Lord, in whom you also are being built together for a habitation of God in the Spirit" (Eph. 2:16, 19-22). Obviously, this Church of Christ is not identical with the Commonwealth of Israel.

THE JEWISH CHURCH OR COMMONWEALTH WAS THE ENEMY OF THE CHURCH

If two men who are enemies are removed from one another their enmity and differences may not be readily seen because the occasion for conflict may not be present. As I wrote above, the Jewish church ended and the Christian church began. However, during the time of Christ there was an overlapping of these two institutions before the destruction of Jerusalem. How did they coexist? If they were the same and the "Commonwealth of Israel was the church" as Hodge wrote; we would expect them to be able to exist in harmony. However, the book of Acts plainly shows that the Jewish "church" was the inveterate enemy of the church Christ called His Church. I don't think examples are necessary. If they are, surely we have the example of one of the followers of Judaism called Paul who said,

> "I am indeed a Jew, born in Tarsus of Cilicia, but brought up in this city at the feet of Gamaliel, taught according to the strictness of our fathers' law, and was zealous toward God as you all are today. I persecuted this Way to the death, binding and delivering into prisons both men and women" (Acts 22:3-4).

The word *ekklesia*, assembly or church, carries a completely different meaning than the Hebrew word *cahal*, which is used to denote the Hebrew assembly or congregation. They were not confused. For instance, when Christ said, "on this rock will I build my *ekklesia*," all realized that He was not speaking of the cahal, the congregation or assembly of Israel which had long before been instituted in the time of Moses and its services defined completely. When Christ said, "Tell it to the *ekklesia*," it was and is evident that he didn't mean tell it to the congregation of Jewish worshippers. Were these enemies and persecutors of the church to mediate their differences? Impossible!

When we read that, "The Lord added to the church daily such as should be saved" it was from the Jewish "church" that the converts were added. When those from the Jewish Commonwealth were saved they were added to the church. It is obvious that the church to which they were added was not the Jewish "church" or assembly to which they had previously belonged.

All these four points prove the Commonwealth of Israel was not the Church. All Jews belonged to the Commonwealth including their children.

However, they did not belong to the Church except by faith. None entered it by birth or descent. It could only be seen and entered by the new birth. "Jesus answered, Verily, verily, I say unto thee, Except a man be born of water and of the Spirit, he cannot enter into the kingdom of God" (John 3:5).

32

The Inconsistencies of Infant Church Membership

The teaching of infant baptism and infant church membership is mainly derived from the Abrahamic Covenant as found in Genesis 17. In Genesis 17 the covenant of circumcision was made with Abraham. From this covenant certain conclusions are arrived at to support infant membership in the Church and infant baptism.

It is said that all Abraham's natural seed until the introduction of the gospel belong to the church but this is false! All his natural seed belonged to the Commonwealth of Israel not to the Church. The Church is not entered by physical birth. The universal Church includes all the elect of God and excludes all others. The visible Church includes all those who profess faith and is defined by Dr. John Murray as follows: "The Church is the company or society or assembly or congregation or communion of the faithful."[*] He defines the *invisible church* as follows,

> "As has just been indicated, the Church is the body of Christ. If so, it is comprised of those who are sanctified and cleansed by the washing of water by the Word, the company of the regenerate, the communion of the saints, the congregation of the faithful, those called effectually into the fellowship of Christ. The Church is therefore circumscribed by the facts of regeneration and faith, facts which in themselves are spiritual and invisible."[†]

---

[*] Murray, *Christian Baptism*, 36.
[†] *Ibid.*

Both definitions exclude all Abraham's natural seed unless they become believers.

After the introduction of the gospel the infant baptism teaching introduces Gentile believers among the covenant seed. This is to change from Abraham's literal or natural seed belonging to the covenant, as in point one above, to his spiritual seed. This is inconsistent. Then this interpretation returns to the literal meaning of seed and introduces the natural seed of believers into the Covenant of Grace and into the Church. Then, unaccountably, this is only followed for one generation and abandoned. The next generation is not necessarily considered to be part of the church as all generations of Abraham's seed are considered to be. This interpretation is inconsistent, confusing and false. The natural seed of believers cannot inherit the literal promises of the Abrahamic Covenant because they are Gentiles. Nor can they inherit the spiritual promises because they are only to believers, Abraham's spiritual seed.

Thus infant baptism and infant church membership teaching is false because it assumes Abraham's natural seed are born into and included in the Covenant of Grace. All infants, whether under the old dispensation or gospel dispensation, are born in Adam and under the covenant of works. No infants are born naturally into the Covenant of Grace. This is to ignore original sin. All infants, being born in Adam, contract original sin. No one is in the Covenant of Grace except those united by faith with that covenant head even Christ.

This teaching says that the Covenant of Grace given to Abraham was with his natural seed. They teach that "to you and your seed" means to you and your descendants but Paul teaches that to you and your seed is not to seeds or descendants but to one seed or descendant, even Christ (see Gal. 3:16).

This teaching errs by failing to distinguish between the covenant of literal circumcision which is the law and the Covenant of Grace which refers to spiritual circumcision. The covenant of circumcision was made with Abraham and his natural descendants but the Covenant of Grace was made with Christ and those "in Him."

The covenant of circumcision that was made with Abraham included all his seed. It had no respect to age. Nor did it only include Abraham's first generation. It was to be "to a thousand generations." The infant seed of all the Israelites was circumcised whether the fathers were godly or ungodly, believers or unbelievers, righteous or wicked. Circumcision of children had nothing to do with the spiritual qualifications of the fathers. It was to all. Every male descendant of Abraham's was to be circumcised. It was not to be based on the parents' faith.

Righteous Archbishop Leighton writes,

> "Touching baptism freely my thought is, it is a weak notion taken up on trust almost generally, to consider so much, or at all, the qualifications of parents. Either it is a benefit to infants, or it is not. If none, why then administer it at all? But if it be, then why should the poor innocents be prejudged for the parents' cause, if he profess but so much of a Christian, as to offer his child to that ordinance? For that the parents' faith gives the child a right to it, is neither from Scripture nor any sound reason."[*]

This is a sound argument and shows the fallacy of basing infant baptism on the parents' faith. To give a concrete illustration: if a man is saved in his later years why shouldn't all his children, grandchildren and great grandchildren be baptized? Why shouldn't all be baptized regardless of age, marital condition, moral walk or spiritual condition? Why this inconsistency if the promise is to believers and all their descendants "to a thousand generations"? Why shouldn't all the descendants of the sixteenth or seventeenth century believers be baptized now? If the Paedobaptist interpretation of the Abrahamic Covenant is consistently followed it leads to such absurd conclusions.

If the covenant made with Abraham was to Abraham's natural descendants how can Gentiles be included in it? They are not in the covenant of circumcision made with Abraham's natural descendants. Rather they are in the Covenant of Grace made with Abraham's seed (singular), even Christ, if they are found in Him by faith. Once again I emphasize the

---

[*] Leighton, *Select Works*, 518.

importance of seeing that two different covenants were made with Abraham and they must not be confused.

Part 6

A Theology of Infants

33

Regeneration of Infants

D
r. Murray commenting on Matthew 19:14 speaks of principles found in this portion pertaining to infants. His second principle is "that little children, even infants . . . are members of his kingdom and therefore have been regenerated."[*]

Dr. Vos explains what is meant by saying that the children of believers are included in the Covenant of Grace. He has four points. His fourth point is "it must be assumed that they are elect and regenerate in the absence of evidence which would lead to the contrary conclusion."[†] There is no contrary evidence in regard to infants since they are unable to act. Therefore, according to Dr. Vos, they are all regenerate.

The Church of England Prayer Book Service for the Public Baptism of Infants says, "Seeing now, dearly beloved brethren, that this child is regenerate . . ."

As quoted above, Paedobaptists believe and teach that the infant children of believers are regenerate. This means then that all the children of believers are regenerate for they were all infants at one time.

First, if this was so then the church everywhere would grow according to physical generation. It is difficult to see then how churches that were full of believers could disappear in a few generations or less or how whole nations that were once bastions of the faith could become spiritual deserts.

---

[*] Murray, *Christian Baptism*, 65.
[†] Vos, 38.

Does the Word of God teach that the church grows by physical generation? I think not. The church does not grow by physical generation but by spiritual regeneration. Those added to the Lord were not added through procreation but through evangelization. "And the Lord added to the church daily those who were being saved" (Acts 2:47). How did the number grow? "Many of those who heard the Word believed; and the number of the men came to be about five thousand" (Acts 4:4). Again we read, "Believers were increasingly added to the Lord." It was believers not infants that were added to the Lord. The verse continues, "multitudes of both men and women" (Acts 5:14). Note that it says nothing of infants or children. Yet when the Word describes the multitudes the Lord fed it says, "Now those who had eaten were about five thousand men, besides women and children" (Matt. 14:21).

The nation of Israel, a type of God's people, grew through physical birth, "the people grew and multiplied in Egypt," but God's spiritual nation grows through the preaching of the gospel. It was "when they had preached the gospel" that they "made many disciples." Disciples are only made one way as the whole New Testament abundantly witnesses. Infants of believers being part of the church is incompatible with the church growing through spiritual means rather than natural means.*

Secondly, if the infants of believers are regenerate there must be multitudes who were regenerated when they were infants. Yet I have never met such a person. I don't know of anyone who has met such a person. I have never heard of anyone saying they were regenerated as an infant. Rather all the testimonies I have heard and read speak of conversion occurring later in life after living ungodly lives. All without exception, as far as I know, would deny they were regenerated as infants. How can this be if believers' infants are regenerate? I rehearse a few narratives of conversions of men who were children of believers who would deny they were regenerate when infants.

Jonathan Edwards' father was a minister at Windsor, Connecticut for 60 years. "He was a man of great piety and usefulness." I copy a few excerpts from Jonathan Edwards's papers.

---

* I am indebted to Greg Nicols for much of the above.

"Indeed, I was at times very uneasy, especially towards the latter part of my time at college, when it pleased God to seize me with a pleurisy; in which he brought me nigh to the grave, and shook me over the pit of hell. And yet it was not long after my recovery, before I fell again into my old ways of sin.

My concern now wrought more by inward struggles and conflicts, and self-reflection. I made seeking my salvation the main business of my life.

The first instance, that I remember, of that sort of inward, sweet delight in God and divine things, that I have lived much in since, was on the reading of those words, 1 Tim. 1:17, 'Now unto the King eternal, immortal, invisible, the only wise God, be honour and glory for ever and ever. Amen.' As I read the words, there came into my soul, and was as it were diffused through it, a sense of the glory of the Divine Being; a new sense, quite different from anything I experienced before. Never any words of scripture seemed to me as these words did. From about that time I began to have a new kind of apprehensions and ideas of Christ, and the work of redemption and the glorious way of salvation by him.'"[*]

David Brainerd's father and mother were also believers. He wrote,

"I was walking again in the same solitary place where I was brought to see myself lost and helpless . . . as I was walking in a dark, thick grove, unspeakable glory seemed to open to the view and apprehension of my soul . . . It was a new inward apprehension or view that I had of God such as I had never had before, nor anything which had the least resemblance to it. I stood still, wondered, and admired."[†]

Many have heard of Charles Spurgeon's conversion. He, too, was raised in a Christian home but was unregenerate until converted in a Methodist chapel when he was 15 years old. The verse, "Look unto me and be saved, all

---

[*] Edwards, 12-13.
[†] Edwards, Volume 2, 319.

the ends of the earth: for I am God, and there is none else" (Isa. 45:22), was the arrow that pierced his heart.

I could write further of John Owen, William Burns, Henry Martyn, Thomas Goodwin, among many others. The list would be endless of men who were children of believers and converted when young men or later. All, of whom I have knowledge, would deny they were regenerate as infants. All would agree that membership of the new covenant people is dependent upon spiritual rebirth not natural birth.

If a person told me that they had no knowledge or experience of conversion but rather that they were regenerated in their unconscious infancy and had never "walked according to the course of this world" but always believed and walked in godliness I would certainly doubt their salvation. Wouldn't you? And yet we are told that there are multitudes of such people who were regenerated as infants. Would it be wrong to ask that one such person should be produced?

It is in times of revival that this whole Paedobaptist doctrine is challenged. It is then that the "regeneration of infants" teaching is seen to be inadequate. I quote from David Kingdon,

> "Schenck shows how the Great Awakening with its emphasis on the necessity of conversion challenged the whole Presbyterian theory of covenant-children. Indeed his third chapter is entitled, intriguingly enough, 'The Threat of Revivalism to the Presbyterian Doctrine of Children in the Covenant.' What happened was this. Many Christian parents, influenced by the Awakening, came to regard their children as in Adam, as under wrath and as not, therefore, in the covenant by birth. Hence they neglected to have them baptised as infants, preferring to wait till there was definite evidence in their lives of the fruits of conversion."[*]

Thirdly, if the infants of the faithful are regenerate then their earliest memories would be of walking in truth and holiness. Is this true? No, rather as Dr. Shedd wrote,

---

[*] Kingdon, 63.

> "It still remains true that the first years of your conscious existence were not years of holiness, nor the first acts which you remember, acts of obedience."[*]

Fourthly, if infants are regenerate they would have no consciousness of conversion. Yet those who are converted are sensible of it. Conversion is the miracle of miracles, the great supernatural work, that is manifest to the man.

> "Some profess they love God with all their hearts, and have ever done so since they can remember; they always believed in Christ, and never doubted that they were ever dear to God. But all this is nothing but a deceitful skimming over the sores of their souls with, 'Peace, peace.' The case that was always so good, was never good at all. No, if you cannot remember the time past, when your state was worse than nothing, I can never be persuaded that it is good for the present. An infidel you once were, a hater of God, an enemy to righteousness; and if you know no change, you are so still. The knowledge of God, the love of God, and faith in Christ, grow not in your own ground; neither is God so prodigal of these as to spread them unsought and unknown. He who has them, knows how he came by them; no man is born a believer nor an heir to heaven; neither can any make purchase or take possession of it, without his own knowledge."[†]

The conclusion is that no infant children of believers are regenerate until born of the Spirit and the Word. And this regeneration is such a mighty transformation that it manifests itself. How soon is it seen? Dr. Murray writes,

> "Regeneration is such a radical, pervasive, and efficacious transformation that it immediately registers itself in the conscious activity of a person concerned in the exercises of faith and repentance and new obedience."[‡]

---

[*] Shedd, *Sermons to the Natural Man*, 409.
[†] Taylor, *Titus*, 245.
[‡] Murray, *Redemption Accomplished*, 104-05.

Thus, until faith, repentance and new obedience is manifested we cannot say that any child (or, in fact, anyone) is regenerate. Regeneration should never be divorced from its fruits. No one should be esteemed regenerate who doesn't evidence it.

34

State of Those Who Die in Infancy

Oone view in regard to infants is that, "All who die in infancy are saved."* This view is that all infants who die in infancy are elect, without any exceptions. This also means that from third world countries where infant mortality is extremely high multitudes are in heaven and probably far more than from countries where the gospel is preached. This means that through infant mortality all tribes, tongues and peoples are represented by millions in heaven. Thus, infant mortality has saved many more than the gospel according to the above teaching. Has abortion been the means of millions of infants being saved? I think not.

The fair inference from Hodge's teaching that there are some from every tribe, tongue, people and nation already in heaven and have been there from early history removes a missionary incentive. An incentive for missionaries to seek to reach the unevangelized of every tribe, tongue, people and nation is that there are no representatives of those unreached peoples in heaven to sing the Redeemer's praise. This argument moved Jim Elliot to leave a field of potential thousands of Quichuas to go to a few hundred Aucas. He wrote,

> "The argument of numbers does not hold entirely, since if my call were to go where a great number are needy, I would not have chosen South America at all, but India. The Scriptures indicate that God intends some from every tribe and tongue and people and nation to

---

* Hodge, *Systematic Theology*, 26.

be there in the glory, sounding out the praises of the Redeemer. This is specific indication that the Gospel must be gotten to tribes who are not yet included in the singing hosts. Hence my burden for cultural groups as yet untouched."[*]

This incentive has been very real to many of us who have sought to go to the unreached. We long to have a part in seeing the body completed; made up of all tribes, tongues, peoples and nations on the earth. We labor to bring back the King. Yet, if all Auca infants who died in infancy were already in heaven it seems Jim Elliot was badly mistaken.

Another view is held by Dr. Vos,

> "We should not entertain the slightest doubt that all covenant children which die before reaching years of discretion are of the elect and are saved by the mysterious operation of the Holy Spirit."[†]

He believes all infants of believing parents who die in infancy are elect.

The only verse I have heard used to support that view is where David speaks of his infant son who had died in infancy, "Can I bring him back again? I shall go to him, but he shall not return to me" (2 Sam. 12:23). The word for the place of death or the unseen state in the Old Testament is *Sheol*. It is translated "the grave" or "hell." All who died went to *Sheol*. David probably was speaking of going to *Sheol*, the unseen state, where his son had preceded him. The NIV study Bible says *Sheol* refers to "the realm of the dead, the nether world."

The narrative of the destruction of Sodom and Gomorrah clearly manifests that all infants dying in infancy are not saved. All infants of Sodom and Gomorrah, without exception, were destroyed. Why were they destroyed? They were destroyed by God because they were wicked. Abraham, seeking to see Sodom spared spoke as follows to God,

> "And Abraham came near and said, 'Would You also destroy the righteous with the wicked? . . . Far be it from You to do such a thing

---

[*] Elliot, *Shadow of the Almighty*, 236.

[†] Vos, 43.

as this, to slay the righteous with the wicked, so that the righteous should be as the wicked; far be it from You! Shall not the Judge of all the earth do right?'" (Gen.18:23, 25).

God approved of this speech and went so far as to say, "I will not destroy it for the sake of ten (righteous)" (see verse 32). But there were not ten righteous in Sodom. All, including the infants, were wicked. And yet as Eliphaz said, "Whoever perished, being innocent? Or where were the righteous cut off?" (Job 4:7).

God when bringing judgment made sure that righteous Lot was delivered even by the intervention of angels. These angels told Lot that they could do nothing until he had safely escaped. If there had been one righteous infant surely he would have been spared. Peter's comment on Lot's deliverance is, "the Lord knows how to deliver the godly out of temptations and to reserve the unjust under punishment for the day of judgment" (2 Pet. 2:9). All the infants of Sodom and Gommorah were "reserved under punishment for the day of judgment." None were saved. I think it is obvious that God did not destroy by his judgment the wicked infants' natural life to save them eternally. They were to be "an example to those who afterward would live ungodly" (2 Pet. 2:6). To take away all doubt Jude writes that the inhabitants of Sodom and Gomorrah "are set forth as an example, suffering the vengeance of eternal fire" (Jude 7).

Time and again God commanded the Israelites not to spare anyone but to utterly destroy their enemies not pitying their infants. When God brought judgment on the Egyptians he killed all their first born. Likewise Israel utterly destroyed Jericho, "They utterly destroyed all that was in the city, both man and woman, young and old . . ." (Josh. 6:21). God's command was,

> "But of the cities of these peoples which the Lord your God gives you
> as an inheritance, you shall let nothing that breathes remain alive, but
> you shall utterly destroy them: the Hittite and the Amorite and the
> Canaanite and the Perizzite and the Hivite and the Jebusite, just as
> the Lord your God has commanded you" (Deut. 20:16-17).

The command of Moses concerning the Midianites was, "Now therefore, kill every male among the little ones" (Num. 31:17). All these citations prove God's displeasure upon those infants and evidence his wrath upon them. They were not his people! Their guilt was not pardoned!

What about the infants of God's people the Jews? Some would call such, "covenant children." Did God show respect to such "covenant children" and spare them. Ezekiel chapter 9 tells of the destruction of Jerusalem that included every infant yet God in His faithfulness spared every true child of the covenant. It is well with the righteous but not an infant was spared.

> "I proceed to take notice of something remarkable concerning the destruction of Jerusalem, represented in Ezekiel 9 when command was given to destroy the inhabitants, ver. 1-8 And this reason is given for it, that their iniquity required it, and it was a just recompence of their sin, (ver. 9, 10). God, at the same time, was most particular and exact in his care, that such as had proved by their behaviour, that they were not partakers in the abominations of the city, should by no means be involved in the slaughter. Command was given to the angel to go through the city, and set a mark upon their foreheads, and the destroying angel had a strict charge not to come near any man, on whom was the mark; yet the infants were not marked, nor a word said of sparing them: on the contrary, infants were expressly mentioned as those that should be utterly destroyed without pity, (ver. 5, 6.) 'Go through the city and smite: let not your eye spare, neither have ye pity. Slay utterly old and young, both maids and little children: but come not near any man upon whom is the mark.'"[*]

The only ones who were spared were those "who sigh and cry over all the abominations that are done within it" (verse 4). That the infants had a "negative righteousness," as the Paedobaptists say, availed nothing. God required a positive righteousness. Thus, the statement is false that says, "It must be assumed that they are elect and regenerate in the absence of

---

[*] Edwards, 176.

evidence which would lead to the contrary conclusion."[*]

> "And it is of importance to observe, that in order to a man's being universally obedient, his obedience must not only consist in negatives, or in universally avoiding wicked practices; but he must also be universal in the positives of religion. Sins of omission are as much breaches of God's commands, as sins of commission. Christ, in Matthew 25 represents those on the left hand, as being condemned and cursed to everlasting fire, for sins of omission, I was an hungred, and ye gave me no meat, &c. A man therefore cannot be said to be universally obedient, and of a Christian conversation, only because he is no thief, oppressor, fraudulent person, drunkard, tavern-hunter, whore-master, rioter, night-walker, nor unclean, profane in his language, slanderer, liar, furious, malicious, nor reviler. He is falsely said to be of a conversation becoming the gospel, who goes thus far, and no farther; but, in order to this, it is necessary that he should also be of a serious, religious, devout, humble, meek, forgiving, peaceful, respectful, condescending, benevolent, merciful, charitable, and beneficent walk and conversation. Without such things as these, he does not obey the laws of Christ, laws that he and his apostles abundantly insist on, as of greatest importance and necessity."[†]

But it is objected that infants have an inability to do righteousness. Just so! Therefore, are they spared? Not at all. God poured out his fury upon them (see Ezekiel 9:8). No infant belongs to God's children until he is born of God's Spirit and evidences such by faith and holiness.

It is surely false to say,

> "We should not entertain the slightest doubt that all covenant children which die before reaching years of discretion are of the elect and are saved by the mysterious operation of the Holy Spirit."[‡]

---

[*] Vos, 38.

[†] Edwards, 315.

[‡] Vos, Jan-March, 1959, *Blue Banner Faith and Life*, 43. Quoted by T. E. Watson in

In the song of Moses is the prophecy of the destruction of Israel that is applied by many commentators to the destruction of Jerusalem.

> "They have provoked Me to jealousy by what is not God; They have moved Me to anger by their foolish idols. But I will provoke them to jealousy by those who are not a nation; I will move them to anger by a foolish nation. For a fire is kindled in My anger, and shall burn to the lowest hell; it shall consume the earth with her increase, and set on fire the foundations of the mountains. I will heap disasters upon them; I will spend My arrows upon them. They shall be wasted with hunger, devoured by pestilence and bitter destruction; I will also send against them the teeth of beasts, with the poison of serpents of the dust. The sword shall destroy outside; there shall be terror within for the young man and the virgin, the nursing child with the man of gray hairs" (Deut. 32:21-25).

So terrible was to be the plight of the Jewish infants and nursing children that Christ declared, "For indeed the days are coming in which they will say, 'Blessed are the barren, the wombs that never bore, and the breasts which never nursed' " (Luke 23:29). Such destruction was to be a clear evidence to other nations that God was angry with the wicked and his wrath was upon infants along with the rest. This is incontrovertible proof that many children of the covenant people were covenant children in name only. They were not children of Abraham but as Christ said to the Jews, "You are of your father the devil" (John 8:44), when they had said, "Abraham is our father." Only those who do the works of Abraham are Abraham's children. "If you were Abraham's children, you would do the works of Abraham" (verse 39).

Baptism Not for Infants.

35

Infants and the Covenant

A major point in the Paedobaptist argument is that all infants of believers are automatically in the Covenant of Grace. For this reason they teach that they should receive the sign of the covenant which they believe is baptism.

The Paedobaptists believe in original sin and agree that all infants are born in Adam and under the Covenant of Law or works. They must therefore believe that all infants are somehow, someway united with Christ and so enter into the Covenant of Grace. Thus they believe all infants dying in infancy are saved. If they die a few minutes after birth they were, according to their reasoning, in that short interval, transferred from being in Adam to being in Christ; from being under law to being under grace. However, there is no scriptural support for this theory. In fact this theory in practice overthrows the doctrine of original sin and the imputation of Adam's sin to every infant.

Practically speaking, these doctrines mean nothing to Paedobaptists since all their infants are immediately removed from that state and transferred into Christ according to their teaching. Although they give lip service to these doctrines do they believe that their infants are condemned and lost? Not at all. They teach that all believers' seed without exception are united to Christ immediately after birth and are in the Covenant of Grace so that if they die they are safe in heaven. Or if they believe all aborted infants go to heaven then sometime after they were "conceived in sin" they must have been translated into God's kingdom before they were aborted. They accept the Bible doctrine that all born according to nature are born unclean and under condemnation (Job 14:4). But it seems that they believe such children are only momentarily "by nature children of wrath even as others" so that practically it has no effect on their standing before God for all without exception are in the Covenant of Grace and have the promise that God will be their God. Certainly this promise is sure to all to whom it is given and cannot possibly fail but it is not given promiscuously to all believers' infants or to all Abraham's seed but only to the spiritual seed.

All in the Covenant of Grace are eternally saved and cannot be anything but saved unless God be unfaithful to his covenant that he made with an oath. It doesn't do to say no, the children may later be unfaithful and take themselves out of the covenant. If that was so the covenant would be uncertain and it would rather be a covenant of works. They say that such may depart from God and so be removed from the covenant but the promise in the covenant is that God "will put his fear in our hearts, that we shall not depart from him" (Jer. 32:40). The Covenant of Grace is a sure covenant "ordered in all things and sure" (2 Sam. 23:5). Away with this talk that "covenant breakers will be cut off and receive the curses of the covenant."[*]

That is works! The Covenant of Grace has only blessing! Amen. Although faith and obedience are required of us by God the whole gospel of Christ teaches us that we are unable of ourselves to fulfill his commands but God in mercy bestows his grace on his elect producing faith and obedience. The above theory takes away all grace from the Covenant of Grace.

---

[*] R. Booth, *Children of the Promise*, 46.

36

Infants In the light of Romans 5

We must look at this in the light of Romans 5. The teaching of Romans 5 is that there is a parallelism in Adam's sin being imputed and in Christ's righteousness being imputed but that there are also great differences. Thus in Romans 5 the results of Adam's sin are contrasted with the results of Christ's obedience, "the free gift is not like the offence" (Rom. 5:15). One contrast is that the condemnation that comes on man through Adam involves the whole race of mankind but justification does not include all men.

Calvin gives the reason for this,

> "The reason for this is indeed evident; for as the curse we derive from Adam is conveyed to us by nature, it is no wonder that it includes the whole mass; but that we may come to a participation of the grace of Christ, we must be ingrafted in him by faith. Hence, in order to partake of the miserable inheritance of sin, it is enough for thee to be a man, for it dwells in flesh and blood; but in order to enjoy the righteousness of Christ it is necessary for thee to be a believer; for a participation of him is attained only by faith."[*]

This rules out all infants unless they receive grace in another way peculiar to them. For this peculiar way there is no scripture to be found. Salvation comes but one way to all. A "participation of him is attained only

---

[*] Calvin, commentary on Romans 5:17.

by faith."

Another difference between the imputation of Adam's guilt and the imputation of Christ's righteousness is that condemnation comes to all involuntarily without an act on their part. However, the righteousness of Christ is imputed to those who believe intelligently. Faith is a voluntary act. None are justified without this intelligent, voluntary act of faith. None enter the Covenant of Grace without their consent.

> "Christ's coming under imputation of guilt was optional and voluntary on his part. And so righteousness is imputed to no soul for justification until that soul freely accepts and chooses it in the act of faith. We must believe in order to be justified. True, it is the merit of the divine substitute, and not the merit of the believing, which justifies; but none the less it is absolutely true that the sinner must believe in order to have that divine merit imputed to him. So that in both the imputations involved in the sinner's redemption, that of his sins to Christ and Christ's merits to him, we find this feature of free consent in the party receiving the imputation to be an essential element.
>
> The subjective righteousness inwrought in the soul in regeneration only becomes a true righteousness as it is accepted and freely preferred by the soul again. The causal source of it is external to the renewed will, almighty and supernatural? Yes, certainly. But none the less is the infused holiness the freely chosen preference of the soul from the very instant it is accounted by God as a true holiness. The rule of the divine work is expressed in the text, 'My people shall be willing in the day of my power.' The very essence of the divine work within the dead soul is that it renews and quickens the will, causing the soul to choose and pursue freely that godliness which, in the days of its bondage and spiritual death, it had as freely rejected."[*]

Just as the ground of Adam's sin being imputed to all is their union with Adam so the ground of Christ's righteousness being imputed to believers is

---

[*] Dabney, *Discussions of Robert Lewis Dabney*, Volume 1, 149-50.

the union between believers and Christ. Some try to avoid this teaching by claiming that the covenant of works has been abolished by Adam's sin. It is true that works cannot be a possible way of justification since Adam sinned but it is the rule by which all will be judged. The covenant of works continues in force.

"The broken covenant of works is still in force over Adam's race as a rule of condemnation. It is for that reason that 'we are all by nature children of wrath, even as others.' God's elect are born under the force of that covenant as a rule of condemnation, 'even as others.' It passes human wit to see how, if the covenant of works were wholly revoked as soon as broken by Adam, sin is still imputed under it in 'this year of grace' 1873; how in the 'year of grace' 1, our Lord Christ was placed under both its preceptive and penal terms as a surety; and how, in thirty-three years thereafter, he so repaired and fulfilled it as thereby to purchase for the elect the very 'adoption of sons' which that covenant had first proposed to Adam. See Gal. 4:5: 'These be the two covenants, the one from Mount Sinai, which gendereth to bondage, which is Agar. For this Agar is Mount Sinai in Arabia, and answereth to Jerusalem which now is, and is in bondage with her children.' Does not every Reformed expositor explain that the Sinai covenant, as perverted, broken, and misapplied by legalists, reverts into the covenant of works? We never heard of any other way of explaining the Epistles to the Romans and the Galatians. They uniformly represent that there are two covenants, and only two: of works, of grace; that all men are born under the first, and born condemned, because they are born under it, its breach in Adam having rendered it a ministry of condemnation; that we all live under it, until, by union to the second Adam, we pass under the other, the Covenant of Grace. The epoch of transition is when we are effectually called and believe. Rom. 7:6: 'But now we are delivered from the law,' etc. When? When we are 'married' to Christ. The truth remains, then, that our natural union to Adam is a union to a corrupted nature; and it is confessed on all hands that such union is one of the essential grounds of the imputation of his guilt to us."[*]

Infants are all involved in the sin of Adam since it is transmitted to all his descendants by nature. However, none partake of Christ's righteousness except those who are united to him by faith. Thus all remain in Adam until engrafted by faith into the second Adam, even Christ. All infants are born in Adam but only those born again are in Christ. Only those in union with Christ are in the Covenant of Grace. None are delivered from the law until they are "married" to Christ and so united to Him. This is the fruit of regeneration which evidences itself in "bearing fruit to God" (Rom. 7:4). And this marriage is entered into not only with full consent but most willingly and joyously. This excludes all infants for as Dabney said above, "And so righteousness is imputed to no soul for justification until that soul freely accepts and chooses it in the act of faith." No infant is in the Covenant of Grace!

All infants are born in sin and are, as the apostle put it, "dead in trespasses and sins." They all without exception are born in Adam their representative head. They are not in Christ but in Adam. Paedobaptists agree with this but then contradict themselves when they talk of infants being children of the Covenant of Grace. If infants are in Adam they cannot at the same time be united with Christ, the head of the Covenant of Grace. Therefore since they do not have the reality, union with Christ, they should not be given the sign of such, *i.e.*, baptism. As J. Murray rightly says, "Where that reality is absent the sign or seal has no efficacy."[†] Why then baptize them if it has no efficacy? G. B. Wilson in *Romans* quotes T. K. Watson, "Circumcision did not guarantee the person circumcised that he was justified in the sight of God, though many of the Jews mistakenly believed this." Sadly Jews are not the only ones so deceived by an infant rite.

---

[*] *Ibid.*, 271-72.
[†] Murray, 86.

JEWISH CHILDREN RECEIVE THEIR MORAL NATURE FROM ADAM, NOT FROM ABRAHAM

Paul in Romans 5 is not only continuing his teaching that justification is only through Christ's imputed righteousness even as sin was imputed through Adam's sin but also dealt with one of the great errors of the Jews. The Jews believed that since Abraham, called the friend of God, was their father they were holy children and since the Gentiles were not Abraham's children they were by nature sinners and unholy. So Paul takes them back to Adam, who is the father of both Jews and Gentiles, so that they are both alike sinners and guilty. It is their relation to Adam, not Abraham, which determined their moral state. Adam is the natural head of all men. Abraham is not the covenant head of anyone so his righteousness is not imputed to anyone. None are counted righteous because they are the natural children of Abraham.

This Jewish error is continued today by those that believe the children of believers are "covenant children" and are holy. Just as the Jews; they believe other children are by nature sinners and unholy but that their children are not. This is not so! All children are born sinners because of their natural relation to Adam. They are not born holy because of their natural relation to believing parents. Believing parents do not transmit righteousness to their children but pass along the original sin of Adam. A circumcised father still begets an uncircumcised child. In short, to use the scriptural phrase, "there is no difference" (Rom. 3:23). There is no difference between children. "All have sinned." Whether they are Jewish children or Gentile children, baptized infants or unbaptized infants, "there is no difference." This was unacceptable and flatly rejected by the Jews. Likewise, there is no difference between believers' children and unbelievers' children. They all stand equally in need of the righteousness of God (verse 24). They too, have all sinned.

Many Paedobaptists cannot accept that there is no distinction between their children and non-covenant children. They are carried along by the old Jewish error that Paul zealously opposed. Does a believer have promises that put his children in a different category to a pagan child? No, "there is no difference."

However, if we go back to the question of verse 1, "What advantage then has the Jew?" We answer, "much every way." Do believers' children have advantages? Yes! Then, "Are they better? No, in no wise, they are all under sin" (verse 9). This could not be so if believers' infants are regenerated, in the Covenant of Grace, members of the church and receivers of the promises. Let us then repeat it again with emphasis, "*There is no difference.*" The promise is no more to children of believers than it was to Ishmael, a "covenant" child. The promise is only to the children of promise who are hidden to all until evidenced by faith and a walk of obedience.

37

Infants and the Church

Calvin wrote, "The children of the godly are born the children of the Church."* John Murray wrote, "Little children, even infants are among Christ's people and are members of his body . . . they belong to the church."†

Paedobaptists believe and teach that the infants of believers belong to the church. Their argument is by inference; what they call "good and necessary consequences."

My argument is that many children of believers evidence by their lives and by their lack of profession that they do not belong to the church. To overthrow the teaching that believers' children are in the Church it is not necessary to show that every child is not in the Church. All that needs to be proved is that any believer's child is not in the Church. If this can be shown then the statement that believers' infants are in the church is false. And if they now do not belong to the church they never belonged to the church and therefore as infants they were not members of the church.

If they were once in the church, which is Christ's body (Eph. 1:22-23) then they were joined to the head. How then can they be separated from the body? Impossible! If once in the church they were the flock of God. But how can any sheep be lost without disparaging their shepherd? If they were in Christ's hand and carried on his shoulders it is not possible for them to be lost (John 10:27-30; Luke 15:5). If they were once in the church how can

---

* Calvin, John-Acts, 1075.
† Murray, 65.

they lead unholy lives since the church is constantly being sanctified and cleansed by Christ (Eph. 5:25-27)? The church is loved by Christ as his own flesh (Eph. 5:30-33). Won't He apply all sorts of remedies to heal? How then can part of his church die? No, infants of believers do not belong to the church until they are born again and evidence it by the new life. That many children of believers are not born again no one can deny.

38

Infants and Scripture

Now I would like to look in greater detail at how various verses apply to infants.

ALL INFANTS ARE BORN IN A STATE OF NATURE

Everyone without exception is born in sin. All begin life in the state of nature. All are born with original sin and all have Adam's sin as the head of our race, imputed to them. Likewise, "death passed upon all men for that all have sinned (in Adam)" (Rom. 5:12). So death reigns over all men, "even over them that had not sinned after the similitude of Adam's transgression" (Rom. 5:14). Death reigned and still reigns over all people and also over a class of people who had not sinned as Adam had. The apostle is teaching that death also comes upon those who have not committed personal sins. They have not violated a positive command. Thus this includes infants. As Hodge writes,

> "The simple doctrine and argument of the apostle is, that there are penal evils which come upon men antecedent to any transgressions of their own; and as the infliction of these evils implies a violation of law, it follows that they are regarded and treated as sinners, on the ground of the disobedience of another. In other words, it was 'by the offence of one man that judgment came on all men to

condemnation.' "[*]

Infants die although not having sinned knowingly as Adam did. They die because they are justly exposed to the punishment that is due to Adam's sin. The ground or reason for being justly charged with Adam's sin is their union with Adam. He is the head and representative of the human race. His sin is the ground of everyone's condemnation just as Christ's righteousness is the ground of the believer's justification.

Death is not limited to the dissolution of the body. It includes spiritual death. Men are born dead in sin, dead spiritually. Both the scriptural use of the term and the context of Romans 5 show that death in Romans 5 is not speaking of merely natural death. Why do some infants die although they have not committed sin against known law? The answer can only be Adam's sin. Why are infants born spiritually dead? Once again the answer can only be because Adam's sin is imputed to all. Thus infants dying before repentance and faith are justly condemned by Adam's sin to eternal death. God is at liberty to save whom he will. It is

> "God's sovereign election to determine . . . to send the news of the gospel to all nations, or only to some; to give every child of Adam, born in a Christian land, opportunity by living, to hear the glad tidings, or only to grant this to some; while others die in infancy, and never hear. Those who die in infancy may as justly be held under law in the next world as those that live may in this world. God is under no more obligation to save those that die, than he is to save those that live; to grant the regenerating influences of His Spirit to them, than he is to these."[†]

God is not unjust if He does not send the gospel to all lands even though this means that whole nations have died in unbelief. God is not unjust if he allows some infants to die before hearing the gospel even though this also means that they die in their sins and in unbelief and are eternally lost. Since

---

[*] Hodge, *Romans*, 161.
[†] Bellamy, *Sin, the Law and the Glory of the Gospel*, 36.

the infants who die are under law and not grace is God unjust to judge them under the law even as he judges those that live?

REGENERATION IS THAT WHICH BRINGS THE ELECT INTO THE STATE OF GRACE

The passage between the state of nature and the state of grace is made through regeneration. Titus 3:3 speaks of the state of nature when "we ourselves were also once foolish, disobedient, deceived, etc . . ." and then opposite to that state he says, "God saved us." How did He accomplish this so great salvation? "He saved us, through the washing of regeneration and renewing of the Holy Spirit" (Titus 3:5). In Ephesians this same transition is called a being made alive. In Colossians it is called a reconciliation, "And you who were once alienated and enemies in your mind by wicked works yet now has he reconciled" (Col. 1:21). 1 Peter 1:3 calls it a begetting again, "Blessed be the God and Father of our Lord Jesus Christ, who according to His abundant mercy has begotten us again to a living hope through the resurrection of Jesus Christ from the dead" and also calls it a "being born again of incorruptible seed" (verse 23).

No one is born naturally into the state of grace. All are born in a state of nature as is stated under point one, above. All are born in Adam and are united to him. They must be united to Christ since, "As in Adam all die so in union with Christ all are made alive" (1 Cor. 15:22). Thus we see that the scriptures again and again insist that all men without exception must be regenerated, born again, reconciled, translated from darkness to light, etc. or they will be eternally lost. As with adults so with children for no children are "innocent." All are born "children of wrath," that is, abiding under the just anger of God and exposed to His punishment, having already been judged and condemned to die. As William Cable writes,

> "If we say that a child is innocent or safe until he reaches that age at which he becomes accountable to God for the choices which he makes, we do not accept the doctrine of original sin in its true

meaning."*

GOD'S ELECT ARE PRESERVED UNTIL CALLED BY THE GOSPEL

God has so ordered the lives of His elect that He preserves them until they are converted. None die before God translates them from darkness to light; from a state of nature to a state of grace. All are "born again by the Word of God" and it is "of His own will that he begat us with the word of truth." Many of God's elect have told of being preserved from certain death and escaping miraculously to live until they were called by the gospel. If a person is elect he is sure to live until he is called. "Moreover whom He predestined, these He also called; whom He called, these He also justified; and whom He justified, these He also glorified" (Rom. 8:30). The "these" in this verse are the same group. All who are predestined to life are eventually effectually called. All those who are effectually called believe and are justified. All those who are justified are glorified. On the other hand if a man dies without being called then he was never predestined to life. He was not of the elect. All those who die before believing in Christ were not "chosen to salvation." Another verse tells us that "as many as were ordained to eternal life believed" (Acts 13:48). All who are ordained to eternal life will believe. If any die without believing they were not ordained to eternal life.

ALL GOD'S ELECT EXPERIENCE AND LIVE IN CONSCIOUS SIN BEFORE HE SAVES THEM

"And you He made alive, who were dead in trespasses and sins, in which you once walked according to the course of this world according to the prince of the power of the air, the spirit who now works in the sons of disobedience, among whom also we all once conducted ourselves in the lusts of our flesh, fulfilling the desires of the flesh and of the mind, and were by nature children of wrath, just as the others" (Eph. 2:1-3).

---

* Kingdon, 93.

Paul is writing to all of the church of Ephesus. All who had spiritual life had previously walked in the lusts of the flesh. Thus this excludes the possibility that infants of believers were regenerate. Not only are God's elect born in sin, they also walk in it for a period of time. They live in conscious sin, "fulfilling the desires of the flesh and of the mind" (Eph. 2:3). Colossians 1:21 makes it clear that God's people "were sometimes enemies in their minds by wicked works." They consciously and purposely opposed God by their sin. He is not speaking of unconscious, uncomprehending infants.

This is not true of some of God's people but of all of God's people. In Ephesians 2:2 Paul says, "You once walked according to the course of this world," and then in verse 3 he says, "Among whom also we all once conducted ourselves in the lusts of our flesh . . ." He first speaks to the Gentiles and then in verse 3 includes himself and all his countrymen the Jews; "we all."

God's elect do not die as infants. They all live in conscious sin before they are delivered but they are all delivered. Paul, speaking of the saved, writes,

> "We ourselves were also once foolish, disobedient, deceived, serving various lusts and pleasures, living in malice and envy, hateful and hating one another. But when the kindness and the love of God our Saviour toward man appeared . . ." (Titus 3:3-4).

All God's elect are born "natural" men and continue in that state until born again to become "spiritual" men. "That which is born of the flesh is flesh, and that which is born of the Spirit is spirit" (John 3:6).

This new birth does not occur before a man comes to the age of discretion. It occurs while a man is willingly and consciously obeying sin and then he is set free and "obeys from the heart that form of doctrine to which he was delivered" (Rom. 6:17). However, previously he was a slave of sin and consciously and willingly "presented his members as slaves to uncleanness and of lawlessness, leading to more lawlessness" (Rom. 6:19). Paul then goes on to say, "So now present your members as slaves of righteousness for holiness." Obeying from the heart and presenting their members to God as slaves of righteousness for holiness is not done ignorantly or without comprehension. Such acts are consciously experienced. They are not the acts of unconscious infants.

GOD SAVES HIS ELECT THROUGH MEANS

David Kingdon, after insisting that infants in order to be saved must be regenerated just as adults, writes,

> "We must, it seems to me, strenuously maintain that God is able to regenerate infants by free and sovereign grace ... We must affirm that no unregenerate person is able to enter into the kingdom of God, and so infants and children must be regenerated in order to enjoy the bliss of heaven, but we dare not maintain that God cannot regenerate a child from its earliest infancy. This being the case, our emphasis must be upon God's grace (his willingness) and power (his ability) to save children. Rather than emphasizing the incapacity of children we must proclaim the capacity of God. In other words, we must place our emphasis upon the power of God through his Spirit to save children. This is what the authors of the Westminster Confession do: 'elect infants dying in infancy, are regenerated and saved by Christ through the Spirit who worketh when and where, and how he pleaseth. Nothing is impossible with God.'"[*]

I don't believe the issue is over whether God *can* or *cannot* save infants. Yes, He can do the impossible. His power and grace are infinite. However, since there are no scriptures given to prove that God in fact saves infants who die in infancy, we should pause. Rather, scripture teaches, contrary to the Westminster Confession, that no elect infants die in infancy but all are brought to faith. Please note the scriptures quoted in point number three of the above "God's elect are preserved until called by the gospel." It is true as the Westminster Confession says, "Christ ... worketh when and where and how He pleaseth." But how, when and where does He please to work? It is

---

[*] Kingdon, 96-97.

only the Word of God that can tell us.

In the Word of God we read that God works through means in saving lost men and women. God uses instruments to save. God uses, as instruments, faith, the gospel, His Spirit and men. We may say that God can save without instruments but is there any scripture that says He actually does? In countries and in peoples and tribes where the gospel has not gone does God save without the gospel? Does He save without missionaries going and preaching Christ? No, He does not. Possibly He could save heathen peoples by His Spirit without faith but He does not. Possibly He could produce faith by sending angels to preach or through dreams or miracles but He is not pleased to. We believe all peoples who have not heard the gospel are lost and this is a great missionary incentive.

> "For whoever calls upon the name of the Lord shall be saved. How then shall they call on Him in whom they have not believed? And how shall they believe in Him of whom they have not heard? And how shall they hear without a preacher? And how shall they preach unless they are sent? As it is written. How beautiful are the feet of those who preach the gospel of peace, who bring glad tidings of good things'" (Rom 10:13-15).

In the very same way all infants who have not heard the gospel are lost. Until they have intelligently turned from their sins in repentance and laid hold of Christ by faith they continue under the law; dead in sins and in the kingdom of darkness. John 3:36, "He who believes in the Son has everlasting life; and he who does not believe the Son shall not see life, but the wrath of God abides on him," is as applicable to infants as it is to adults. If this is not so and infants of believers are born in the Covenant of Grace and regenerated, as many Paedobaptists teach, then,

> "There is no more required of any to be saved than a continuance in the estate wherein he was born (that is, in covenant, actually restored by Christ thereunto), when the whole Word of' God crieth out that

all such as so abide shall certainly perish everlastingly.'"*

---

* Owen, Volume 10, 399 (writing against a book entitled *The Universality of God's Free Grace*).

39

Infants and the Promises

The great desire of Christian parents is for the salvation of their children. For this they pray, labor and teach. The natural affection of parents for their children is strengthened by grace. Because of this love and sentiment infants are often baptized. As Dr. Murray admits, "Often there is little more than sentiment and tradition behind it (infant baptism)."*

We fervently desire the salvation of each of our children. Because of this fervent desire many Christian parents are open to the teaching that all their children receive the promises of God. Wanting it to be so leads some to say it is so. We agonize in prayer for them and follow their lives with concern and sometimes trepidation. Our children are part of ourselves and we pray to our father just as Abraham did concerning his first born son Ishmael, "Oh, that Ishmael might live before you."

However, God's answer was, "No" (Gen. 17:18-19). Ishmael, although the son of God's friend Abraham, was never included in the Covenant of Grace and died a stranger to the promises. Abraham, himself, had no promise that all his children would be redeemed nor do any Christian parents today. (It seems all Abraham's children were unsaved except Isaac). The Paedobaptist says that believers do have such promises in regard to their children. They say to Christian parents God has made such promises to you and your seed. This is what we all long to hear. Many accept such teaching readily and with rejoicing.

---

* Murray, 1.

"Parents of all generations have enjoyed these promises of God to redeem their children and their children's children. God has been pleased to embrace the households of his people in the Covenant of Grace from the beginning until now. What a delight it is to know that we may stand fully and securely on the promises of our covenant-keeping God and, by his grace, expect the fulfillment of those promises in our children and our children's children."[*]

We know that God's promises cannot fail. He is God who cannot lie. "He is faithful that promised" (Heb. 10:23). But has God promised to save all our children? Has He promised to redeem them, forgive their sin and give them the inheritance? I have written under my last heading, "The Ill Effects of Infant Baptism," that most children of the Old Testament saints were ungodly. Paedobaptists do not deny that many children who were baptized in their infancy live ungodly lives.

"It may appear to be an argument of some weight to appeal to the sad record of so many who have been baptized in infancy—they have grown up to be indifferent to the baptismal engagements and have often lived lives of infidelity and godlessness. This record cannot be denied."[†]

How can this be? We cannot for a moment entertain the thought that God has not been faithful to His promises. Not one of His promises can fail.

Mr. Booth says, "The children of believers who are faithful to God's covenant will know the individual blessing of personal salvation. Covenant breakers will be cut off and receive the curses of the covenant."[‡]

But does this really answer anything? We know that all faithful children "will know the individual blessing of personal salvation," because we read "that whoever (children of unbelievers as well as children of believers) believes in Him should not perish but have everlasting life" (John 3:16). But

---

[*] R. Booth, 133.

[†] Murray, 75.

[‡] R. Booth, 46.

what about the ones he calls "Covenant breakers"? Were the promises to them and their Christian parents? If so, how could they become covenant breakers who receive curses? Others say the promises are good but the parents must be faithful to teach, discipline and pray. If they do not the promises will fail. However, God does not make promises founded on the faithfulness of man in the Covenant of Grace nor do his promises fail. Such teaching is cruel for it blames the parents and puts great guilt on those who have unbelieving children.

The verses that Mr. Booth uses to establish that "parents of all generations have enjoyed these promises of God to redeem their children and their children's children" are,

> " 'The Redeemer will come to Zion, and to those who turn from transgression in Jacob,' says the Lord. 'As for Me,' says the Lord 'this is My covenant with them: My Spirit who is upon you, and My words which I have put in your mouth, shall not depart from your mouth, nor from the mouth of your descendants, nor from the mouth of your descendants' descendants,' says the Lord, 'from this time and forevermore'" (Isa. 59:20-21).

He says this teaches that God "makes a promise to parents about their children's place in his new covenant." However, the promise is made to a single person. This person is the Redeemer, our blessed Lord Jesus, the head of the church. Matthew Henry in his *Bible Commentary* on these verses wrote,

> "The Spirit promised to the church was first upon him, and from his head that precious ointment descended to the skirts of his garments; and the word of the gospel was first put into his mouth; for it began to be spoken by the Lord. And all believers are his seed, in whom he prolongs his days. Isa. ch. 53:10."

God also says that "this is My covenant with them," that is with them that the Redeemer comes to who turn from transgression. Thus, Isaiah 59:20-21 has nothing to do with the natural offspring of believers, but with the offspring (seed) of Christ which is the church and the continuing offspring of the church. There will always be the Word of the gospel in the church. Paedobaptists always jump at the phrase, "to your seed," to mean the children of believers. But this promise is not to parents concerning their natural children but to Christ concerning his spiritual children.

> "And this ministration of the Spirit is by virtue of a covenant made (Isa. 59:21) with Christ; that Spirit that was in him, and word that was in his mouth, to wit, the gospel, should not depart out of the mouth of his seed's seed forever, but it should accompany his elect."[*]

What has God promised to our natural seed? Has He promised to redeem them all? Certainly not. Has he promised them the eternal inheritance? Again, no. As Dr. Berkhof, a Paedobaptist wrote, "Christ is a surety only for the elect . . . The covenant promises will be surely realized but—only in the lives of the elect."[†]

Since believers and their seed includes the non-elect there is some inconsistency here with the Paedobaptist. Thus, God has not made promises to children of believers. The proof is that many die in unbelief even as Ishmael did.

Dr. Murray wrote on Acts 2:38-39: "the promise is to the children . . . children are embraced with their parents in God's covenant promise . . . (They) are the possessors of God's covenant promise."[‡]

He pulls the phrase "to you and your children" out of Acts 2:38-39 without regard to the context. Peter is *not* speaking to believing parents. It is an exhortation to unsaved Jews to repent and on that basis the promise is to them and their children that is "to as many as the Lord our God shall call." None who are not called by the gospel will receive the promise. Only those who repent will receive the promise. To take it in the sense of Dr. Murray that all infants of believers "are the possessors of God's covenant promise" is to go beyond scripture. This is most dangerous for it is evident that many

---

[*] Goodwin, 4:245.

[†] Berkhof, 276.

[‡] Murray, 70-71.

who are the offspring of believers and were baptized as infants are ungodly and evidence it by their walk. The promises are not realized to them. This is freely admitted by Dr. Murray,

> "Though circumcision and baptism are the signs and seals of covenant union and communion, it does not follow that everyone who bears this sign and seal is an actual partaker of the grace signified and sealed and is therefore an heir of eternal life . . . many who bear the sign and seal do not possess the blessings of the covenant itself. . . . It must be admitted that this appears very anomalous, and it presents us with great difficulty."[*]

Dr. Murray is saying that infants of believers are "possessors of God's covenant promise,"[†] but this is inconsistent with the statement that the "many . . . do not possess the blessings of the covenant itself."[‡] How can this be? There are only two possible answers. Either God has been unfaithful to his promises (a horrid, blasphemous thought that cannot be entertained for a moment), or the promises are not to those infants. Paedobaptists refuse to say the promises are not to parents and their infant seed.

Charles Hodge makes a surprising admission in that

> "the great majority of those who have been baptized in the name of Christ, and who call themselves Christians, and are included in the external organization of his followers, are not true Christians. This external society, therefore, is not a company of believers; it is not the Church which is Christ's body; the attributes and promises do not belong to it."[§]

He admits that the "promises do not belong" to the majority of those baptized. Since most of those baptized in Paedobaptist churches were baptized as infants his statement is overthrowing their whole case for infant

---

[*] Murray, 54-55.

[†] *Ibid.*, 71.

[‡] *Ibid.*, 55.

[§] Hodge, *Princeton Review*, 674.

baptism built on the promises being to all believers' infants. He also plainly says that the great majority of those baptized do not belong to the Church. This includes infants. Then why were they baptized? He is contradicting his whole position.

John Owen when writing on infant baptism said, "This covenant was, that God would be 'a God unto Abraham and to his seed,' which God Himself explains to be his infant seed, Genesis 17:12."*

However, when Owen is writing on the doctrine of the saints perseverance he disagrees with his statement above and says that God will be a God to Abraham and his faithful seed not his infant seed. He wrote this in his chapter on the Covenant of Grace,

> "For our present purpose, the producing and vindicating of one or two texts of Scripture, being unavoidably expressive towards the end aimed at shall suffice.
>
> The first of these is Gen. 17:7, 'I will establish my covenant between me and thee and thy seed after thee in their generations for an everlasting covenant, to be a God unto thee, and to thy seed after thee.' This is that which God engageth himself unto in this Covenant of Grace, that he will for everlasting be a God to him and his faithful seed. Though the external administration of the covenant was given to Abraham and his carnal seed, yet the effectual dispensation of the grace of the covenant is peculiar to them only who are the children of the promise, the remnant of Abraham according to election, with all that in all nations were to be blessed in him and in his seed, Christ Jesus. Ishmael, though circumcised, was to be put out, and not to be heir with Isaac, nor to abide in the house for ever, as the son of the promise was, Gal. 4:22-23, 30. Now, the apostle tells you, look what blessings faithful Abraham received by virtue of this promise, the same do all believers receive. Chap. 3:9, 'They which be of faith are blessed with faithful Abraham;' which he proves (in the words foregoing) from Gen. 12:3, because all nations were to be blessed in him. What blessing, then, was it that was here made over to Abraham? All the blessings that from God are conveyed in and by his

---

* Owen, 16:261-62.

seed, Jesus Christ (in whom both he and we are blessed), are inwrapped therein. What they are the apostle tells you, Eph. 1:3; they are 'all spiritual blessings.' If perseverance, if the continuance of the love and favour of God towards us, be a spiritual blessing, both Abraham and all his seed, all faithful ones throughout the world, are blessed with it in Jesus Christ; and if God's continuing to be a God to them for ever will enforce this blessing (being but the same thing in another expression), it is here likewise asserted."[*]

Please notice that when he is defending infant baptism he identifies the seed of Abraham in Genesis 17 as "his infant seed." But when he defended the perseverance of the saints he identifies the seed of Abraham as "his faithful seed," and that the blessings are to "Abraham and all his seed, all faithful ones throughout the world." Dr. Owen repeats this in a later chapter on the mediation of Christ to prove the perseverance of the saints. He wrote,

"The persons to whom this promise is made are called 'thee' and 'thy seed;' that is, all those and only those with whom God is a God in covenant. God here minds them of the first making of this covenant with Abraham and his seed, Gen. 17:7. Now, who are this seed of Abraham? Not all his carnal posterity, not the whole nation of the Jews; which is the last subterfuge invented by our author to evade the force of our argument from this place. Our Saviour not only denies, but also proves by many arguments, that the Pharisees and their followers, who doubtless were of the nation of the Jews and the carnal seed of Abraham, were not the children of Abraham in this sense, nor his seed, but rather the devil's, John 8:39-44. And the apostle disputes and argues the same case, Rom. 4:9-12, and proves undeniably that it is believers only, whether circumcised or uncircumcised, whether Jews or Gentiles, that are this seed of Abraham and heirs of the promise. So, plainly, Gal. 3:7, 'Know ye therefore that they which are of faith, the same are the children of Abraham;' and then he concludes again, as the issue of his debate, verse 9, 'So then they which be of faith are blessed with faithful

---

[*] *Ibid.*, 11:205-06.

Abraham.'"*

This is significant for if Abraham's seed are not his natural descendants but his spiritual descendants the case for infant baptism has evaporated since Paedobaptists argue that since Abraham's natural seed was in the Covenant of Grace and so were circumcised all believers natural seed are also in the Covenant of Grace and so are to be baptized. However, Dr. Owen wrote that Abraham's carnal seed were not the seed of Abraham spoken of in Genesis 17 that he covenanted with but his spiritual seed or believers.

Why did Owen argue that way? His opponent was a Mr. John Goodwin, an Arminian theologian, (not to be confused with Thomas Goodwin whom I often quote) who denied that all believers persevere but rather taught that some through unfaithfulness are lost. Volume eleven of Owen's Works addresses this doctrine and defends the doctrine of the perseverance of the saints against Mr. John Goodwin. As all of Owen's writings it is worthy of high esteem.

John Goodwin's argument was that the promise was made to all Israel and it was evident that they did not persevere in faith and holiness. Thus the whole argument concerning the doctrine of perseverance turned on who are the seed in Genesis 17 and Isaiah 59:20-21. Owen answered Mr. Goodwin referring to Isaiah 59:21:

> "The force, then, of this promise, and the influence it hath into the establishment of the truth we have in hand, will not be evaded and turned aside by affirming 'that it is made to the whole people of Israel:' for besides that the Spirit of the Lord could not be said to be in the ungodly, rejected part of them, nor his word in their mouth, there is not the least, in text or context, to intimate such an extent of this promise as to the object of it: and it is very weakly attempted to be proved from Paul's accommodation and interpretation of the verse foregoing, 'And the Redeemer shall come to Zion,' etc, in Rom. 11:26; for it is most evident and indisputable, to anyone who shall but once cast an eye upon that place, that the apostle accommodates

---

* *Ibid.*, 11:312.

and applies these words to none but only those who shall be saved, being turned away from ungodliness to Christ; which are only the seed before described."[*]

Therefore, if seed means natural descendants of Abraham then the perseverance of the saints cannot be established. It seems that the Paedobaptists can either hold to infant baptism or the perseverance of the saints but not to both. Mr. John Goodwin argued against the saints' perseverance as follows,

> "That though God undertake to be our God in an everlasting covenant, and upon that account to bless us with the whole blessing that is conveyed by the promised seed, yet if we abide not with him, if we forsake him, he will also cease to be our God, and cease to bless us with the blessing which on others in Jesus Christ he will bestow."[†]

Some Paedobaptists argue much the same. "Remember, a covenant is a conditional promise. Each covenant that God made with man promised certain blessings for covenant keepers and curses for covenant breakers."[‡]

They speak of "duties of remaining in the covenant"[§] with the implication that those in the covenant can fall out of it which is just another way of saying all the saints may not persevere. They believe those in the Covenant of Grace can be eternally lost. These are called "covenant breakers." They seem to make our eternal salvation to be suspended on us fulfilling conditions. This is to turn the Covenant of Grace into a covenant of works. Dr. Owen's answer to such is,

> "If there be a necessity to smite this evasion so often as we shall meet with it, it must be cut into a hundred pieces. For the present, I shall only observe two evils it is attended withal: First, It takes no notice that God, who hath undertaken to be a God unto us, hath, with the

---

[*] *Ibid.*, 11:312-13.
[†] *Ibid.*, 11:206.
[‡] R. Booth, 60.
[§] *Ibid.*, 141.

like truth, power, and faithfulness, undertaken that we shall abide to be his people. So is his love in his covenant expressed by its efficacy to this end and purpose, Deut. 30:6, 'The Lord thy God will circumcise thine heart, and the heart of thy seed, to love the Lord thy God with all thine heart, and with all thy soul, that thou mayest live.' Secondly, It denies the continuance of the love of God to us to the end to be any part of the blessings wherewith we are blessed in Jesus Christ; for if it be, it could no more be suspended on any condition in us than the glorification of believers that abide so to the end.

This, then, is inwrapped in this promise of the covenant unto the elect, with whom it is established: God will be a God to them for ever, and that to bless them with all the blessings which he communicates in and by the Lord Jesus Christ, the promised seed. The continuance of his favour to the end is to us unquestionably a spiritual blessing (if any one be otherwise minded, I shall not press to share with him in his apprehension); and if so, it is in Christ, and shall certainly be enjoyed by them to whom God is a God in covenant."[*]

All this is written to prove that the seed in the Covenant of Grace are only believers, not the natural seed of believers. Thus, none should be baptized who are not believers and evidence it in their lives. Are the promises given to the children of believers? No, they are only to believers.

"Whilst a man lives without regeneration, he is also without promise: Eph. 2:12, 'He hath now quickened you, who in times past were strangers to the covenant of promise.' And what are promises but the golden veins or rivulets that mercies run into, as the dust and sand of the purest gold use in several rills to do? Which promises, though they were bequeathed before by God's eternal decrees, and purchased by Christ's death, yet the right to them, the *seisin*, the possession of them, is given at conversion: 2 Pet. 1:3, 4, after he had said that 'his divine power had given to them all things belonging to life and godliness' (that is, furnished us with all requisite abilities thereunto), 'through the knowledge of him that called us to glory and

---

[*] Owen, 11:206-07.

virtue,' he adds, 'Whereby are given to us (delivery of *seisin* thereby is made) 'exceeding great and precious promises;' so as the youngest convert may upon regeneration go over and run through all the Scriptures, and view and lay claim to whatever is promised of spiritual blessings therein.'"*

Note the phrase "given to us," the called, in 2 Peter 1:4. A person may be an heir of the promise but that is hidden until revealed by regeneration and calling. He receives no promise until, "the kindness and love of God appeared" (Titus 3:4), and it appeared when "he saved us, by the washing of regeneration" (verse 5).

The promises are only to believers. Men must see the promises with opened eyes and be assured of them before they can be embraced and so welcomed and received. "These all died in faith, not having received the promises (*i.e.*, the things promised) but having seen them afar off were assured of them, embraced them . . . " (Heb. 11:13). Thus the promises are not to any infants. As Goodwin wrote, "Whilst a man lives without regeneration, he is also without promise: Eph. 2:12, 'He now hath quickened you, who in times past were strangers to the covenants of promise.'"

Until a person is called he has not obtained mercy:

> "that you may proclaim the praises of Him who called you out of darkness into His marvelous light, who once were not a people but are now the people of God, who had not obtained mercy but now have obtained mercy" (1 Pet. 2:9-10).

It is very upsetting to me to hear it being said and written that infants of believers have the promises for it implies that God is unfaithful since those supposed promises are unfulfilled in numerous cases. This is even admitted by Calvin commenting on Deuteronomy 5:9-10,

> "But here a difficult question arises, for the history of all ages shews that a great proportion of the progeny of the holy have been rejected

---

* Goodwin, 6:406.

and condemned; and that God has inflicted upon them weightier manifestations of His curse and vengeance, than upon strangers. We must, however observe, that in these words grace is not promised severally to all the posterity of the saints, as if God were bound to each individual who may derive their race and origin from them. There were many degenerate children of Abraham, to whom it profited nothing that they were called the offspring of the holy patriarch; nor indeed is the promise restricted to individuals, for many who are the children after the flesh, are not counted for the seed—but God in His free election adopts whom He will, yet so governs His judgments, as that His paternal favour should always abide with the race of believers."*

Please note that he wrote, "Grace is not promised severally to all the posterity of the saints." How then can the baptism of the posterity of the saints be justified?

---

* Calvin, 2:112.

40

One Way of Salvation

The Word of God everywhere teaches that there is only one salvation and only one way of salvation. If infants are saved in a different way than adults then we have at least two ways of salvation. In a book that defends infant baptism by Uuras Saarnivaara, a Lutheran, he writes of an imaginary conversation between a Baptist and a Paedobaptist:

> "PAEDOBAPTIST: According to your doctrine, infants cannot be born again since they are not able to understand the Gospel. Do you, then, believe that infants have no possibility of being saved? In my view, that is the only possible conclusion from the baptistic doctrine.

> "BAPTIST: No, we do not believe that infants are lost. Those who die in their infancy are saved by the atonement of Christ.

> "PAEDOBAPTIST: Don't you believe that we sinners become partakers of the blessings of Christ's atonement through faith, in the new birth?

> "BAPTIST: We do, but children are saved directly by the atonement of Christ.

> "PAEDOBAPTIST: Then you have two entirely different ways of salvation: infants and adults are alike sinful and lost. The adults are saved through faith and the new birth, but infants are saved without

faith and without the new birth. How do you reconcile this doctrine of yours with the words of Christ which I quoted: all men are born of the flesh, and cannot enter into the kingdom of God without the new birth, or birth of water and the Spirit? Do you make these words of Christ null and void in the case of infants?

"BAPTIST: I don't want to reject any words of Christ, or the Bible, but I cannot understand how an infant can believe, as he is incapable of understanding the Word of God. Repentance and faith belong together. Man must be convicted of his sins, pray for pardon, and believe the Gospel. 'Faith cometh by hearing, and hearing by the word of Christ.' You have two different conditions of coming to faith, one for the infants and another for the grownups.'"[*]

My comment is that both the Baptist and the Paedobaptist pointed out inconsistencies in the other's belief. Anyone who believes infants are saved, whether with baptism or without, holds to two ways of salvation. This is directly contrary to the teaching of the Bible. Isn't the Paedobaptist correct when he accuses the Baptist of having "two entirely different ways of salvation"? Yes, he is if the Baptist believes "infants are saved without faith and without the new birth." However, isn't the Baptist also correct to accuse the Paedobaptist of having "two different conceptions of coming to faith, one for infants and another for adults"? Yes, he is if the Paedobaptist believes that infants are regenerate but without knowledge or understanding.

Dr. John Murray accepted two ways of salvation for the sake of infant baptism but it cannot be. He wrote,

"In the case of adults intelligent repentance and faith are the conditions of salvation. But intelligent repentance and faith are not the conditions of salvation in the case of infants."[†]

He excludes infants from the conditions of repentance and faith for

---

[*] Saarnivaara, 61-62.
[†] Murray, 73.

salvation and makes an assertion of such. However, he gives no scripture and does not base his assertion on scripture. Scripture does not exclude anyone from the necessity of exercising repentance and faith for salvation. Dr. Murray is putting an exception to all God's commands to repent and believe with the implication that God is not speaking to everyone but is excluding infants. "Except ye repent ye shall all likewise perish" does not have the added qualification "unless they are infants." "Whoever does not believe stands condemned" (John 3:18) means just that. Whoever includes everyone. It does not say, "Whoever does not believe stands condemned unless they are infants." These verses are to all and exclude none.

If infants cannot exercise faith it is inconsistent to believe they are saved. Dr. Berkhof was quite right to argue as he did,

> "The Baptist . . . argues as follows: Active faith is the prerequisite of baptism. Infants cannot exercise faith. Therefore infants may not be baptized. But in that way these words might also be construed into an argument against infant salvation, since they not only imply but explicitly state that faith (active faith) is the condition of salvation. To be consistent the Baptist would thus find himself burdened with the following syllogism: Faith is the *conditio sine qua non* of salvation. Children cannot yet exercise faith. Therefore children cannot be saved. But this is a conclusion from which the Baptist himself would shrink."[*]

We must not shrink from saying that infants cannot be saved before they believe. Regeneration cannot be divorced from repentance and faith. As soon as a person is regenerated his eyes are open so that he repents and believes. There is no time span between regeneration and faith any more than there is a time span between when a person's eyes are opened and he sees. Regeneration is the work of the Spirit in which He gives seeing eyes, hearing ears, understanding hearts, and of course, that is living faith. Where there is no faith there is no life, no regeneration.

J. C. Ryle asks the question,

---

[*] Berkhof, 637.

"But may it not be true that all baptized persons receive the grace of regeneration in baptism, and that it remains within them like a dormant seed, alive, though at present bearing no fruit? Certainly not. The Apostle St. John expressly forbids us to suppose that there can be such a thing as dormant or sleeping grace. He says, 'Whosoever is born of God does not commit sin, for his seed remaineth in him, and he cannot sin because he is born of God.' (1 John 3:9). This witness is true. When there can be light which cannot be seen, and fire without heat, then, and not till then, there may be grace that is dormant and inactive."*

There are absolutes in the Word of God in regard to salvation. One absolute is repentance. None can be saved without repentance since repentance is unto life (Acts 13:24). Without repentance men are lost. "Unless you repent you will all likewise perish" (Luke 13:3, 5).

Another absolute is faith. "Whoever does not believe will be condemned." To have the Spirit of God is to have all spiritual blessings. Without Him there is no life. Yet all receive the Spirit only through faith (Gal. 3:14). Too, unless a person is justified he can never be accepted by God. Yet justification is only through faith "just as Abraham believed God, and it was accounted to him for righteousness" (Gal. 3:6). None are accepted by God apart from faith. Indeed, "Without faith no one can please God" (Heb. 11:6), regardless of what operations a person may be subject to.

It is also true that God saves only through the gospel. "The gospel . . . is the power of God unto salvation" (Rom. 1:16). All saved people are "begotten through the gospel" (1 Cor 4:15). Unless a person is called he will never come and it is by the gospel all are called, "He called you by our gospel" (2 Thess. 2:14).

If infants are elect we can be sure that the gospel will come to them in power. But until it does we have no reason to believe they are elect. How did Paul know the Thessalonians were elected of God?

"Knowing, beloved brethren, your election by God. For our gospel

---

* Ryle, *The Upper Room*, 357.

did not come to you in word only, but also in power, and in the Holy
Spirit and in much assurance, as you know what kind of men we were
among you for your sake" (1 Thess. 1:4-5).

Until the word of God comes to a person in power, in the Holy Spirit and in
much assurance we can have no confidence that that person is elected of God
to salvation.

Thus we see that God uses means to save. He does not work without
instruments. As far as we know no children are saved until they hear the
gospel in faith. No children are saved until they come to the only Savior, our
Lord Jesus Christ. What brings them? God uses motives to move intelligent
beings. He draws them with fear, hope, love and by the warnings, invitations
and promises of His Word that produce such desires and emotions. He
draws by that which is suitable to thinking beings with hearts, minds and
conscience. "I drew them with cords of a man, with bands of love" (Hos.
11:4). These terms exclude infants. God has a willing people.

This does not mean that faith is impossible for young children as
opposed to infants. We should realize that a child's faith is a simple faith.
Their understanding may be small compared to an adult's but still be
genuine faith at an early age. I have read Jonathan Edwards' account of Phebe
Bartlett's faith and conversion when she was four years old with joy and
wonder. Just last week I held a conversation with a teen-aged boy who said
he was converted when he was four years old. He bore a good testimony by
my observation.

What then of infants of believing parents who die in infancy? We cannot
claim that they are regenerate because of birth for they are born in Adam.
Nor can we believe they are regenerate without faith and repentance any
more than we can believe those who have not heard the gospel may be
regenerate without faith and repentance. Both infants and the unreached
have an inability to believe. Is the infant culpable being born in sin? Yes.
Death comes to infants not through their own sins but through the sin of
Adam. "Death reigned . . . even over those who had not sinned according to
the likeness of the transgression of Adam (a conscious sin)" (Rom. 5:14).

Although all of us want to think the best and many are moved by their sentiments I don't see the scriptures giving any hope for the salvation of such. But of this we can be sure, the judge of all the earth will do right. Salvation is in his hands but that He passes by many is evident. Let us submit to Him. I think of the testimony of Eli who upon being told the prophecy of the death of his two ungodly sons and the bringing of his whole household to ruin said, "It is the Lord. Let Him do what seems good to Him" (1 Sam 3:18). He graciously submitted to God and to God's purpose although he knew it meant his two sons entered eternity lost and without hope.

Objections are many to this. The example of John the Baptist is given. He was filled with the Holy Spirit from the womb (Luke 1:15). Does this mean he was regenerate from birth? I don't know. Yet we do know that Christ said of John that "among those born of women there is not a greater prophet . . ." (Luke 7:28). There was only one person who was spoken of by God to his Son, "Behold, I send my messenger before your face, who will prepare your way before you" (Luke 7:27). He was absolutely unique. We cannot use John as a pattern for others. The fact that John was unique means that God made him so and did in him what he did in no others.

41

A Body of Truth

There is only one way of salvation and this one way of salvation is defined by a body of truth. This body of truth is a whole and if any part of the truth is missing it affects the whole such that what remains is another message. The various doctrines that make up this whole are mutually dependent on one another so that if one truth or doctrine is omitted or denied the other doctrines will be made void.

To give one example: Christ exercises three offices in saving His people. These are called His priestly office, His prophetical office and His kingly office. Christ is prophet, priest and king. As a prophet He reveals or proclaims salvation. As a priest He procured salvation. As a king He applies salvation. Christ's foundational work is as a priest. The other two offices depend on His priestly work.

If Christ had not purchased and procured salvation there would be no salvation to proclaim or apply. If infants are saved without hearing and believing the gospel proclaimed by Christ through His servants then the gospel itself is not necessary. If faith is not necessary then the object of faith, the gospel, is likewise needless. And if the gospel is not necessary, Christ's death, the crux of the gospel is not necessary. Christ's priestly office is overthrown and as Paul writes, "Christ died in vain" (Gal. 2:21). If His death was not necessary then instead of it being an exhibition of the wisdom of God it would depict God as going to great pains and cost to do a needless work. If infants can be saved without faith in the gospel then everyone can be saved without faith in the gospel and then the gospel is no longer needed.

Everything is overthrown. If infants are heirs without faith then "faith is made void" (Rom. 4:14). "It is of faith that the promise might be sure to all the seed" (Rom. 4:16). If it is not of faith the promise is not sure and everything falls to the ground. I realize that those who teach infant salvation do not accept that these are the ramifications and consequences of their teaching but I believe it overthrows the gospel of grace. It sets aside the grace of God if salvation comes by birth and makes Christ's death to be in vain (see Gal. 2:21). Indeed it is teaching another way of salvation.

We must stand against such teaching by proclaiming the whole counsel of God. O, may we preach our precious Lord Jesus Christ and His death as absolutely necessary, "determining not to know anything among you except Jesus Christ and Him crucified."

Part 7

THE DOCTRINES IN REGARD TO INFANTS

42

The Doctrine of Election and the Remnant

God chose the nation of Israel. He bypassed greater nations and set his love on Israel.

> "For you are a holy people to the Lord your God; the Lord your God has chosen you to be a people for Himself, a special treasure above all the peoples on the face of the earth. The Lord did not set His love on you nor choose you because you were more in number than any other people, for you were least of all peoples" (Deut. 7:6-7).

This was a national election. It was not a personal election. It could not be said of each individual Jew as it was said to the Thessalonian church,

> "God from the beginning chose you for salvation through sanctification by the Spirit and belief in the truth to which He called you by our gospel for obtaining of the glory of our Lord Jesus Christ" (1 Thess. 2:13-14).

The Jewish nation was rather known for its unbelief and ungodliness.

During the Mosaic period the nation as a whole is in the forefront. The history written in the Word of God is the history of Israel from its inception until its apostasy. In the early period we read of its ordinances and the sacrifices which were offered for the whole nation. We go on to the period of the judges who judged the nation and legislated for Israel as a whole. Then the period of David and the kings continues this emphasis as a whole. After

Solomon died the nation was divided and Israel, the northern kingdom, apostatized which left Judah as the remnant of Israel. Because of the sin and idolatry of Israel the Lord destroyed Israel through the Assyrians. "So the Lord was very angry with Israel and removed them from his presence. Only the tribe of Judah was left" (2 Kgs. 17:18).

However, the very next verse reads, "And even Judah did not keep the commands of the Lord their God." Thus Judah, the remnant, was a mixed group. So we later read of God's threatening to Judah,

> "Therefore thus says the Lord God of Israel: 'Behold, I am bringing such calamity upon Jerusalem and Judah, That whoever hears of it, both his ears will tingle. So I will forsake the remnant of My inheritance and deliver them into the hand of their enemies; and they shall become victims of plunder to all their enemies'" (2 Kgs. 21:12, 14).

This leads to a further shrinking of the remnant. Yet, God would always preserve his people as a remnant even though they be few.

> "Thus says the Lord: 'As the new wine is found in the cluster, And one says, 'Do not destroy it, for a blessing is in it,' so will I do for My servants' sake, that I may not destroy them all. I will bring forth descendants from Jacob, and from Judah an heir of My mountains; My elect shall inherit it, and My servants shall dwell there'" (Isa. 65:8-9).

God would sift the house of Israel and shake and scatter them among all the nations to separate the chaff from the wheat yet He promised that the righteous would be preserved. The least grain would not fall to the earth though the sinners of God's people would die. "Behold, the eyes of the Lord God are on the sinful kingdom, and I will destroy it from the face of the earth; yet I will not utterly destroy the house of Jacob," says the Lord. "For surely I will command, and I will sift the house of Israel among all nations, as grain is sifted in a sieve; yet not the smallest grain shall fall to the ground" (Amos 9:8-9).

The idea of a faithful remnant became more and more prominent in the history of Israel. There was a dwindling of the remnant as God sifted them so that at times there seemed to be no remnant left as when Elijah said, "I am the only one left" (1 Kgs. 19:10). Yet, he was wrong. God had preserved a remnant for himself.

In the early days of Israel the processes of sifting and dividing were not so evident and their apostasy had not been evidenced to reveal the true people of God within the nation. Even in the time of the patriarchs, however, as seen in the narrative of Ishmael and Isaac and then again in the narrative of Esau and Jacob there were hints that the people of God were not born after the flesh but after the Spirit. In other words the people of God were not Israel but a people within Israel. There is an election within an election or as Paul puts it, "they are not all Israel who are of Israel" (Rom. 9:6).

The idea of a remnant or a small faithful body within Israel is particularly spotlighted in Elijah's time.

> "It is introduced in one of the most solemn and impressive narratives of that history. The prophet is taken into the desert to commune with God; he is taken to Sinai, the mountain of God, which played such a large part in the tradition of His people, and he receives the Divine message in that form which has ever marked off this as unique amongst theophanies, the 'still small voice,' contrasted with the thunder and the storm and the earthquake. And the idea that was introduced marks a stage in the religious history of the world, for it was the first revelation of the idea of personal as opposed to national consecration. Up to that time it was the nation as a whole that was bound to God, the nation as a whole for which sacrifices were offered, the nation as a whole for which kings had fought and judges legislated. But the nation as a whole had deserted Jehovah, and the Prophet records that it is the loyalty of the individual Israelites who had remained true to Him that must henceforth be reckoned. The nation will be chastised, but the remnant shall be saved.
>
> The idea is a new one, but it is one which we find continuously from this time onwards, spiritualized with the more spiritual ideas of the later prophets. We find it in Amos (9:8-10), in Micah (2:12; 5:3),

in Zephaniah (3:12-13), in Jeremiah (23:3), in Ezekiel (14:20, 22), but most pointedly and markedly in Isaiah.

This doctrine of a Remnant implied that it was the individual who was true to his God, and not the nation, that was the object of the Divine solicitude; that it was in this small body of individuals that the true life of the chosen nation dwelt, and that from them would spring that internal reformation, which, coming as the result of the Divine chastisement, would produce a whole people, pure and undefiled, to be offered to God (Isa. 65:8-9).

The idea appealed with great force to the early Christians. It appealed to St. Stephen, in whose speech one of the main currents of thought seems to be the marvelous analogy which runs through all the history of Israel. The mass of the people has ever been unfaithful; it is the individual or the small body that has remained true to God in all the changes of Israel's history, and these the people have always persecuted as they crucified the Messiah. And so St. Paul, musing over the sad problem of Israel's unbelief, finds its explanations and justification in this consistent trait of the nation's history. As in Elijah's time, as in Isaiah's time, so now the mass of the people have rejected the Divine call; but there always has been and still is the true Remnant, the Remnant whom God has selected, who have preserved the true life and ideal of the people and thus contain the elements of new and prolonged life.

And this doctrine of the 'Remnant' is as true to human nature as it is to Israel's history. No church or nation, is saved en masse, it is those members of it who are righteous. It is not the mass of the nation or church that has done its work, but the select few who have preserved the consciousness of its high calling."*

Paul's comment on this is found in Romans 9-11. Note his quotations of Isaiah in Romans 9:27-29,

> "Isaiah also cries out concerning Israel: 'Though the number of the children of Israel be as the sand of the sea, the remnant will be saved. For he will finish the work and cut it short in righteousness, because

---

* Sanday and Headlam, *Romans*, 316-17.

the Lord will make a short work upon the earth.' And as Isaiah said before: 'Unless the Lord of Sabaoth had left us a seed, we would have become like Sodom, and we would have been made like Gomorrah.'"

The doctrine that Paul thus distills from Israel's history and develops in Romans 9 is that of the personal election of men to eternal life, not to external privileges as with the nation of Israel.

Hodge makes the same point,

> "Paul teaches clearly the doctrine of the personal election of men to eternal life, an election not on works, but on the good pleasure of God. If this election is to eternal life, it is, of course, a choice of individuals, and not of communities, because communities, as such, do not inherit eternal life. This is still further proved by the cases of Isaac and Ishmael, and Jacob and Esau, between whom, as individuals, the choice was made. From the illustration derived from the case of Pharoah. From the objection presented in verses 14, 19. From the answer to these objections in verses 15-16, 20, 23, especially from the passage just referred to, which speaks of the vessels of mercy prepared unto glory; which cannot be applied to nations or communities."[*]

Also, because it is a choice of individuals and not of any social group it is not an election of families but of individuals within families, clans, tribes and nations. It is not of the flesh. The sons of God are "born, not of blood, nor of the will of the flesh, nor of the will of man, but of God." Blood relationship is left out.

Physical birth does not unite with Christ.

> "And it was told him by some who said, 'Your mother and your brothers are standing outside, desiring to see you.' But he answered and said to them, 'My mother and my brothers are these who hear the word of God and do it'" (Luke 8:20-21).

---

[*] Hodge, *Romans*, 323.

"The very mother that bore Jesus, and his nearest kindred, could attain to no peculiar place in his kingdom by reason of their earthly connection with him: not these, he said, but every one that heareth the word, and doeth the will of my Father in heaven, is my mother and sister and brother. Thus the fleshly bond was broken at the centre, and it must vanish to the farthest circumference; everything founded on natural relationships and genealogical descent was, with the handwriting of ordinances, nailed to the cross of Christ and buried in his grave, as a part of that bondage to the elements of the world from which the Church had at length escaped, and which should never more be heard of in her borders. The one relationship to be accounted of is union to Christ, which renders all who possess it children of Abraham, and heirs according to the promise—heirs, that is, of all that was given to Abraham in promise; more even, if more could be, for they are heirs of God and joint heirs with Christ himself."[*]

Thus, when the Paedobaptist argues for "the inclusion of all the members of the family in the redemptive purposes of God,"[†] he is arguing directly against personal, unconditional election. Booth further writes, "If God continues to deal with us as families in his covenant, then we need to give some very serious consideration to what we are doing if we leave our children unbaptized."[‡] But Romans 9 and in fact the illustrations found in Romans 9 taken from Israel's history prove conclusively that God does not deal with us as families but as individuals. "For he says to Moses, 'I will have mercy on whomever I will have mercy, and I will have compassion on whomever I will have compassion.'" The word whomever is singular. To do this God splits families as Paul has just illustrated. "Descent from pious parents does not secure admission into the Kingdom of Christ."[§] Nor in the Covenant of Grace, I may add.

Christ clearly taught that God does not deal with families as units but

---

[*] Fairbairn, *Ezekiel*, 200.

[†] R. Booth, 149.

[‡] *Ibid.*

[§] Hodge, 323.

with men and women as individuals when he said, "A man's foes will be those of his own household" (Matt. 10:36). Natural ties are broken down by the gospel. Did Christ come to bring peace in the family by uniting all in baptism?

> "Do not think that I came to bring peace on earth, I did not come to bring peace but a sword. For I have come to 'set a man against his father, a daughter against her mother, and a daughter-in-law against her mother-in-law.' And 'a man's foes will be those of his own household.' He who loves father or mother more than Me is not worthy of Me. And he who loves son or daughter more than Me is not worthy of Me" (Matt. 10:34, 37).

Often the gospel brings intense ill feeling into families even as Paul writes of one godly family, "But, as he who was born according to the flesh then persecuted him who was born according to the Spirit, even so it is now" (Gal. 4:29). The gospel brings strife, discord, and persecution into all relationships, not least the family.

One of the major reasons infant baptism has been insisted on by government authorities was to bring about an homogenous society. They wanted a sacral society. That is, a society "bound together by a common religious loyalty." It means a society held together by a religion that all the members follow. As Verduin wrote, "All pre-Christian society is sacral."[*] Old Testament religion was sacral and pre-Christian. New Testament Christianity is based on personal faith and never includes everyone in a locality. There is no state church in New Testament Christianity. Infant baptism is a relic of sacral societies and is after the pattern of Old Testament nationalistic election not New Testament personal election.

Heathen cultures are sacralistic. They desire uniformity and peace so much pressure is put on the individual to conform in religion to the whole. Mr. Booth, in his book, quotes from a letter to him,

> "In modern times, there are incidents where the tribal chief

---

[*] Verduin, 22.

announces that, 'We are becoming Christians,' and the whole tribe asks to be baptized. Individualistic Americans are not used to this type of procedure, but it is not rare or absurd.'"

He is right; it is not rare. Nor is it absurd from a natural viewpoint. Rather it is good worldly policy to keep the peace. I have spent most of my life as a missionary to a tribal society. Often whole groups desire baptism because they think it to be a good policy. Sometimes it is a desire for education or prestige or material goods that they think baptism will help to obtain. Sometimes they think it will get their names written "in the book."

Most superstitiously believe that the water of baptism has power to wash away sin. Their old belief in spirits that was passed on to them by their ancestors is that the spirits dwell in swamps, the forest, in stones, trees, etc., and that certain stones, bark, wood and plants have mysterious power to ward off sickness, or to cause sickness and even death. Such inanimate things they believe cause gardens to grow, children to be strong, etc. Thus they readily accept that the water of baptism has mysterious, inherent power. Everyone wants baptism in this culture.

The reason that they want baptism as units, families, clans, and tribes is to keep the social structures intact and to keep individuals from going contrary to the body of the people. It takes great courage for a believer to go against his family, or clan but it is necessary as Christ said when

> "great multitudes went with Him. And He turned and said to them, 'If anyone comes to Me and does not hate his father and mother, wife and children, brothers and sisters, yes and his own life also, he cannot be My disciple. And whoever does not bear his cross and come after Me cannot be My disciple'" (Luke 14:25-27).

Although multitudes followed Christ only a few were the true Israel. Never is the whole mass good. It is only the salt within the mass that preserves it from corruption.

We see over and over again on the mission field that not only the

---

* R. Booth, 148.

"unbelieving, abominable, murderers, sexually immoral, sorcerers, idolators and all liars shall have their part in the lake which burns with fire and brimstone," but also, "the cowardly" (see Rev. 21:8). People fear their families and their clans. Only Almighty grace can enable a man to turn his back on his society and come out from among them and be separate. Of course, such a public profession by the believer does not pertain to infant baptism.

I have had to always oppose mass baptism. Why? Because the people's desire was not a work of the Spirit but rather worldly prudence. If there was a revival and families and whole clans were gloriously saved and gave credible professions I would delight to see them baptized. Sadly, I have not seen such a revival and all the mass baptisms I have been acquainted with in the country in which I live and work have hardened men and women in their unconverted state and produced thousands upon thousands of men and women carnally secure in their sin. In this country the answer to the question, "Are you a Christian?" is usually, "Yes, I have been baptized by such and such a Mission." Baptism in most cases has sounded the death knell for those baptized. Very few of those baptized ever see the light and die in total darkness. Baptism, both infant and adult, has deceived them and they will curse the missionaries who gave it to them when they cry out in anguish in that fire that never shall be quenched.

43

Reconciliation

We must be reconciled to God if we are ever to be saved. All who are regenerate are also reconciled to God, for it cannot be that anyone born again can continue to be an enemy to God. Reconciliation has two parts.

God's part. God moved first towards reconciliation by the death of Christ. "God was in Christ reconciling the world to himself" (2 Cor. 5:19).

Man's part. There is reconciliation on our part and this is necessary for salvation. This was the exhortation of the apostle, "We implore you on Christ's behalf: Be reconciled to God" (2 Cor. 5:20).

There is a necessity that men (including little children) hear the message of the gospel and obey it to be saved. God will doubtless destroy all who have not obeyed the gospel "in flaming fire taking vengeance on those who do not know God and on those who do not obey the gospel of our Lord Jesus Christ" (2 Thess. 1:8). This includes infants as well as adults. God can accept no one who is unreconciled to Him in his heart and life and disobeys the gospel. There can be no reconciliation unless it is on both sides. God was in Christ reconciling the world unto Himself but man must throw down his weapons of warfare and "kiss the Son" to be reconciled. God's love must be answered by man's or God's love is thrown away and is for naught. He loved us that we might love Him. This is the aim of God's love. God desires love answering to His but if He saved and regenerated without an answering love His love would be despised and not valued. There can be no true marriage unless there is love on both sides.

Thus, there is no salvation until the love of God begets a reciprocal love in our hearts. Surely God and Christ cannot delight in us until our hearts are won and we delight in them. As enemies we were reconciled to God through the death of His Son but it is as reconciled that we shall be saved (Rom 5:10). Unrequited love is most bitter. How sweet is love when it is returned!

Previous to a man being reconciled it is necessary for him to see himself as an enemy to God, and to realize that God accounts him as His enemy. It is necessary that a man sees the great danger of being an enemy to God or he will not seek to be reconciled. And yet he will not seek such a reconciliation unless he also sees a possibility of being reconciled. As he hears and learns of the Father's love in sending His Son as a propitiation he sees a way and has hope. As Christ said, "Every man that hath heard and learned of the Father, comes to me" (John 6:45).

He comes as an unworthy sinner, even as one condemned, to seek the Father's favor and forgiveness. Even so,

> "He shall pray to Him, and He will be gracious and say, 'Deliver him, I have found a ransom.' He looks upon men and if any say I have sinned, and perverted that which was right, and it profited me not he will deliver his soul from going into the pit, and his life shall see the light" (Job 23:24, 26-28).

The sinner will do this seeking with mourning and confession of sin and this is necessary to reconciliation. For

> "God will have men know when He pardons, that he knows what he pardons, and therefore will have them acknowledge what they deserve, 'that every mouth might be stopped, and become guilty,' and obnoxious in their own acknowledgment before him (Rom 3:19). As if a man will become wise, he must become a fool; so that a man that will become a friend to God, must turn enemy against himself and judge himself worthy of destruction. And God will have the freeness and glory of his grace acknowledged in pardoning; and therefore will have us confess our evil ways and deservedness of

destruction."[*]

The sum of what is here written is that hand in hand with regeneration goes reconciliation and reconciliation on the sinner's part includes an acknowledgment of sin and a seeking for pardon to God as the gracious God who has shown forth His love through His Son. Thus, if an infant knows nothing of being reconciled with God and dies in that state he is not regenerate and not one of the elect. As there is but one road, so all who are saved, without exception, have walked that road that leads to eternal life. None get to heaven in the dark with the shades down and asleep in a carriage during the journey. It is a journey that is on foot. None arrive in ignorance, not seeing the ways of God in saving sinners. All arrive with some knowledge of the way with thankfulness to their Savior and rejoicing in so great a salvation. All have consciously experienced sin and likewise experienced grace as a revelation of God's undeserved love and mercy. All know something of the sweetness of the pardon and the wonder of their escape even from the outer darkness where there is weeping and gnashing of teeth. All will be able to sing the new song for they learned it on the road. There will be none who are silent in heaven; none left out from declaring free and sovereign grace to the glory of God.

THE JUSTICE AND MERCY OF GOD IN HIS CONDEMNATION OF INFANTS WHO DIE IN INFANCY

God's Justice

Infants who die in infancy die because of Adam's sin. "Therefore, just as through one man sin entered the world, and death through sin, and thus death spread to all men, because all sinned" (Rom. 5:12). Infants, being born in Adam, experience death, disease and misery, yes, even eternal death. They participate in the guilt of Adam's sin and since they are guilty they justly come under condemnation and punishment. They are not innocent

---

[*] Goodwin, Volume 6, 128-29.

although they have not committed actual transgression against known law. As is written, "Whoever perished being innocent? or where were the righteous cut off?" (Job 4:7). No, infants are neither innocent nor righteous. Death passes on all men because all at birth are sinners. Adam's sin is as truly the sin of everyone of his descendants as if it had been personally committed by them. Adam's sin is imputed to all those in him just as Christ's righteousness is imputed to all those united to Him.

God's testimony is,

> "Therefore, as through one man's offense judgment came to all men, resulting in condemnation, even so through one Man's righteous act the free gift came to all men, resulting in justification of life. For as by one man's disobedience many were made sinners, so also by one Man's obedience many will be made righteous" (Rom. 5:18-19).

We may not be able to understand this. It is repugnant to natural reason. How this is, and how it can be, we may not be able to comprehend. That should not be our concern. We are not to believe based on our human reason. That is not faith at all. We are to believe God's testimony because it is His testimony, not because we understand it.

Haldane's statement concerning this is helpful and precious,

> "The Christian ought to be accustomed to submit to God's testimony without question, and without reluctance, even in things the furthest beyond the reach of the human mind. 'Speak Lord, for Thy servant heareth,' ought to be the motto of every Christian. Yet how few follow out to their full extent the plain statements of the word of God on these subjects; and while many utterly deny and abhor every representation of the imputation of sin and righteousness, others hide its genuine features by an attempt to enable men to understand the reasons for it, and to justify the Divine procedure. This is altogether improper. The ways of God are too deep for our feeble minds to fathom them, and it is impious as well as arrogant to make the attempt. Against nothing ought Christians to be more constantly and earnestly guarded, than the opinion that they

ought to be able to comprehend and justify what they believe on the authority of God.

The true ground on which to vindicate it is the explicit testimony of God in the Scripture. This is so clear, that no man can set it aside, we need not say, without wresting the Scriptures, but, we may assert, without being conscious of violence of interpretation. Our defence of this doctrine, then, should ever be, 'Thus saith the Lord.' This method of defence, which we are taught in this same Epistle, ch. 9:20, is not merely the only scriptural one, but it is the one that will have the greatest success. As long as a reason is alleged by the wisdom of man in support of the doctrine, so long, from the same source, an argument will be produced on the other side. But when the word of God is appealed to, and upon it all the stress of evidence rested, the Christian must submit. The writer knows from personal experience the effect of this method of teaching this doctrine.

'You cannot comprehend,' says Luther, 'how a just God can condemn those who are born in sin, and cannot help themselves, but must, by a necessity of their natural constitution, continue in sin, and remain children of wrath. The answer is, God is incomprehensible throughout; and therefore His justice, as well as His other attributes, must be incomprehensible. It is on this very ground that St Paul exclaims, '0 the depth of the riches and the knowledge of God! How unsearchable are His judgments, and His ways past finding out!' Now His judgments would not be past finding out, if we could always perceive them to be just.' "*

Rather than God being unjust to punish infants He would be unjust to pass them by. Let us rejoice in the justice of God who will "by no means clear the guilty" (Num. 14:18).

God's Mercy

It is just for God to cut off infants before they come to understanding. It also has mercy in it for Him to cut off such whom He has not chosen, (and

---

* Haldane, 225-26.

it is only non-elect infants He does cut off), not allowing them to add to their condemnation by a life of sin. If such non-elect infants had lived then they would be continually adding to their judgment every moment. They would be "treasuring up wrath in the day of wrath and revelation of the righteous judgment of God" (Rom 2:5). They would be adding to their treasure every day and accumulating wrath; the just anger and judgment of God against sin.

Any judgment of God is a fearful thing but nevertheless infants cut off in their infancy will find the judgment more tolerable than if they had lived many years in ungodliness. Although the judgment of Sodom will be terrible, those who have lived in sin under the light of the gospel will find the truth of Matthew 11:24, "But I say to you that it shall be more tolerable for the land of Sodom in that day of judgment than for you." As Christ taught,

> "And that servant who knew his master's will, and did not prepare himself or do according to his will, shall be beaten with many stripes. But he who did not know, yet committed things worthy of stripes, shall be beaten with few. For everyone to whom much is given, from him much will be required; and to whom much has been committed, of him they will ask the more" (Luke 12:47-48).

There is a difference in judgment. All sinners are not rewarded the same. All will be judged justly according to their works. Each shall receive according to what he has done. However, even those "who did not know, yet committed things worthy of stripes, shall be beaten," but "with few."

Sins of ignorance even in Old Testament times were not overlooked by God and had to be atoned for,

> "Speak to the children of Israel, saying: 'If a person sins unintentionally (ignorantly) against any of the commandments of the Lord in anything which ought not to be done, and does any of them, if the anointed priest sins, bringing guilt on the people, then let him offer to the Lord for his sin which he has sinned a young bull without blemish as a sin offering.' " (Lev. 4:2-3).

Thus we see that infants who die in infancy are justly punished for their sin but even then God has been merciful by taking them away from a more intolerable judgment; even many stripes.

GOD'S PURPOSES IN ALLOWING HIS ELECT TO CONTINUE FOR A PERIOD OF TIME IN A STATE OF NATURE BEFORE SAVING THEM

For the Glory of God's Grace and the Joy of His People

Sin is the black background that makes God's grace even more glorious and amazing in the same way that a black velvet background reveals the splendor and brightness of a precious diamond. If God saved an infant who had never consciously and purposely walked in sin much of the brilliance and glory of God's grace would not be seen. But when God allows an elect child of His to continue in sin even unto a fullness and then converts him the luster of free grace is seen.

This is illustrated for us in the story of the Prodigal Son. When his son returns the father gives the reason why they should feast and be merry, "For this my son was dead and is alive again, he was lost and is found" (Luke 15:24). The son's lost condition increased the joy that he was found more than if he had never gone to the far country and lived the life of a prodigal. This is also taught by Christ in the story of the lost sheep, "I say to you that likewise there will be more joy in heaven over one sinner who repents than over ninety-nine just persons who need no repentance" (Luke 15:7).

Many commentators have shown how God's love is magnified in Romans 5:6-10. In verse 6 it is said that our condition was "ungodly," that is breakers of the first table of the law. Just as, "They did not glorify Him as God neither were thankful" (Rom. 1:21), so we dishonored God and would not worship Him but, "worshipped and served the creature rather than the Creator." We are also described as "sinners" (verse 8), who had also transgressed the second table. But God's love is further heightened and glorified since it came to us "when we were enemies" (verse 10). But even our malice and hatred of God could not quench His love. O, how great is the love of God who loved us while we hated and rebelled against Him. "Herein is the love of God, not that we loved God but that He loved us" (1 John

4:19).

I think it could be easily shown that all God's gracious attributes; mercy, love, grace, patience, etc., are all magnified and exalted by God's allowing His elect to continue for a time in the state of nature. As the apostle says, "God has shut up all under unbelief that He might have mercy upon all." (Jew and Gentile). He shuts men up in unbelief for a time that He may have the more mercy on them.

Just as a physician shows his skill more in curing a deadly disease than in curing a lesser one so God shows His pardoning grace and mercy more in pardoning great and multiplied sins. This was the conviction of the Psalmist, "For your name's sake, O Lord, pardon my iniquity, for it is great" (Psa. 25:11). O Lord, he says, make your fame great and glorify your name by pardoning my great iniquity. Do it for your mercy and for your goodness sake (see verse 7).

As a Testimony to Others

God saves men who have the reputation of sinners before others to the advantage and help of the saints. Such salvation causes those saved to testify to God's mercy. What great blessing the churches received from Paul's conversion when they heard, "He who formerly persecuted us now preaches the faith which he once tried to destroy." And Paul wrote, "And they glorified God in me" (Gal. 1:23-24). By that very method God makes men fit instruments to take the gospel to men and women who are living in sin. Saved sinners are the only ones able to preach convincingly, lovingly and effectively to sinners. God has left this work of evangelism in our hands. Rather than God saving infants by some exceptional means or in a way unknown to us He saves through us. Knowing what a great motive our own salvation from sin would be God has left us the joy of bringing others to Him through the gospel. He gave the law by angels but God has left the preaching of the gospel solely to us. He knew what a great joy it would be for a father to win his child and for a wife to win her husband (see 1 Cor. 7:16).

This way of God's also gives hope to sinners when they see sinners like themselves converted. Paul saw that he was just such an example to those yet unsaved for since God saved him, the chief of sinners, others could take hope of a like salvation.

> "This is a faithful saying and worthy of all acceptance, that Christ Jesus came into the world to save sinners, of whom I am chief. However, for this reason I obtained mercy, that in me first Jesus Christ might show all longsuffering, as a pattern to those who are going to believe on Him for everlasting life" (1 Tim. 1:15-16).

To humble and strengthen His people when they remember their former sinful state and misery One of the things all God's people are told to remember is their life before their salvation "Wherefore remember that ye were sometimes Gentiles in the flesh" (Eph. 2:11). "Remember that you were a slave in Egypt and that the Lord your God brought you out" (Deut. 5:15). In Ezekiel 16:5-6 God reminds the nation of Israel what they were:

> "No eye pitied you, to do any of these things for you, to have compassion on you; but you were thrown out into the open field, when you yourself were loathed on the day you were born. And when I passed by you and saw you struggling in your own blood, I said to you in your blood, 'Live!' Yes, I said to you in your blood 'Live!'"

He then gives as a cause of their abominations, "You did not remember the days of your youth, when you were naked and bare, struggling in your blood" (Ezek. 16:22).

The remembrance of our former state will humble us, make us thankful and produce a return of love to our Lord and Savior. What a great motive it is to holiness and service.

> "For when you were slaves of sin, you were free in regard to righteousness. What fruit did you have then in the things of which you are now ashamed? For the end of those things is death. But now having been set free from sin, and having become slaves of God, you have your fruit to holiness, and the end, everlasting life. For the wages of sin is death, but the gift of God is eternal life in Christ Jesus our

Lord" (Rom. 6:20-23).

A man would not have these motives unless he had experienced the state of nature and sin and spent some time in them. Infants who die in infancy have no knowledge of these things and

> ". . . without knowledge, there is no remembrance; and without remembrance, there is no repentance; and without repentance, there is no remission or forgiveness."[*][†]

---

[*] John Welch (1570-1622).

[†] I acknowledge my indebtedness to Thomas Goodwin for much of what I have written above from his *Works*, Volume 6, Book 3.

44

Regeneration, Calling, and Faith

Many Paedobaptists seek to divorce regeneration from its fruits by a period of time. For instance, Professor Berkhof labors to prove that God generates the new life without employing "the word of scripture or the word of preaching as an instrument or means."[*] They do this so that they can claim infants may be regenerated but not be called by the gospel until years later or even never if they die in infancy. They want to make regeneration to be without any concurrent evidence. Since infants are not conscious and have no intelligent faith they desire to make regeneration in the subconscious with no conscious experience of conversion and excluding repentance and faith. Calvin wrote that infants "are baptized into future repentance and faith; for though these graces have not yet been formed in them, the seed of birth lies hid in them by the secret operation of the Spirit."[†]

This is a grave error. All the graces are formed in the regenerate person at regeneration. If this was not so the following verses would not be true. "Whoever has been born of God does not sin, for His seed remains in him; and he cannot sin, because he has been born of God" (1 John 3:9). "For whatever is born of God overcomes the world. And this is the victory that has overcome the world—our faith" (1 John 5:4). "We know that whoever is born of God does not sin; but he who has been born of God keeps himself, and the wicked one does not touch him" (1 John 5:18). These verses prove

---

[*] Berkhof, 474.
[†] Calvin, *Institutes*, IV, XVI:20.

that these graces are in the regenerate and not to be formed sometime in the future. The Paedobaptist is making regeneration to be far less than it is. It is nothing less than life from the dead, a new creation, a resurrection, a being born again. It is a radical transformation, a complete change. It cannot be hidden.

"The regenerate person cannot live in sin and be unconverted. And neither can he live any longer in neutral abstraction. He is immediately a member of the kingdom of God, he is spirit, and his action and behaviour must be consonant with the new citizenship. In the language of the apostle Paul, 'if any man be in Christ, he is a new creature; the old things have passed away, behold they have become new', 2 Cor. 5:17. There are numerous other considerations derived from the Scripture which confirm this great truth that regeneration is such a radical, pervasive, and efficacious transformation that it immediately registers itself in the conscious activity of a person concerned in the exercises of faith and repentance and new obedience. Far too frequently the conception entertained of conversion is so superficial and beggarly that it completely fails to take account of the momentous change of which conversion is the fruit. And the whole notion of what is involved in the application of redemption becomes so attenuated that it has little or no resemblance to that which the gospel teaches. Regeneration is at the basis of all change in heart and life. It is a stupendous change because it is God's recreative act. A cheap and tawdry evangelism has tended to rob the gospel which it proclaims of that invincible power which is the glory of the gospel of sovereign grace. May the church come to think and live again in terms of the gospel which is the power of God unto salvation."[*]

Since men are dead in sin regeneration logically comes first. However, calling and faith come with regeneration and they come immediately. They are concomitant, they occur along with and at the same time as regeneration. There is no period of delay. There is no such thing as a regenerate unbeliever

---

[*] Murray, *Redemption Accomplished and Applied*, 104-05.

or an unrepentant son. Professor Berkhof opposes this by teaching that regeneration has two parts. The first part he calls the masculine begetting and the second stage he likens to the feminine giving birth to children.

Between these two stages he implies there is an indeterminate period of time.[*]

It is true, as he says, "that the verb *gennao* does not always refer to the masculine begetting, but may also denote the feminine giving birth to children."[†] In fact, this one verb is used for both the begetting of children and bearing children. The Greek does not make a distinction. One Greek word is not used for begetting and another Greek word for giving birth. *Gennao* is used for both actions. It is used to refer to women giving birth in such passages as Luke 1:13, 57; 23:29; John 16:21; Galatians 4:24 and of men begetting children in Matthew 1:2-16. It is also used in referring to Christ as the "only begotten." This begetting is not an event in time. This same Greek word is also used for the act of God in imparting life or being born of God; John 3:3, 5, 7; 1 John 2:29; 3:9; 4:7; 5:1, 4, 18. And it is used in reference to begetting children by the gospel, 1 Corinthians 4:15; Philemon 10. Thus the new birth is not in two stages.

We see that scripturally there are not two parts of regeneration separated by a period of time as there is nine months between human begetting and the bearing of children. Regeneration is an "instantaneous change from spiritual death to spiritual life."[‡]

Thus, when 1 Peter 1:23 speaks of believers as "being born again, not of corruptible seed, but of incorruptible, by the Word of God, which liveth and abideth forever," he is teaching that regeneration, the new birth, is through the Word of God. None are regenerated apart from the Word. True, the new birth is by the Spirit but His instrument or weapon is the Word. For it is the Word of God which is the sword of the Spirit. No child is regenerate until begotten by the Word.

Calvin answering Servetus, one of the Anabaptists, in regard to this says,

---

[*] See his *Systematic Theology*, 475.

[†] *Ibid.*

[‡] Hodge, Volume 3, 5.

"I must again repeat, what I have so often remarked, that the doctrine of the Gospel is the incorruptible seed to regenerate those who are capable of understanding it but that where, by reason of age, there is not yet any capacity of learning, God has his different degrees of regenerating those whom He has adopted."[*]

Degrees of regeneration are not found anywhere in the scriptures. There is either death or life, no in between. Calvin let infant baptism push him into such an untenable position and so to err on a most fundamental doctrine, the doctrine of regeneration.

---

[*] Calvin, Book 5, Chapter 16, paragraph 31, subparagraph 16.

45

Regeneration, Faith, and the Holy Spirit

The Paedobaptist, in regard to the infants of believers, severs regeneration and faith. For instance, Bannerman wrote of infant baptism as "a prospective seal in connection with the faith which he has not at the moment, but which he may have afterwards."[*]

This would mean that this regenerate infant would not have received the Holy Spirit since the Spirit is received by faith. The purpose of the crucifixion was "that we might receive the promise of the Spirit through faith" (Gal. 3:14). The receiving of the Spirit by the Gentiles was on condition of faith. Peter said,

> "... God chose among us, that by my mouth the Gentiles should hear the word of the gospel and believe. So God, who knows the heart, acknowledged them, by giving them the Holy Spirit just as He did us" (Acts 15:7-8).

How can there be regenerate infants without them receiving the Spirit? This is utterly impossible! "If anyone does not have the Spirit of Christ, he is not His" (Rom. 8:9). Sensual and having not the Spirit are joined together. "Sensual persons ... not having the Spirit" (Jude 19). All the regenerate have the Spirit without exception. All without the Spirit are unregenerate.

---

[*] Bannerman, *The Church of Christ*, 116.

46

Faith and Union With Christ

The natural man is separated from Christ and indeed, alienated from Christ. On the other hand believers receive all Christ's benefits by being "in Him." Apart from Him they are dead but joined to Him they receive life and all that means even as a branch partakes of the sap and life of the tree to which it is vitally joined. To have Christ is to have life. "He that has the Son has life" (1 John 5:12). "In Him was life" (John 1:4) and as Hendricksen writes, "This life . . . is the cause, source, or principle of all life, physical as well as spiritual."[*]

The union of the members of the body with the head is the ground of their life. They partake of the life of the head. This relation between Christ and His brethren, between the teacher and His disciples, between the bridegroom and His wife is entered into by faith. Faith is the true Christian's part whereby he is actively engaged in coming into this relationship with Christ. This uniting act is by faith which we call union with Christ. This union is often represented in the scriptures by the marriage bond. The bride accepts the bridegroom to take him for her husband and to give herself to him, renouncing all others. Without this act there is no union. Faith is the necessary act for union on the part of the true disciple.

> "(Faith) is that by which the soul, which before was separate and
> alienated from Christ, unites itself to him, or ceases to be any longer
> in that state of alienation, and comes into that fore-mentioned union

---

[*] Hendricksen, *John*, 72.

or relation to him; or, to use the scripture phrase, it is that by which the soul comes to Christ, and receives him: this is evident by the Scriptures using these very expressions to signify faith: 'He who comes to me shall never hunger, and he who believes in me shall never thirst . . . All that the Father gives me will come to me . . . And this is the will of him who sent me, that everyone who sees the son and believes in him may have everlasting life' John 6:35,37,40).

God does not give those that believe an union with or an interest in the Saviour as a reward for faith, but only because faith is the souls active uniting with Christ, or is itself the very act of union, on their part. God sees that in order to an union being established between two intelligent active beings or persons, so as they should be looked upon as one, there should be the mutual act of both, that each should receive other, as actively joining themselves one to another."*

Without faith there is no union. Without union there can be no receiving of Christ's benefits. Without union there is no justification since faith precedes justification. If that was not so John 3:18 that says, "He that believes not is condemned already," would be false. Further, as the footnote to Edwards that is given on page 626 says,

"From the premise it follows, that the generally received theological maxim is perfectly just and plain, vis., that justification and regeneration are simultaneous—union is the immediate cause of both."

The conclusion from the above is that all infants are not united to Christ because they are without faith. This being so they have no life and are yet dead in sin. Without union they are not justified or regenerated since they occur simultaneously.

As Professor John Murray says, "It should not surprise us that the beginning of salvation in actual possession should be in union with Christ."[†] Again,

---

* Edwards, 1:625-26.
† Murray, 163.

"Union with Christ is the central truth of the whole doctrine of salvation . . . It is adoption into the family of God as sons and daughters of the Lord God Almighty that accords to the people of God the apex of blessing and privilege. But we cannot think of adoption apart from union with Christ."[*]

In other words without union with Christ none are children of God. Thus all infants are children of the evil one. It is in union with Christ that God's people are created. "We are his workmanship created in Christ Jesus" (Eph. 2:10). Effectual calling, that always results in a response, is a call "into the fellowship of His son, Jesus Christ our Lord" (1 Cor. 1:9).

"An effectual call, however, must carry along with it the appropriate response on the part of the person called. It is God who calls but it is not God who answers the call; it is the person to whom the call is addressed. And this response must enlist the exercise of the heart and mind and will of the person concerned."[†]

A call without a response is not an effectual call. Thus since no infants have responded none have been effectually called and united to Christ. All Paedobaptists acknowledge that infants do not have faith. Calvin said, infants "are baptized into future repentance and faith."[‡]

Yet union with Christ is only by faith. Paul prays that, "Christ may dwell in your hearts by faith" (Eph. 3:17). After writing that, "You have been saved by faith," Paul continues to say, "we are . . . created in Christ Jesus" (Eph. 2:8, 10). Only believers will "be found in Him" at that great day. "In Christ" is the phrase that everywhere speaks of union. This union is illustrated and compared to the union of the branches to the vine, to the relation of stones in a building to the corner stone, to the union that exists between Adam and his posterity, to the union of man and wife, to the relation of members to the head of the body and even to the union of the trinity. This is a great mystery.

---

[*] *Ibid.*, 170.
[†] *Ibid.*, 95.
[‡] Calvin, 4:16,20.

It is the mystery of the life of faith. Without faith there is no union with Christ. How can anyone be regenerated but not "in Christ"? How can it be that an infant can be regenerated and not be in union with Christ? Impossible!

The Word of God also links justification with union with Christ and with faith. It is in Christ we are justified. "There is therefore now no condemnation to them which are in Christ Jesus . . ." (Rom. 8:1). And justification is by faith. "Therefore we conclude that a man is justified by faith without the deeds of the law" (Rom. 3:28). What about adoption? Dr. Murray writes, "It is never separable from justification and regeneration.""

Also, *calling* is intimately related to regeneration. Calling is from death to life. "(He) called you out of darkness into his marvelous light" (1 Pet. 2:9. Professor Berkhof said,

> "Logically, the external call in the preaching of the Word, (except in the case of children) generally precedes or coincides with the operation of the Holy Spirit, by which the new life is produced in the soul of man."[†]

It is significant that he makes infants an exception. However, I overlook this now. The main point is that calling which addresses itself to the consciousness is given as closely allied to regeneration. In Romans 8:30, "Moreover, whom He predestined, these He also called; whom He called, these He also justified; and whom He justified, these He also glorified." It seems to be that calling is the initial act in the application of redemption.

All the above proves that all the applications of redemption go together. They cannot be divorced. Regenerated unbelievers, children of God uncalled, regenerate not in Christ, etc. would be monstrosities. There are no such beings. All regenerate are believers. All regenerate have been called by the gospel. All regenerate are united to Christ. All have been justified by faith. Obviously, this means that no infants are regenerate.

---

[*] Murray, 132.
[†] Berkof, 471.

47

Conversion and Repentance

Another great doctrinal term is *conversion*. Conversion occurs after regeneration and calling. Conversion can be described as repentance and faith. Professor Berkhof writes that "*metanoia* is the most common word for conversion in the New Testament."[*] This word is translated repentance in the English Bible. It is translated as repentance everywhere in the KJV. Repentance is a conscious experience. Professor Berkhof continues,

> "while maintaining that the word (metanoia) denotes primarily a change of mind, we should not lose sight of the fact that its meaning is not limited to the intellectual, theoretical consciousness but also includes the moral consciousness, the conscience . . . it includes a conscious opposition to the former condition. This is an essential element in it, and therefore deserves careful attention . . . The converted person becomes conscious of his ignorance and error, his willfulness and folly. His conversion includes both faith and repentance."[†]

> "The sinner consciously forsakes the old sinful life and turns to a life in communion with and devoted to God."[‡]

---

[*] *Ibid.*, 480.
[†] *Ibid.*, 481.
[‡] *Ibid.*, 485.

"1. God the author of conversion. 2. Man co-operates in conversion. But though God only is the author of conversion, it is of great importance to stress the fact, over against a false passivity, that there is also a certain co-operation of man in conversion. That man is active in conversion is quite evident from such passages as Isa. 55:7, Jer. 18:11, Ezek. 18:23, 32, 33:11, Acts 2:38, 17:30.'"

Here is a serious problem for the Paedobaptist. Since conversion is a conscious experience how can an unconscious infant be converted? Since conversion includes both faith and repentance how can infants be converted, when "they are not yet psychologically capable of such?" [†] How do Paedobaptists answer these questions? Most do not. Professor Berkhof seeks to and writes,

"The Bible speaks in absolute terms of the necessity of regeneration; not so the necessity of conversion. The passage that comes nearest to an absolute declaration is found in Matt. 18:3, 'Assuredly, I say to you, unless you are converted and become as little children, you will by no means enter the kingdom of heaven.' But even in this case one might insist that this refers only to the persons addressed. The expressed or implied exhortations to turn about, found in scripture, come only to those to whom they are addressed and do not necessarily mean that every one must pass through a conscious conversion, in order to be saved."[‡]

These statements are quite astonishing. Matthew 18:3 does not come near to an absolute declaration of the necessity of conversion; it is an absolute declaration of the necessity of conversion. To say that Christ's words, "unless you are converted you will by no means enter the kingdom of heaven," do not necessarily mean that everyone must pass through a conscious conversion in order to be saved seem to be against the obvious meaning since Dr. Berkhof has emphasized that conversion is a conscious

---

[*] *Ibid.*, 490.

[†] Murray, 90.

[‡] Berkhof, 490.

experience. Notice Christ's emphasis, "Assuredly . . . by no means." If what is spoken or preached is only valid to the ones addressed what is valid for us in the Bible? This effectively does away with Christ's statement, "you must be born again," with Peter's exhortation, "repent and be baptized" and Paul's promise, "Therefore let it be known to you, brethren, that through this Man is preached to you the forgiveness of sins; and by Him everyone who believes is justified from all things from which you could not be justified by the law of Moses" (Acts 13:38-39), if they "are only to those who are addressed."

We are left with little scripture that applies to us if we accept Professor Berkhof's argument. Why does he use this argument? Because "those who die in infancy . . . cannot very well experience conversion."* His argument here is to make exceptions so that infants may be considered saved without conversion and thus affirm that infant baptism is valid.

---

* *Ibid.*, 491.

Part 8

THE ILL EFFECTS OF INFANT BAPTISM

48

It Opposes the Doctrines of Grace

I realize this is a serious charge. I made a similar statement in the introduction and have tried to verify it throughout my writing. I think I have but the reader will judge. Sometimes the Paedobaptist writers contradict themselves because their doctrinal statements in regard to salvation differ with their statements on infant baptism. I have documented this in regard to a number of writers. In other cases the consequences of infant baptism in regard to doctrines related to salvation are overlooked. I will sum it all up with a few of the issues that I have mentioned.

(1.) The Scriptures teach that no one is saved without repentance and faith. The advocates of infant baptism believe infants are saved without repentance and faith.

(2.) The Scriptures teach that there is only one way of salvation. The advocates of infant baptism believe infants are saved in a different way to adults.

(3.) The Scriptures teach that all are born in sin and under the covenant of works. The advocates of infant baptism teach that infants are born in the Covenant of Grace.

(4.) The Scriptures teach that all in the Covenant of Grace persevere and are saved. The advocates of infant baptism say that some who are in the Covenant of Grace may "contract out" and become covenant breakers and be eternally lost.

(5.) The Scriptures teach that it is through the knowledge of the truth people are saved. The advocates of infant baptism believe that infants are saved without the knowledge of the truth.

(6.) The Scriptures teach that regeneration manifests itself immediately. The advocates of infant baptism believe that infants are regenerate although they do not manifest it.

(7.) The Scriptures teach that "as many as were ordained to eternal life believed." The advocates of infant baptism believe that all believers' infants are ordained to eternal life although many die without believing.

(8.) The Scriptures teach that all who enter the Covenant of Grace enter freely and willingly of their choice. The advocates of infant baptism believe that infants enter it without their choice.

(9.) The Scriptures teach that a participation in Christ is only by faith. The advocates of infant baptism believe infants participate in Christ apart from faith.

(10.) The Scriptures teach that all are born under the law. The advocates of infant baptism teach infants are born under grace.

(11.) The Scriptures teach that only believers belong to the church. The advocates of infant baptism say that believers and their children belong to the church.

(12.) The Scriptures teach that "unless you are converted . . . you will by no means enter the kingdom of heaven." Some advocates of infant baptism say there is not a necessity for conversion.

(13.) The Scriptures teach that all are saved by effectual calling. The advocates of infant baptism believe infants are saved although not called.

(14.) The Scriptures teach that the church grows through evangelization. The advocates of infant baptism believe it grows through physical generation.

(15.) The Scriptures teach that a spiritual birth is necessary to enter God's kingdom. The advocates of infant baptism believe believers' infants enter it through physical birth.

(16.) The Scriptures teach God imputes righteousness to believers. The advocates of infant baptism believe that believers' children are born holy and so righteous.

(17.) The Scriptures teach that God's election is of individuals. The advocates of infant baptism believe God elects families and family lines to a thousand generations.

(18.) The Scriptures teach that being born the children of God is "not of blood." The advocates of infant baptism say it is of blood.

49

It Brings the Unregenerate Into the Church

The ground for infant baptism was given by Dr. A. A. Hodge,

> "The children of all such persons as, on the ground of their own credible profession of faith, are received as members of the visible Church are to be baptized as members of the visible Church, because, presumptively, heirs of the blessings of the Covenant of Grace. The divinely appointed and guaranteed presumption, is, if the parents, then the children. This is not an invariable law binding God, but it is a prevailingly probable law, basing the authorized and rational recognition and treatment of such children by the Church as heirs of the promises."[*]

He said it is by divine appointment which is what is in dispute between us. He also said it was a "guaranteed presumption." This is a bit of double talk. Who guaranteed it? He continued,

> "This presumption is rendered exceedingly probable by the fundamental constitution of humanity as a self-propagative race . . . and thus the character and destiny of families, races and nations have always been predetermined by the deeds and experiences of their ancestors."

This presumption is not borne out by the Old Testament history. The

---

[*] A. Hodge, *Evangelical Theology*, 329.

presumption is that the children of the faithful will be faithful children, therefore they should be baptized. This is hardly true. It is true that Abraham had an Isaac but he also had an Ishmael. Edwards writes of his posterity,

> "Yes, and the far greater part even of Abraham's posterity, the children of Ishmael, Ziman, Joksham, Medan, Midian, Ishbak, and Shuah, and Esau, soon forgot the true God, and fell off to heathenism."[*]

Likewise, Isaac had a Jacob but he also had an Esau. Fifty per cent is hardly considered an "exceedingly probable" outcome. And as we continue in history the percentage of faithful children is even less. Jacob had twelve sons. Joseph was faithful. The others are doubtful. David had many children. Solomon seems to have been a believer but of the rest we have no evidence of faith. Absalom was an ungodly son as was Amnon and Adonijah. Many godly kings had ungodly sons. As to the priests; Aaron's two sons Nadab and Abihu were ungodly men. Eli's two sons were ungodly. Samuel's two sons were ungodly (1 Sam. 8:1-4). None of the great early leaders of Israel were replaced by their sons; such as Moses, Joshua, Gideon, Barak, Samson, Jeptha and Samuel. As to the godly kings; Solomon's son Rehoboam was an ungodly man. Jehosaphat's son Jehoram was ungodly. Jotham's son Ahaz was ungodly. Manasseh's son Amon was an ungodly man. Josiah's son Jehoahaz was ungodly. We can say that the children of the faithful usually were not faithful children. Besides this, surely we should not baptize on presumption or probability even if there was such, which there is not. Therefore, if the children of believers are baptized, many unregenerate will be brought into the church. We must do nothing that will knowingly bring the unsaved into the church. We should seek to have local churches made up only of believers.

Booth objects by saying,

> "Baptists have maintained their well-intentioned belief in, and desire

---

[*] Edwards, 1:163.

for, a fully regenerate church membership. We all must abhor a nominal church. Nevertheless, as admirable as the desire may be, such an idyllic situation does not exist now, nor do we see it in Scripture. The invisible church consists of the spiritually faithful, who 'abide' in Christ (John 15). Nevertheless, the members of the visible church are marked out by baptism and actual membership in a local church. Regeneration and faith are spiritual and invisible realities, and therefore, as John Murray says, 'No man or organization of men is able infallibly to determine who are regenerate and who are not.'"*

Mr. Booth's quote of Dr. Murray's is on page 34 of Murray's *Christian Baptism*. However, Mr. Booth failed to quote Dr. Murray on page 37 where he wrote, "Union with Christ and the faith through which that union is effected, though in themselves invisible and spiritual facts, are, nevertheless, realities which find expression in what is observable." This changes the thrust of Mr. Booth's previous quotation of Dr. Murray's.

It is true as John Murray says that men are unable to infallibly determine who are regenerate but that does not mean that the attempt should not be made to discern if a person is regenerate before being accepted into church membership. A church should be made up of those who have a common faith in Christ and living faith will evidence itself. Shouldn't everyone be examined before being admitted into the visible church concerning this faith? Undoubtedly! Entrance into the church should be on a credible profession. Dr. Murray wrote,

> "Mere lip confession, contradicted by other evidence either in the realm of faith or conduct, could not be accepted for entrance into or continuance in the fellowship of the saints. We may, therefore define the confession as an intelligent and consistent profession of faith in Christ and of obedience to him. It is obvious that such confession falls within the orbit in which human discrimination and judgment may be exercised. It is not the prerogative of man to search the heart

---

* Booth, 88.

of another. But it is the prerogative of man to judge in reference to public confession or profession. This, therefore, is the criterion in accord with which human administration is exercised. And what needs to be emphasised here is that this is so by divine institution. It is not the expedient of proven experience. And it is not simply a necessity arising from the limitations inherent in human nature. It is by divine institution that the church, as a visible entity, administered by men in accordance with Christ's appointment, must admit to its fellowship those who make a credible profession of faith in Christ and promise of obedience to him."[*]

Wouldn't this exclude all infants? R. R. Booth says,

"The attempt to know people's hearts has led to many excesses in the search and demand for evidence of true conversion. As a Baptist minister, I was always troubled when called on to judge the genuineness of someone's 'conversion experience.' It was all so subjective on the part of the convert, as well as on the part of those who were evaluating the experience."[†]

But wouldn't Mr. Booth if he is a careful and prudent Paedobaptist pastor have to judge whether the parents of the children presented for baptism are believers? A faithful man will not turn away from this difficult but necessary task of judging the genuineness of people's profession. Be that as it may we are not to judge "conversion experiences" or to "attempt to know people's hearts" but we are to judge whether a person is a believer by his profession and walk. Mr. Booth is relieved that as a Baptist converted to the Paedobaptist position he no longer needs to judge whether people are genuine believers to enter into the church. However, if there are conversions or professed conversions in his church judgment will have to be made. It is only in dead churches that have no conversions that judgment does not have to be made. As Christ taught, a tree is known by its fruit so that Christians

---

[*] Murray, 39.
[†] Booth, 89.

can be discerned (although admittedly not infallibly.) Unconverted persons are not entitled to church membership. They do, however, enter and obtain membership through human fallibility and sometimes carelessness. Surely this is a blight and needs to be diligently guarded against and prayed over.

Often Paedobaptist churches do not adequately screen those applying for church membership. A. A. Hodge wrote,

> "A 'credible profession' does not mean a profession of faith which compels credence, or which convinces the observer that it is genuine: but it is simply the opposite of incredible, it is a confession that can be believed."[*]

Such judging will admit everyone and anyone unless the profession is "incredible." If the profession doesn't compel credence and doesn't convince the one who hears the profession but the professor is still received into the church many false professors will enter the church. In the same quotation, A. A. Hodge adds that the person seeking admission to ordinances of the church "does not need to prove his way in."

We have only one account of judging professions to receive baptism. This is the account of John the Baptist refusing multitudes that came out to be baptized by him, Luke 3:7-14. They had not proved their profession by their deeds or as they are called in Luke 3:8, "fruits worthy of repentance." Doubtless this account is given to be followed.

I work among tribal people who are uneducated and illiterate. A few weeks ago I sat in on an examination for baptism. After a young woman gave her profession of faith one of the church leaders asked her unsaved husband, who was present, whether he had seen a change in his wife's behavior. Another young man, after he told of his conversion, was asked who he had told about his conversion. Both these questions were wise questions to determine if there were "fruits worthy of repentance." Although the church leaders are uneducated by our standards they have been taught by the Lord. They realize the great importance of discerning "between the righteous and

---

[*] A. Hodge, 329.

the wicked" (Mal. 3:18).

If the examination for church membership is allowing unregenerate into the church it is an inadequate examination. It is not true that "the criteria we are given in scripture for adult membership in the visible church, whether in the Old Testament or the New, are such that anyone, at least for a time, may meet them outwardly."* Can anyone "bear fruits worthy of repentance"? Listen as Jonathan Edwards speaks of scriptural judging:

> "When I speak, in the question, of being godly or gracious in the eye of a christian judgment, by christian judgment I intend something further than a kind of mere negative charity, implying that we forbear to censure and condemn a man, because we do not know but that he may be godly, and therefore forbear to proceed on the foot of such a censure of judgment in our treatment of him: as we would kindly entertain a stranger, not knowing but in so doing we entertain an angel or precious saint of God. But I mean a positive judgment, founded on some positive appearance, or visibly, some outward manifestations that ordinarily render the thing probable. There is a difference between suspending our judgment, or forbearing to condemn, or having some hope that possibly the thing may be so, and so hoping the best; and a positive judgment in favour of a person. For having some hope, only implies that a man is not in utter despair of a thing, though his prevailing opinion may be otherwise, or he may suspend his opinion. Though we cannot know a man believes that Jesus is the Messiah, yet we expect some positive manifestation or visibility of it, to be a ground of our charitable judgment: so I suppose the case is here."†

Since "a fully regenerate church membership does not exist now nor do we see it in scripture" (Booth) does this mean we should not seek it? Not at all. This is the ideal that we should strive for. It is true that we do not live without sin. We will not come up to the ideal of living without sin in this world. Should we therefore give up the struggle? In the same way all diligence

---

* Booth, 88.
† Edwards, 1:345.

should be used to seek to have pure churches.

It seems quite probable that some local churches have attained to a fully regenerate membership. We have known some small assemblies where all the members evidenced the new birth and persevered in the faith. Admittedly these were small churches where everyone was personally well known to one another. But to say that a fully regenerate church membership does not exist now seems to be a statement that would be difficult, if not impossible, to prove. Does Mr. Booth know as a fact that there are no churches throughout the world with a fully regenerate membership?

However, that a fully regenerate church membership is to be sought and is the norm I believe is attested by the word. The apostles judged that the churches they wrote to were made up of the regenerate. Paul wrote to the Philippian church, "Being confident of this very thing that He who has begun a good work in you will complete it . . . it is right to think this of you all" (Phil. 1:6-7). John judged that the ones he wrote to were regenerate, "I write to you little children because your sins are forgiven . . . to you fathers because you have known Him who is from the beginning . . . to you young men because you have overcome the wicked" (1 John 3:12-13). Peter wrote, "You have purified your souls in obeying the truth" (1 Pet. 1:22). Paul wrote to the Thessalonian Church, "Knowing beloved brethren your election of God" (1 Thess. 1:4). He wrote to the Hebrews, after warning them about some people who fell away, "But beloved, we are confident of better things concerning you, yes, things that accompany salvation" (Heb. 6:9). I have chosen just a few verses out of scores that could be quoted. In all the salutations the churches are greeted as gracious persons.

I do not mean that there were no counterfeit Christians, false professors or hypocrites among the churches. There were but they "crept in unnoticed" (Jude 4), or were "secretly brought in" (Gal. 2:4). Such were not accepted by the saints of the New Testament churches as members with them but they came in "secretly" or "crept in." When they entered they were thought to be genuine believers. Our difference isn't over whether some hypocrites were in the churches. I acknowledge this. Our difference is over whether such was allowed by the apostles and whether the churches were so constituted by them. The verses I have written above defend my statement that the churches under the apostles' authority according to the guidance of the Holy Spirit were constituted of true believers and that anything else was an anomaly, a deviation from the rule. The proper qualification was a profession of faith evidenced by a new life. It is true as Mr. Booth wrote of Baptists that this is our "belief in and desire for a fully regenerate church membership."

If the churches were ordinarily made up of believers and unbelievers why did the apostles make no distinction and write as the above verses indicate?

"Why do they never direct their speech to the unconverted members of churches, in particular, in a manner tending to awaken them, and make them sensible of the miserable condition they were in, and press them to seek the converting grace of God? It is to be considered, that the apostle Paul was very particularly acquainted with the circumstances of most of those churches to whom he wrote; for he had been among them, was their spiritual father, had been the instrument of gathering and founding those churches, and they had received all their instructions and directions relating to Christianity and their soul-concerns from him; nor can it be questioned but that many of them had opened the case of their souls to him. And if he was sensible, that there was a number among them who made no pretensions to a regenerate state, and that none had reason to judge them to be in such a state, he knew that the sin of such—who lived in the rejection of a Saviour, even in the very house of God, in the midst of gospel-light, and in violation of the most sacred vows—was peculiarly aggravated, and their guilt and state peculiarly dreadful. Why should he therefore never particularly and distinctly point his addresses to such, applying himself to them in much compassion to their souls, and putting them in mind of their awful circumstances? But instead of this, we observe him continually lumping all together, and indifferently addressing the whole body, as if they were all in happy circumstances, expressing his charity for them all, and congratulating them all in their glorious and eternal privilege. Instead of speaking to them in such a manner as should be a tendency to alarm them with a sense of danger, we see him, on the contrary, calling on all without distinction to rejoice."[*]

That a fully regenerate church is the ideal to be sought is taught by the scriptures describing the glory of the New Covenant church when "all your people shall be righteous" (Isa. 60:21a). God says it is then that the church will be "for the display of my splendor" (60:21b). It is when Zion clothes herself with strength and puts on her garments of splendor that "the uncircumcised and defiled will not enter again" (Isa. 52:1). This is the great promise to the New Testament Church "all your sons will be taught by the Lord" that the Lord quoted in John 6:45 from Isaiah 54:13 and applied it to gospel grace. When it is so then the church is in peace and unity as the next phrase tells us, "Great shall be the peace of thy children." Surely we should seek such blessing.

A "mixed multitude" came out of Egypt with the Israelites (Exod. 12:38). These people soon proved to be a stumbling block. "The mixed multitude that was among them fell a lusting" (Num. 11:4). Matthew Henry called them, "the scabbed sheep that infected the flock, the leaven that leavened the whole lump," and so it proved to be. The children of Israel were drawn into the same sin. They said, "Who shall give us flesh to eat?" The people of Israel learned the way of these discontented and evil people. How often this happens in churches. A few unregenerate can divide and defile a whole church.

Again, in Nehemiah 13:3 we hear of a "mixed multitude." This mixed multitude was made up of Ammonites and Moabites who were the enemies of Israel. God had commanded that "an Ammonite or Moabite shall not enter the congregation of the Lord" (Deut. 23:3). The Israelites had disobeyed this command. The unconverted should not be allowed to enter the congregation of the Lord.

When infants are baptized and brought into the church God's directive is ignored to the church's harm. How much harm did Tobiah the Ammonite try to do? Although he was a great enemy to God's people the high priest, Eliashib, did much evil by "preparing him a chamber in the courts of the

---

[*] Edwards, 1:456.

house of God." He was allied to Tobiah by marriage. We read in Nehemiah 6:18 that both Tobiah and his son had married daughters of Israel. Doesn't this often happen?

In many Paedobaptist churches there is much intermarrying. Since all the infants of these marriages are baptized and brought into the church unconverted church members are multiplied. Also, because of family loyalties these unconverted people have much influence and are often voted into office. This is a fact. Although such men have no spiritual life and adversely effect and even cripple the church they are in good standing among the churches because of their attendance. Since their mothers and fathers, sisters, brothers, uncles, aunts, brothers-in-law and sisters-in-law, etc. also belong to the assembly discipline is unimaginable. R. R. Booth writes,

> "Again, every local church faces the potential problem of having baptized members, regardless of their age when baptized, who never manifest the fruit of repentance. That's why, in addition to the formative discipline of instruction from the Word of God, the church must also perform its duty of corrective discipline from the Word, even to the point of excommunication."[*]

This is not realistic. Most Paedobaptist churches never excommunicate for the above reasons. It is extremely hard to put out unregenerate church members. Most Paedobaptist churches would agree with the Directory of Worship, Chapter 10, section 1,

> "If they be free from scandal, appear sober and steady, and to have sufficient knowledge to discern the Lord's body (they are to be acknowledged as members in good standing) they ought to be informed it is their duty and their privilege to come to the Lord's Supper."[†]

Most churches would only require such a negative righteousness. They

---

[*] Booth, 158.
[†] Words in parentheses are mine.

would not deal with them if they did not "manifest the fruit of repentance." It is true that unregenerate enter Baptist churches too, but the numbers are usually far less because manifesting the fruit of repentance is a qualification for baptism with good Baptist churches even as it was for John the Baptist who preached, "Produce fruit in keeping with repentance" and required it as a condition of baptism. As John Reisinger wrote,

> "(Paedobaptism) allows a congregation to deliberately and consciously include both believers and known unbelievers in its membership. Baptist churches may have unregenerate people as members, but it is never with a conscious knowledge and consent. Charles Hodge, in his section trying to prove infant baptism, argues that it is not even God's purpose to have only regenerate members in the so called 'visible' church:

> > 'Second Proposition. The Visible Church does not consist exclusively of the Regenerate. It is no less clearly revealed that it is not the purpose of God that the visible Church on earth consist exclusively of true believers . . .' Chas. Hodge, Systematic Theology, Vol. 3, p. 548.

> A false profession of faith and a non-profession of faith are two different things. Accepting a hypocrite (only because we cannot see his heart) who has made a false confession of faith is a totally different matter than knowingly saying unbelievers may be church members. The Baptist concept of 'visible/invisible' church is radically different than a Paedobaptist's view. The Church as 'believers only' and the church as 'believers and their children' are two totally different concepts that have far-reaching consequences. A Covenant Theology concept of the Church is absolutely essential to the practice of infant baptism."[*]

If there is no profession of faith and no manifestation of repentance required to gain admittance into a church, as in the case of infants who are

---

[*] Reisinger, 66.

baptized, unconverted church members will, of course, be multiplied. Through the chink of infant baptism the unregenerate will pour into the churches. With such a chink it is impossible to even approach a pure church.

Professor David Engelsma, a Paedobaptist of the Protestant Reformed Church wrote,

> "One of the strongest objections of the Baptists against infant baptism is that it fills the church with young people, and finally with adults, who are manifestly unspiritual, worldly, and immoral. Nor can it be denied that some Reformed churches expose the truth of the covenant to this charge by their tolerance of the ungodliness of the young people and by their refusal to discipline even the most blatant transgressors among them. All are presumed to be regenerate and saved. The result of this presumption is the death of the church as the carnal, profane seed come to dominate the church, finally driving the spiritual children out. These churches do not take election seriously. Not all the children are included in the covenant and church of God, but the elect only. The elect manifest themselves by holiness of life. Those who are unholy must be disciplined both by sharp preaching and by church censure."[*]

However, this does not plug the chink.

A pertinent portion concerning only true saints being added to the church is 1 Corinthians 3:10-15.

> "According to the grace of God which was given to me, as a wise master builder I have laid the foundation, and another builds on it. But let each one take heed how he builds on it. For no other foundation can anyone lay than that which is laid, which is Jesus Christ. Now if anyone builds on this foundation with gold, silver, precious stones, wood, hay, straw, each one's work will become manifest; for the Day will declare it, because it will be revealed by fire; and the fire will test each one's work, of what sort it is. If anyone's work which he has built on it endures, he will receive a reward. If

---

[*] Engelsma, *The Covenant of God and the Children of Believers*, 22.

anyone's work is burned, he will suffer loss; but he himself will be saved, yet so as through fire."

Paul defines the ones who build on the one foundation, which is Jesus Christ, in verse 9, "we are God's fellow workers," that is Paul himself, Apollos, other fellow laborers, and those church builders who would follow them. The materials of the building are given in verse 12, "gold, silver, precious stones, wood, hay and straw." What do these materials signify? Most commentators understand the materials to signify doctrine. For instance Hodge, "In consistency with the context: gold, silver and precious stones can only mean truth; and wood hay and stubble, error," on 1 Corinthians 3:12-13.

However, I believe the building materials are not doctrine but people. I will give four reasons why I believe this is the proper meaning.

The Context

In verse 9 Paul wrote, "You are God's building." The Corinthians were the building built on the foundation. Then immediately following this portion Paul wrote, "You (plural) are the temple of God" (verse 16). The building, the temple of God, is built of people.

The Usual Scriptural Representation

The New Testament represents the church as a building made up of individual saints or believers. The stones are living stones, people with the life of God indwelling them. As Paul wrote, "the Spirit of God dwells in you" (verse 16). "You are fellow citizens with the saints and members of the household of God . . . being built together for a habitation of God in the Spirit" (Eph. 2:19-22). "You also, as living stones, are being built up a spiritual house . . ." (1 Pet. 2:5).

The Saints are So Pictured

True saints are represented in scripture as stones, "living stones," (1 Pet. 2:5), precious jewels (stones) "on the day that I make them my jewels" (Mal. 3:17), and gold, "sons of Zion, comparable to fine gold" (Lam. 4:2). The foundation of the building rather than the building itself seems to be doctrine. Paul laid the foundation, even Jesus Christ, by preaching the gospel.

The Scriptures Represent People Being Tested by Fire Rather than Doctrines

"I will try them as gold is tried" (Zech. 13:9). "Many shall be purified, made white, and refined" (Dan. 12:10).

If this is the meaning of this portion what a solemn warning we have to God's ministers to build the church only of the regenerate. How solemn is the exhortation, "Let every man take heed how he builds." If an orthodox man would build on the true foundation but bring into the church the unregenerate, his work will be lost. He himself will escape but he will lose everything in the fire. The church is not added to and built up by the "wood, hay and stubble." What a glaring light this puts on the duty of discerning between the righteous and the vile. Lax and careless examinations for baptism and church membership will produce buildings of wood, hay and stubble; to be burnt up in the great day.

Great imposing churches that are made up of multitudes who enter through their infant baptism but do not evidence changed lives will be burnt up to the great loss of the builders. Such builders who through fear of man accepted all who applied for membership will see their works burnt up. Men like John the Baptist, who refused the multitudes by insisting on "works worthy of repentance," will receive a reward when their work endures the fire. What wisdom and self-sacrifice it takes to build with gold, silver and precious stones! What courage and fortitude it takes to reject wood, hay and stubble as building material. "Let each one take heed how he builds."

50

It Produces Carnally Secure Hypocrites

Natural men look on the things that can be seen and touched. Natural religion is founded on the physical, not the spiritual. In baptism the natural man will see the physical sign but fail to see the spiritual meaning. This is especially true in a rite like infant baptism that is performed on an infant who has no qualification for baptism except heredity. This is a real danger. It is compounded by the fact that the natural man will tend to trust in anything, particularly an ordinance of the church, rather than the person and work of Christ. Thus, an infant who has been baptized when he becomes mature will tend to trust in his baptism. This is reinforced by his parents. They are taught as follows,

> "Viewing their children as God's covenant children, believers must approach them as elect children in their teaching and discipline, even though there may indeed be reprobate and unregenerated children among them."[*]

The parents are taught to view their children as God's elect children even though, as Dr. Engelsma says, they may not be. This is a very strange directive. Murray wrote about infant baptism principles,

> "These principles are: (1) that little children, even infants, are among Christ's people and are members of his body; (2) that they are

---

members of his kingdom and therefore have been regenerated; (3) that they belong to the church.'"[*]

If a baptized unbeliever believes this he will have no concern to be converted. He will continue asleep and secure.

Further, the Directory for the Public Worship of God prepared by the Westminster Assembly includes this statement regarding the children of the faithful. "That they are Christians and federally holy before baptism and therefore are they baptized." Why then should the young person who has been baptized strive to enter the narrow gate? He is already a "Christian."

Dr. Murray wrote, "Baptized infants are to be received as the children of God and treated accordingly." Is that honest? What could be more calculated to dispel all fear and to make such into hypocrites? Are they not treated as children of God by the church? Surely then they will think they are. How difficult it would be to bring such a person under conviction of sin and to cause him to arise and flee for his life. Every Sunday the preaching assumes all who have been baptized are God's children and it is never directed to such calling them to repentance and faith.

Do the parents earnestly pray for the conversion of their baptized children? Not likely. Do they warn them of the judgment to come? As Professor Engelsma wrote,

> "Let us admit that there is a danger that the important place of conversion in the life of the covenant child is neglected both by Reformed parents and by the Reformed church and therefore also by the child."[†]

---

[*] Murray, 65.
[†] Engelsma, 19.

51

Discipline Is lacking

I f all the children of church members are automatically accepted into the church the "world" comes into the church and destroys the church as a spiritual body. When a church is no longer looked upon as a gathering of confessing believers, changed men and women, a constant pressure will be exerted to accept a lower standard than a pure church. Please take note of Luther's statement below.

During the Reformation the Anabaptists were accused of holding to Perfectionism because of their desire for holiness in the church and because of their assault on a church that included converted and unconverted. Paedobaptist churches are at peace with having tares in the church and even use that parable as an excuse for allowing the unconverted to continue in fellowship. The parable is not speaking of tares in the church. Christ explained that "the field is the world" where Satan sows the tares. The place of togetherness is the world not the church. Concerning the wicked in the church the direction is not "let both grow together" but "expel the wicked man from among you" (1 Cor. 5:13).

However, even if this parable refers to the visible church it gives no support to the idea of bringing the unregenerate into the church nor allowing them to continue if their lives are inconsistent with true grace in the heart. As Jonathan Edwards wrote,

> "(1) the parable shows plainly, that if any are introduced into the field of the householder, or church of Christ, who prove to be not wheat (*i.e.*, not true saints), they are brought in unawares or contrary

400

to design; (2) this parable plainly shows, that those who are in the visible church, have at first a visibility or appearance to human sight of true grace, or of the nature of true saints. For it is observed tares have this property, that when they first appear, and till the products of the field arrive to some maturity, they have such a resemblance of wheat, that it is next to impossible to distinguish them.'"*

Infants do not have this "visibility or appearance to human sight of true grace." A visibility of grace should be a qualification for church membership and the rule for the church. Luther wrote in regard to these things,

"From the beginning of the Church heretics have maintained that the Church must be holy and without sin. Because they saw that some in the Church were servants of sin they denied forthwith that the Church was the Church, and organized sects . . . This is the origin of the Donatists and the Cathars . . . and of the Anabaptists of our times. All these cry out in angry chorus that the true Church is not the Church because they see that sinners and godless folk are mixed in her and they have separated from her . . . It is the part of wisdom not to be offended at it when evil men go in and out of the Church . . . The greatest comfort of all is the knowledge that they do no harm but that we must allow the tares to be mixed in . . . The 'Schwarmer,' who do not allow tares among them, really bring about that there is no wheat among themselves—by this zeal for only wheat and a pure Church they bring about, by this too great holiness, that they are not even a Church but just a sect of the devil."[†]

Yet in regard to this "too great holiness" even

"the Reformed preachers at Berne admitted as much (conversation such as becometh saints), in a letter which they sent to the City Council, 'The Anabaptists have the semblance of outward piety to a far greater degree than we and all the other churches which in union

---

[*] Edwards, 1:468.
[†] Quoted by Verduin, 107.

with us confess Christ; and they avoid the offensive sins that are very common among us.'"[*]

So prevalent was the difference in conduct between the Reformed national churches and the Anabaptists that those who seriously sought to live godly lives were given the name Anabaptist even when they were not.

> "Henry Bullinger declared, 'There are those who in reality are not Anabaptists but who do have a pronounced aversion to the sensuality and frivolity of the world and for that reason reprove sin and vice and are as a consequence called or misnamed Anabaptists by petulant persons.' Schwendfeld complained, 'I am maligned by preachers and otherwise, with the charge that I am an Anabaptist, even as all who lead a true and devout Christian life are almost everywhere given this name.'"[†]

I would suggest two main reasons for the good testimony of the Anabaptists even among their enemies, the Paedobaptists. The first is that they only accepted believers with a credible profession into their membership, excluding all infants, and secondly, they disciplined their members and excluded those who did not conduct themselves as Christians. The Paedobaptists did not.

The inclusivist policy of the Reformed Paedobaptist churches even led such a good man as Calvin to say, "We must think so highly of the Word and the Sacraments that wherever we see them we are to conclude without a doubt that the church is there, regardless of how much vice and evil there may be in the corporate life of men."[‡] Again, "Often no distinction can be made between God's children and the ungodly; between His own flock and wild beasts."[§] He gives as a reason why "very many ambitious, greedy, envious persons, evil speakers, and some of quite unclean life" exist in the

---

[*] William J. McGlothlin, *Die Berner Taufer bis*, 1532, quoted by Verduin, 109.

[†] Verduin, 109.

[‡] *Ibid.*, 125.

[§] Calvin, 4:1:2.

church; "Such are tolerated for a time either because they cannot be convicted by a competent tribunal or because a vigorous discipline does not always flourish as it ought."*

---

* *Ibid.*, 4:1:7.

52

It Encourages A Trust In the Name

Natural mankind will trust in a name rather than the reality, in the shadow before the substance, in the outward rather than the inward in regard to religion. How difficult to bring the blind to see the uselessness of all such trust and to turn the unregenerate from such trust in the symbol which is empty without the thing symbolized. Infant baptism greatly encourages the trust in the former which leads to neglect of the latter.

Infant baptism confirms many parents in their negligence of seeking to win the souls of their children. If baptism was denied to infants the godly parents of such would be stirred up to more concern and desire for their salvation. Prayer would be more fervent and urgent.

And what about the baptized infants? As they grow up and live in ways of wickedness, whether outward or more hidden, they will be much more likely to be at ease with little concern because of the outward sign of their baptism which they will be strongly tempted to believe made them God's children. They are very likely to be hardened and often have a contempt for true godliness. How difficult it is to see such aroused to a concern for their soul's salvation.

How does it effect unsaved relatives? When infants are baptized unsaved relatives throng to the church to witness it and celebrate the occasion. Then they are never seen at the worship services again. Such baptisms strengthen and confirm such people's deadness and irreligion. Edwards writes of this emphasis on the sign rather than the reality,

"Now why is it looked upon so dreadful, to have great numbers going without the name and honourable badge of Christianity, when at the same time it is no more resented and laid to heart, that such multitudes go without the thing, which is infinitely more dreadful? Why are we so silent about this? What is the name good for, without the thing? Can parents bear to have their children go about the world in the most odious and dangerous state of soul, in reality the children of the devil, and condemned to eternal burnings; when at the same time they cannot bear to have them disgraced by going without the honour of being baptized? A high honour and privilege this is; yet how can parents be contented with the sign, exclusive of the thing signified? Why should they covet the external honour for their children, while they are so careless about the spiritual blessing?

. . . No religious honours, to be obtained in any other way than by real religion, are much worth contending for. And in truth, it is no honour at all to a man, to have merely the outward badges of a Christian, without being a Christian indeed; any more than it would be an honour to a man that has no learning, but is a mere dunce, to have a degree at college; or than it is for a man who has no valour, but is a grand coward, to have an honourable commission in an army; which only serves, by lifting him up, to expose him to deeper reproach, and sets him forth as the more notable object of contempt."[*]

---

[*] Edwards, 476.

53

It Tends to Formalism

"Having a form of godliness, but denying the power thereof" (2 Timothy 3:5).

My mother's family came from Holland so she was brought up in a Dutch Reformed church. They are Paedobaptist. She told me that they didn't teach salvation and its necessity. "Repent" was not preached. Evidence of the new birth was not required or sought. All had been baptized as infants and all were assumed to be God's people. Searching preaching was unknown. It was formalism. She was saved outside of that church. Apparently there was a moving of the Spirit among a number of people at that time that led to her and their salvation. They later began a new church. It was an independent baptistic church not affiliated with a Baptist denomination. It was mainly made up of Dutch people. I was brought up in that church from a child. In doctrine it was weak but basically it was Arminian in doctrine.

I was of the Arminian persuasion until I entered into missionary training where I heard for the first time the doctrines of grace as they are called or nicknamed "Calvinism." Later when I shared the teaching I had come to believe and love with my church one man said to me, "Cliff, that is what we came out of." What he meant was that Calvinism was dead formalism that they had rejected and come out of after their conversion. They knew of none other. A major cause of such deadness among Calvinists is infant baptism that eventually brings unregenerate into the church by the scores and all are presumed Christian.

Another cause of formalism among Paedobaptist churches is that a spontaneous profession of faith is not required. Instead young people go to confirmation classes and learn the right doctrinal answers by rote. They then follow a form when making a public profession which is nothing more than saying, "I do," in answer to the question, "Do you believe . . . etc." This is formalism.

What is formalism? It is when people are Christians in name only. It is when religion is something that is outward. It is not living heart religion. It has no power. Such people know nothing of experimental religion. They do not experience it. It is only a form. Church attendance is a custom. Their daily living is not influenced by their religion. They live as the world and love the world and the things of it. It isn't a disease found only among Paedobaptists. We are all subject to it but infant baptism is a fertile breeding place for it as the following quote shows:

> "I was contending for regeneration as a super-natural act wrought upon the souls of the elect alone by the eternal Spirit, and the Church of England was thanking God for regenerating every child that was sprinkled with a little water . . . I saw it was so by her teaching every child to say he was made in his baptism 'a member of Christ, a child of God and an inheritor of the kingdom of heaven.'"[*]

I have before me a copy of Roland Allen's letter of resignation from the ministry of the Church of England because as he said, "I believe we ought always at all costs to act according to the dictates of our conscience." He believed he could no longer continue in his duties with a clear conscience. He rebelled against ungodly people requiring him to baptize infants and bury their dead as believers although they had lived in unbelief all their lives. He wrote in 1907,

> "Ignorant men speak as if Christ and his Church had nothing to offer which is not the natural inheritance of every Englishman . . . People think and speak as if the services of the Church were 'mere forms.'"

---

[*] Philpot's letter of resignation 1835.

Infant baptism tends to lead to such formalism and the liturgical forms of Paedobaptist churches reinforce it.

54

It Tends to Superstition

When people believe in four leaf clovers, lucky stones or various charms or talismans we call it superstition. We work among a people who were primitive tribes people with many fetishes. These objects are believed to have magical powers to protect and also to aid against sickness, produce fruitful gardens, healthy pigs, etc. Their old religion was animistic, believing that spirits were continually at work doing both good and evil. They believed, and many still believe, that the spirit of a man impregnates things such as his hair, nail parings, excreta, partly eaten food, etc. so those things if obtained can be used to bring sickness and death upon the ones whose hair, etc. it is. They also believe that spirits live in certain rocks, trees, swamps and certain places in the forests so that intrusion or "molesting" by anyone will bring on them or their family various ills.

On the other hand, as said above, they believe in certain plants, bark, wood, etc. having magical qualities that cause gardens to grow, children to be protected, and so on. Thus many believe that the water of baptism has magical qualities such that it can wash away sin and make a person acceptable to God. This superstition is strengthened when they see infants baptized and they are taught that something has happened to the infants. Reason tells them it is the water that does it. All desire baptism and many will go to great lengths to get it. However, if they see a person changed and converted and then hear them at their baptism profess that God has saved them it does not encourage such superstition.

This is particularly so if it is publicly preached that baptismal water of itself has no power but that baptism is only a picture of the baptized person being identified with Christ in his death and resurrection, a picture of the death of the old life and a resurrection to the new. Baptism is a major problem here in church work. Baptism wrongly given has produced much counterfeit religion.

This is of course true in other places, too. Some who want their infants baptized have the essentially pagan superstition that the water has power and effects some good. To be safe they baptize their infant children. This is particularly evident when there has been haste to have a weak or sickly infant baptized before death. Since there is a consciousness that infants are conceived and born in sin, baptism is trusted in to wash away that sin. The rite, which is only a sign, merges with what is signified.

Often infant baptism is "just in case." It is thought that it can do no harm and it may do good. Quite the contrary; infant baptism can do no good and it may do great harm. Giving the sign of conversion to the unconverted is to do them great harm. It tends to harden them in their unbelief, confirm them in their lost state and give them a carnal security that is usually never shaken until death sweeps them away into the pit and they awake with a lie in their right hand.

> "To give that which is holy to those who are profane . . . is not the way to make them better but worse. It is the way to have them habitually trample holy things under their feet, and increase in contempt of them, yea, even to turn again and rend us, and be more mischievous and hurtful enemies of that which is good, than otherwise they would be."[*]

---

[*] Edwards, 1:477.

55

Children Are Regarded As Safe

Paedobaptists treat their children as converted. E. M. B. Green writes,

> "In none of these instances (referring to evidence of the presence of Children in the New Testament church) is there any suggestion that direct evangelising is necessary or fitting in a Christian house. Indeed, the children of believers are already treated as being in the Christian fellowship unless they contract out; like the child of a proselyte to Judaism they are regarded as within the covenant unless they determine to cut themselves off from it. And even then they do not need to be converted in the sense which we examine in Chapter 6; rather they need to be corrected by their parents and brought back to the Christian way from which they had strayed."[*]

Please note his phrase, "they do not need to be converted." Paedobaptists believe the baptized child is to be treated and instructed on the assumption that it is a child of God. Engelsma wrote, "Believers must approach them as elect children in their teaching and discipline."[†]

Charles Hodge,

> "Since the promise is not only to parents but to their seed, children are, by the command of God, to be regarded and treated as of the

---

[*] Green, *Evangelism in the Early Church*, 220; quoted by Kingdon, 99-100.
[†] Engelsma, 18-19.

number of the elect . . ."*

A.A. Hodge,

". . . the child is taught and trained under the regimen of his baptism—taught from the first to recognize himself as a child of God, with all its privileges and duties, trained to think, feel and act as a child of God . . ."†

What if the child is not a child of God and yet is "trained to think, feel and act as a child of God"? Then the church is training hypocrites. What a dreadful thing to baptize a baby and then lead him to believe as he grows up that by baptism he has been saved and will go to heaven although he has never experienced repentance and faith. Infant baptism no doubt sends multitudes to hell clutching a lie in their right hand.

To teach unbelievers as if they are believers not only makes such teaching useless but causes great harm. One of the greatest errors that a preacher or pastor can make is to treat an unbeliever, an unregenerate person, as a Christian and so confirm and even comfort him in his way that will lead to destruction. Unbelievers must be dealt with as unbelievers; believers as believers, convicted sinners as convicted sinners, etc. A major part of the ministry is to discern so as to be able to "take forth the precious from the vile" (Jer. 15:19). In the congregation they must be distinguished by their character and each given their portion. Only a quack doctor would give all the same medicine. Preaching is powerful when it is directed to the person according to his need. Comfort and promises must be given to the saints but warnings and exhortations must be directed to the wicked along with the gospel promises for repentant sinners. When a king reigns in righteousness then "no longer will the fool be called noble, nor the scoundrel be highly respected" (Isa. 32:5). O, may our glorious King reign in His churches! The godly priests were "to teach my people the difference between

---

* C. Hodge, *The Church Membership of Infants in the Biblical Repertory and Princeton Review*, 375.

† A. Hodge, *Evangelical Theology*, 337.

the holy and the common and show them how to distinguish between the unclean and the clean" (Ezek. 44:23). If a teacher of the Word does not distinguish these differences he is an unfaithful man and his ministry will be of little worth.

It is vital that evangelistic preaching that is meant to save souls is seen to be a particular kind of preaching. It is a separate category. To preach to the unsaved is far different than to God's people. A preacher should know to whom he is preaching. It must be directed to the particular needs. To reach the hearts of the baptized children, who are unregenerate, it needs to be awakening. It must pierce the heart with a sense of urgency and danger. The child that is carnally secure must have all his false refuges searched out and swept away. Not least his baptism must be laid before him as giving no hope; as being useless to save and powerless to take away sin. He must be stripped of all that he trusts in to lead him to see his utter nakedness before God. His sins should be revealed. But not only his sins but his sinfulness so that he cries, "Behold I am vile." He needs to be exhorted to strive to enter the narrow gate, to repent lest he perish, to flee to the only Savior and to do it immediately.

Far too much preaching is based on the assumption that all the hearers are Christian. They are not. Children need to be converted. Their need must be pointed out, repentance must be urged; the necessity of the new birth must be emphasized, conviction of sin must be aimed at. Baptized young people who do not evidence the new birth are to be treated as unsaved sinners. They must be converted! They must consciously experience repentance. Parents should earnestly pray for such conversion. Pastors should seek to be instruments in the hand of God for such conversion. Preachers and teachers should aim for conversion. It should be their great object.

Finally, I have written, I trust, for the good of the church and not to further contention and strife. We are fellow soldiers in a great war. In the task of the gospel to every creature how much we need to stand together and fight shoulder to shoulder. In union and through his strength we have abundant hope that "the ends of the world shall remember and turn to the Lord, and all the kindreds of the nations shall worship before him." The gospel must triumph! By his grace the church must succeed. "Grace be with all those who love our Lord Jesus Christ in sincerity."

www.ingramcontent.com/pod-product-compliance
Lightning Source LLC
Chambersburg PA
CBHW062146080426
42734CB00010B/1578